SERENDIPITY

The Story of Building a Dream Ship

Peter L. Murray

Table of Contents

Forward

Between 1965 and 1967, during my years as a law student, my then wife Anita and I had the experience of building a 30' cruising schooner in a field behind my parents' home in Wilbraham, Massachusetts, 100 miles from the sea. The boat was completed enough to be launched on August 30, 1967. For the last 50 years, *Serendipity*, her completion and care, as well as the many cruises and adventures that we have shared, have loomed large in my life. She has brought me great pleasure and satisfaction. Although I have let her down many times, she has never let me down.

For decades, friends have urged me to write the story of how *Serendipity* came into being in that field in Wilbraham. They wanted me to convey how a law student and his spouse were able to build and launch a cruising schooner under those conditions. My first attempt to do this was in 1986 on the eve of a planned world voyage. That account was not completed and the project sat for almost 30 years. A few years ago, another draft was started from the beginning. Late in the writing process, the first draft was rediscovered. This text combines material from both drafts.

Much of the text may seem overly detailed to many readers. An effort is made to explain the process so that readers who are not experienced boat-builders will be able to get an idea of what needs to be done to create a substantial traditionally built sailing yacht. It will also describe how we accomplished, at least after a fashion, each of the numerous steps that were required.

The mid-1960s was not a good time to try to build a traditional wooden vessel. By then, wooden boatbuilding had been relegated to history in favor of molded fiberglass. Traditional materials, tools, and fittings were almost

1

impossible to obtain. Skilled wooden boat-builders had retired without training successors. These circumstances, along with our lack of proper tools, building place, knowledge or experience, combined to make the process even more challenging.

Fortunately, since that time there has been a remarkable revival of interest in wooden boats and how they are built. The skills we had to learn by doing are now taught at boatbuilding schools and other programs. Materials and fittings that were virtually unobtainable in the 1960's have since become readily available from multiple sources. For this, we and many other traditional wooden boat enthusiasts are grateful.

During our building project, we took numerous photographs with our Brownie and Instamatic cameras. With these, and a few pictures taken by my mother on her 1930's-era box camera, we documented our project in an album largely created and maintained by Anita, who wrote the captions on the pages of the album. Over the last half-century, that album has been the only written record of the project. Many of these snapshots now reappear here, as illustrations of the accompanying text.

Although attention has been focused on our project as an accomplishment of two individuals working together with single-minded purpose, in fact, a good number of people helped us in various ways. Without their help, and the encouragement of many others, it is hard to imagine that we would have ever been able to do it. First of all were my parents, Samuel and Josephine Murray, who provided us with the place to build the boat, who made room for us during the building under their roof and at their table, who generously contributed key items such as our fruit-ladder and the Volvo diesel auxiliary engine, and whose faith in us and continuous encouragement lent us strength to carry on. Other family members, such as my siblings, Paul and Alison Murray, Anita's parents, Chester and Anne Jones, and her cousin, John Lyman were also generous with their interest and encouragement. We were assisted immeasurably by various individuals who lent us their skills and specialized tools, compensated and not, to enable us to do things that otherwise we were not equipped to accomplish. Charles Merrick and his large cabinet planer were invaluable resources at many key points in the project. Wilbraham Academy gave us the use of its gym as our loft floor. Suppliers and vendors who extended trade discounts on otherwise extremely expensive materials, supplies and fittings made it possible for us somehow to afford it all. Of these individuals and organizations, Sargent, Lord and Company, Ralph Travers of Travaco Labs., Rostand Manufacturing Company, and Al Pendleton, were particularly helpful. Other suppliers and vendors provided us with their fine products at reasonable prices. These included Harold Koncitek, of Hampden, MA, Massachusetts Foundry, Cambridge, MA, Winde McCormick Lumber Company, of Charlestown, MA, Reid Foundry of Amesbury, MA, and Roy Lumber Company of Willimantic, MA, among others.

Many friends helped us in many ways, mainly by lending a hand on some task or other in the building project. The text contains the names of many such helpers. Those who helped, but were not mentioned, please forgive my poor memory. All your help and encouragement meant a great deal to the builders of *Serendipity* and contributed to the successful completion of the project.

This book is dedicated first to Anita B. Jones, my first spouse, who worked side by side with me to make the dream of *Serendipity* come true. She was also *Serendipity's* crew for those early years exploring the Maine Coast. It is dedicated second to Peter Marshall Murray and Anne Lawrence Murray, my children and the second crew of *Serendipity*, who helped maintain and upgrade her for over ten years and who sailed with me on many cruises and on her most ambitious voyages. It is dedicated third to Deborah Dunn Murray, my wife now for more than 25 years, who lovingly accepted *Serendipity* as a part of our life together, and has sailed her with me the length of the Maine Coast and beyond for two and a half decades.

Portland, Maine

August, 2016

Chapter 1

The moment of conception of a dream ship is an event that often cannot be fixed with certainty. The raging forest fire, the obsession to build one's own ship - with one's own hands - to sail the seven seas - often cannot be traced to any single spark. Indeed, once kindled, the notion might smolder virtually unnoticed for years, or wax and wane, fanned by the changing winds of chance, and then, at some point, often without any discernible reason, burst into a bright and devouring flame.

For many, the image of a dream ship may gently warm the cockles of the soul for years, making bearable many tedious hours of work. The little flames of fantasy often become embers and die when the dusty plans are put away with only a wistful sigh. But in some cases, the progress from the merest notion to a full-blown obsessive project is fast and direct. The idea, once ignited, fueled by energy and imagination, soon devours the soul. In others, the dream is kept alive despite the coldest winds of adversity and only reaches its full-blown development many years after coming into being.

It is difficult to find a place to start this story of my dream ship. If we start with the earliest stirrings of some idea of sailing around the world, I probably was less than 10 at the time, a pudgy boy with a fascination for books about the sea. Undoubtedly, I dreamed of sailing some strange craft upon the world's seven oceans . . .

Shall we begin perhaps with the happy chance of learning to sail at the summer home of a childhood friend at Martha's Vineyard? Or we could start, I suppose, in the dusty attic of our barn where my first sailboat, _Te Amo_, was laboriously reconstructed from a rotten skiff dragged from behind a neighbor's garage. Or maybe it would be more realistic to advance to the Prout's Neck Yacht Club, on the coast of Maine, where a child's fantasies developed into the more mature longing of a young law student to sail the coast of Maine in a small cruising yacht.

The germ of the idea was likely there all along. The experiences of the years, both at sea and ashore, somehow provided the conditions to keep alive and nurture the dream, despite an otherwise conventional middle class upbringing and education. But to try to trace the thread of the fantasy through these many years of childhood and youth would be to labor excessively before the birth. And so, for want of a better time, we will start on a slushy cold morning in February 1965, in Harvard Square, Cambridge, Massachusetts.

I was in my first year of law school at the time. During the preceding summer, I had graduated from college, reached the age of 21, become married, and started my first job all within a single week! That job was as the manager of the yacht club at Prout's Neck, a summer community south of Portland on the Maine coast. There, for the first time, I was really exposed to the pleasures of sailing the Maine coast in small cruising yachts. Some of the most pleasant hours of that summer were spent sailing the *Sally*, a 30-foot Yankee-class sloop graciously made available by one of the members for my new bride, Anita, and me to use on days off. That fall, as I started my first year at law school, I somehow knew that my life would never be complete without a small cruising boat of my own.

In those days, buying a cruising sailboat of 30 feet or so was simply out of the question for an impecunious law student. Our sole sources of support were my wife's earnings and meager savings from summer jobs over the years. But the lurking spark of an idea that I could actually build my own cruising sailboat, somehow came into being during that fall. By Christmas-time, almost unconsciously, I found myself talking with Anita about how we could build a 30 or 35 foot ketch or something. From a lifetime of reading of books on ships, voyages and the sea, I had come to the conclusion that probably a ketch was the most suitable vessel for coastwise and long distance voyaging. And so it was that I began to "keep my eye out" for designs we could at least look at . . .

But I was unprepared for what happened on that February morning in grey and slushy Harvard Square. I don't remember where I was going or what I was doing. Whatever it was, I found myself near "Nini's", a small news and fruit stand on the very corner of Boylston Street and Massachusetts Avenue where they meet at the Square. As I passed by, a small paperback magazine caught my eye - *20 Boats You Can Build*. I only paused for a second. The cover was a grid work of tiny snapshots of the craft featured inside, small runabouts, outboards and perhaps a cabin cruiser. But something in the subtitle intrigued me, "Skiffs, Schooners, Sailboats, Runabouts, . . ." "Schooners?" I could scarcely imagine that such a nondescript little rag would feature a design for a homebuilt schooner.

After all, schooners are large and able seagoing vessels. The typifying feature of the rig is two or more masts with the forward mast shorter than the main. Schooners are the sailing ships of romance. The *Hispaniola* of *Treasure Island* was a schooner. The *America*, of America's Cup fame, was a schooner. Schooners were, for many generations, the draft horses of working sail, beating up and down the coasts of the continents right up to the twentieth century.

But by 1965, schooners had become real rarities. Modern materials, modern rigs and the growth of the large fore-triangle had pretty much banished this romantic anomaly from the ocean. In those days, it was highly unusual to find any kind of an amateur boat-builder publication featuring a schooner.

7

I picked up the magazine from the rack and flipped through the pages. And then, suddenly, there it was. Like a swan amid ducklings, like a dove amid sparrows, the plans,

Nimble

Want a real boat? Build this sweet and salty 30 ft. schooner!

By V. B. Crockett

ONE OF THE SMALLEST schooners to sail the Maine coast, this "big-little" thirty footer is fun to sail and a joy to own. Designed and built for the rugged waters of Maine, she is at home in deep water anywhere. Strongly and heavily built, she sails well in light air and when it is really blowing she can take it with the best of them. With her saucy sheer and down-easter look she reminds many people of the old timers that were once so plentiful on the coast.

The accommodations in this little schooner are very spacious for her size. She has an extra-large galley with sink, icebox and stove and ample space for dishes and stowage. Her toilet room is good size and includes a large linen locker and wash basin. Forward of the toilet and galley are the main cabin berths which double as seats. Upper berths may be added to sleep four in the main cabin. In the forward cabin there are two berths and ample storage space.

In Nimble, V. B. Crockett has captured the saucy "down-easter" look of the old timers.

designs and photographs of *Nimble*, a 30-foot gaff-rigged

schooner, sprang from the pages to my amazed and delighted eyes.

One of the keynotes of this design is the lack of frills or gimcracks. She was designed for comfort and sea-going ability with the accent on common sense design.

The engine is a 16 HP Palmer which gives a good honest 5½ knots without any fuss. Her sail plan is moderate and it has to be really blowing before reefing is thought of.

Although this boat was designed, and the plans drawn, for professional builders there have been many of the plans purchased by amateur builders and there is no reason why, if one is patient and takes his time, the amateur builder could not build a boat to be proud of.

The laying down of the lines, and the making of the patterns and molds from them, is one of the most important steps in the building of any design and it should be emphasized that this step must be carefully done. To do the job right the lines should be laid down on a floor long enough and wide enough to fair all the lines. The offsets given with the plans are corrected offsets, but if you want to do the job right you should make the lines full size as shown, so that your patterns and molds are as perfect as you can get them. I would suggest that you make your iron keel pattern after the lines are laid down. While you are waiting for your iron keel to arrive get out the patterns for the rudder, keel, stem, deadwood, etc.

I am not going into detail about the steps in building this boat as I believe the person who builds the schooner will know the basic facts of building. How-

The 30-ft. Nimble is 24 ft. long at water line: 4-ft. 8-in. draft, a 9-ft. 6-in. beam.

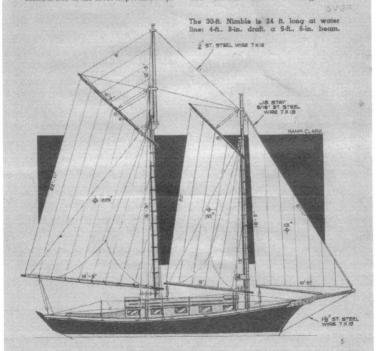

9

ever, there are many books on boat building which could be of help and I strongly urge that at least one be kept at hand for reference.

Following are the complete specifications.

The object of these specifications is to supplement the drawings. In case any item is mentioned in these specifications and is not shown in the drawings or vice versa, it is to be considered that such items are shown in both the specifications and drawings. The fact that ANY item ESSENTIAL to the SEAWORTHINESS or safety of the boat is not shown, or described in the drawings or specifications shall not be considered as an excuse for the elimination of such items on the completed boat.

All lumber shall be of good quality, free from knots, shakes, checks or warps, with the exception that tight knots of not over ½″ diameter will be permitted. Marine glue of approved quality shall be spread on every faying surface adjacent to the water. All fastenings and other hardware to be either hot-dipped galvanized iron or brass, bronze, Everdur or other non-ferrous metal. Throughout the construction only articles of approved marine-type will be permitted.

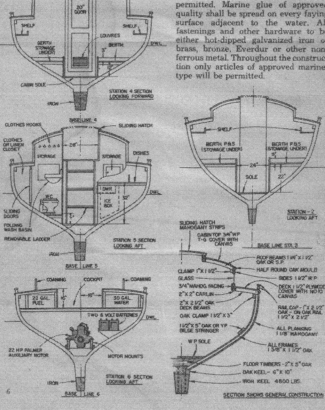

6

10

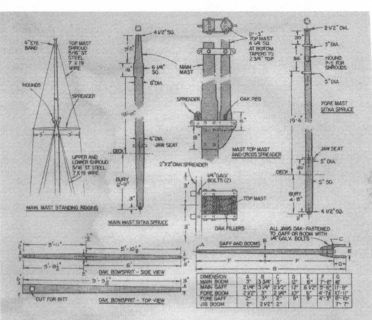

DIMENSION	A	B	C	D	E	F	G
MAIN BOOM	3"	3 3/4"	5"	2"	8"	7'-6"	16'
MAIN GAFF	2 1/4"	3 1/4"	2 1/2"	12"	6 1/2"	5'-6"	11'-9"
FORE BOOM	2 1/2"	3"	2 3/4"	10"	5"	4-7/8"	9'-11"
FORE GAFF	2"	3"	2 1/2"	9"	5"	4-3/4"	8'-9"
JIB BOOM	2"	2 1/2"	2"				7'-7"

The lines of the boat are to be laid down full-scale on the shop floor from the accompanying *table of offsets*. Although the Table was prepared as carefully as possible slight variations may be found and will be permitted for fairing purposes only.

Where more than one material is specified, they are given in the order of preference. Wherever a part is actually dimensioned on the drawing or specified by size, such dimensions are to be used in preference to those obtained by scaling.

WOOD KEEL: Oak. 6"x10" and molded as shown on plans. Fastened to iron keel with 3/4" galv. bolts, staggered and spaced as shown.

IRON KEEL: To be cast as shown on plans. 4800 lbs. approx.

STEM: Oak. Sided 4" and molded as shown. Fastened with 1/2" galv. carriage bolts.

STEM KNEES: Oak. Sided 4" and molded as shown. Fastened with 1/2"

galvanized carriage bolts to the keel.

HORN TIMBER: Oak. Sided 5" and molded as shown. Fastened with 1/2" galv. drift bolts as shown on plans.

CUPRINOL: Bilge-backbone-behind ceiling.

SHAFT LOG: 6" oak bored for 1" shafting. Through fastened with 1/2" galv. drift bolts as shown on plans.

DEADWOOD: White oak sided 4" and molded as shown. Through fastened with 3/8" galv. bolts as shown. All joints locked.

TRANSOM: Mahogany or oak 1 1/4" thick. On the forward outer edges of transom 7/8" x 2" oak cleats must be screwed to form an extra backing for plank ends. If preferred, the cleats may be set in from edge of transom so that end grain of planks will not show. In this case, increase thickness of cleats to 1 1/8". Transom to be fastened to stern post with through bolts of at least 3/8" diameter.

STOPWATERS: There will be stop-

11

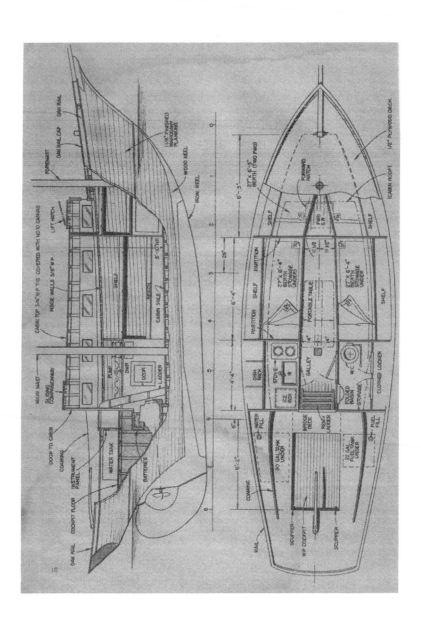

12

waters at all necessary points. Same to be ½″ pine dowels set in marine glue. BREAST HOOK: Oak 2″ thick. Fitted as shown.

FRAMES: White oak 1⅜″ x 1½″ steam bent. To be boxed into keel and securely fastened. Frames to be spaced 9″ on center.

FLOOR TIMBERS: Oak 1½″ x 6″. In way of engine bed and cabin floor mold to suit. Floor timbers to be bolted through wood keel with ⅜″ diameter galv. bolts.

LIMBERS: There will be limber holes in each floor timber of ¾″ dia.

DECK BEAMS: Oak 2″ x 2½″ cut to a crown of ⅜″ to 1′-0″. Deck beams to be fastened to clamp with ¼″ carriage bolts and nailed to frames.

MAIN CLAMP: Oak or L. Pine 1½″ x 3″. To be fastened to frames and through bolted to deck beams with ¼″ galv. carriage bolts. At the ends the clamp will box into the stem and stern cleats and fillers will be arranged between the planking and clamps at the extreme ends.

PLANKING: Mahogany to finish ⅞″. Planks do not necessarily have to be in single lengths but no strakes should have more than 3 pieces. Butts should come about 4″ forward or aft of the frames and should be braced with oak butt blocks ¾″ thick fitted tightly against the frame at one end. Length of butt blocks shall not be less than 8″. Butts adjoining planks should not come within the same frame space and when two butts come within the same space, there must be three other planks in between. Planks are fastened with Anchorfast Monel Everdur nails with heads countersunk or bunged—1¾″ No. 12. Frame fastenings should not be over 3″ apart. To be well caulked.

BILGE STRINGERS: Oak 1½″ x 5″ fastened to frames. At ends box into stem and stern cleats. Use ¼″ galv. bolts at each frame.

DECKING: ⅜″ plywood. Decking to be covered with 10 oz. canvas; plywood to be fastened to beams with nails.

CARLINS: Oak 2″ x 2″ as shown on plans. To be fastened to beams. ¼″ tie rods to be used spaced every third frame to tie carlin and clamp together.

CEILING: White pine ⅜″ T & G. In the cabin to extend to floor. The same in the cockpit. Nail fastened.

FACING PIECE: Mahogany or oak ½″ thick to extend length of cabin. Screw fastened to carlin and cabin sides. Use ¾″ No. 8 screws.

CABIN SIDES: Pine 1½″ to be fastened to deck with ⅜″ galv. tie rods.

CABIN TOP: White pine or cedar T & G ¾″ covered with 10 oz. canvas. Fasten galv. boat nails.

CABIN BEAMS: Spruce 1¼″ x 1½″ cut to a crown of 1½″ to 1′-0″. Notched over and fastened to clamp with 1¾″ No. 10 screws.

CABIN CLAMP: Spruce 1″ x 1½″. Fastened to cabin side with 1½″ No. 8 screws.

WINDOWS: Three stationary windows P & S sizes as shown on plan.

PORTLIGHTS: Two 5″ portlights on forward end of cabin.

CABIN FLOOR: ¾″ white pine. To be screw fastened with 1¼″ No. 8 screws to floor timbers. There will be loose boards in the center to be used as hatches.

COCKPIT FLOOR: ¾″ white pine to be watertight with self-bailing scuppers. Fasten with 1¼″ No. 8 screws.

COCKPIT FLOOR BEAMS: Oak 1¾″ x 2″ to be fastened to frames and clamp. Use 3″ No. 10 screws.

GRAB RAIL: Along the edges of the cabin roof there will be an oak grab rail. 1″ x 2½″ shaped as shown in plan and fastened by screws to the roof.

MAIN RAIL: Oak 3″ high, 2½″ at deck and tapered to 1½″. Scuppers shall be cut as shown on plan. To be securely fastened to deck beams and sheer strake with ¼″ drift bolts.

RAIL CAP: Oak 1″ x 2½″. Screw fastened to rail with 1¾″ No. 12 screws.

MOLDING: There will be 2″ Hf. rd., oak molding extending from stem to stern and screw fastened to planking just under rail.

COMPANIONWAY HATCH: ¾″ mahogany sliding companionway of usual construction, thoroughly watertight. Instead of doors under hatch, slides may be used for entrance to cabin.

FOR'D HATCH: Hatch 1½″ pine, as shown in plans, with sliding hatch and

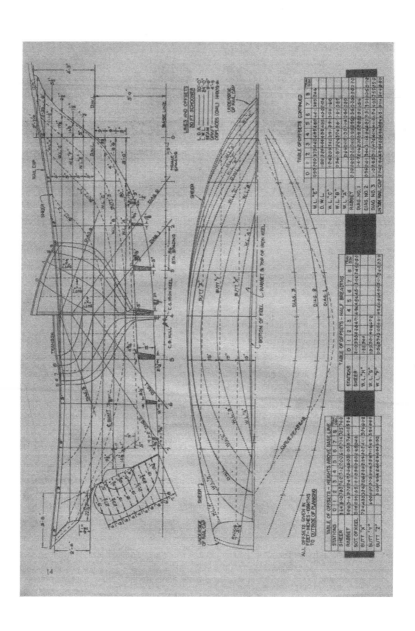

14

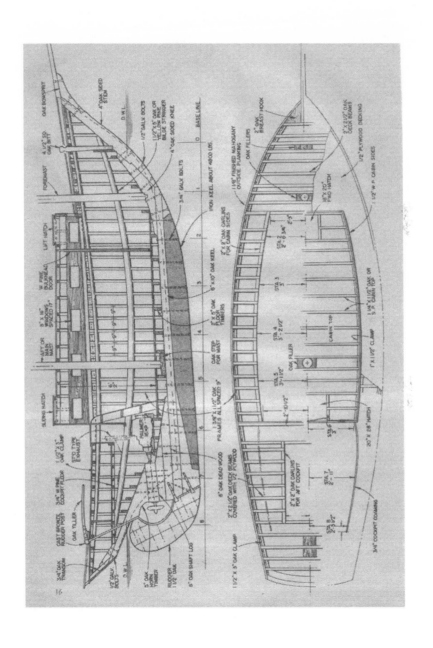

slides same as those on companionway. BULKHEADS: White pine or plywood ¾" thick. Located as shown. STEPS: As shown on plan. Removable to gain access to engine. FILLERS: Oak fillers are to be placed tightly between deck and roof beams under every item of deck equipment to help carry strain to the beams. To be approximately 2" thick and not less than 6" wide. RUDDER PORT: 1½" inside dia. pipe. Galv. or bronze. RUDDER: Oak 1½" thick and tapered. Shaped as shown on plans and through fastened with ½" galvanized bolts. RUDDER POST: 1⅜" bronze rod. RUDDER GUDGEONS & PINTLES: To be bronze, similar to those on plan. TILLER: Oak of suitable size, shaped as shown. Securely fastened to the rudder. ENGINE: *Palmer 16 H.P.* 1" shaft and a 16" x 8" two-blade propeller. To be securely fastened to 2" oak engine beds which are notched over floor timbers. Located as shown on plans. Exhaust to be arranged to suit engine. VENTS: Cowl vent port & stb'd as shown on plan.

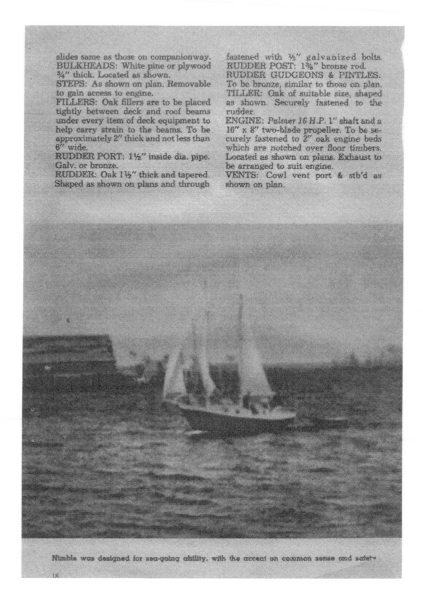

Nimble was designed for sea-going ability, with the accent on common sense and safety

18

For long minutes, I stood there oblivious to the chill and slush as I gazed at and pored over the plans and designs filling several pages of the pulpy periodical. That February morning in 1965 was the one and only time in my life that I felt love at first sight.

Everything about the little schooner pleased and delighted me. The *Nimble* was 30 feet long, 9-1/2 feet broad and drew 4 feet, 8 inches. These were dimensions that promised a degree of commodious comfort, but modest enough for us to handle. Her sheer was saucy. Everything seemed to be in good proportion. She sported a bowsprit, gaff fore and main and even a gaff tops'l.

The long trunk cabin promised a roomy interior - the plans boasted of over 6 feet headroom below. The small square watertight cockpit and the bridge deck promised safety in heavy seas. The layout was conventional with galley and head in the after corners of the trunk cabin, then settee berths to either side of a folding table, a bulkhead, and a V-berth forward.

The designs called for a completely traditional build, steam-bent oak frames, mahogany planking and a fiberglass-covered plywood deck. To my then relatively untutored eyes, the scantlings looked impressive. The oak keel was specified as 21 feet long, 6 inches deep and 10 inches wide at its widest point. Below was bolted a heavy iron keel running almost the full length of the vessel. It was to weigh 4800 pounds. A 16 horsepower Palmer gas engine tucked under the cockpit was the auxiliary power.

The article in the magazine even contained a complete set of "lines and offsets" that define the actual shape of the hull. Boat shapes are not generally square or rectangular. Ordinary measurements will not suffice to capture the complex shape of the hull and it multiple simple and complex curves designed to facilitate its passage through the water. Boat plans, therefore, contain drawings that show the contour of the hull at various slices of the hull form - horizontal "waterlines" and vertical "buttocks". The intersection of the hull surface with these waterlines and buttocks at various cross-sectional "stations" along the keel can be measured and recorded in a "table of offsets". These measurements ultimately can be recreated full size in the process of "lofting," which is the first step in the building process.

In actuality, the article in the magazine, which included a complete "table of offsets", contained all of the information needed for someone to construct the boat without having to purchase actual plans. However, the magazine contained the name and address of the designer and advised that a complete set of plans and specifications for *Nimble* could be purchased for the sum of $50.

There were pages of specifications setting forth more details about how this cute little schooner was to be constructed. I pored over every one of them devouring the details of the construction of the spars, the cross sections of the hull, the listing of the kinds of fastenings, lumber and metalwork that would be required.

The spark had ignited and rapidly became a consuming flame. I bought the magazine and hurried off to the university library where my wife was then employed. She was checking out books. Impatiently, I waited in line, eager to spread before her the excitement of my discovery. Understandably, she was startled at how suddenly the vague imaginings of some sort of cruising ketch had developed into a passionate obsession for a miniature schooner. She nonetheless cheerfully and willingly adapted, and became a vital and integral part of the undertaking.

That evening, back at our tiny apartment, we pored over the plans again and again, discussing and rationalizing the suitability of this craft as our dream ship. I say "rationalizing", for even at that time I was well aware that a schooner is not the most efficient rig. The arrangement of the masts, with the smaller one forward, reflected the limitations on design and building of prior generations. Modern technology had made it possible to erect and stay large masts forward and, thereby, achieve large and efficient airfoils in the fore-triangle. A schooner, particularly a "gaffer", could never work to

18

windward with the efficiency of a Marconi rigged sloop or cutter. Even a ketch could probably develop more power on the wind than could a schooner. But it didn't take us long to agree that the beauty, the duck-like seaworthiness and the dainty nostalgia of the little schooner more than made up for any possible shortcomings in its windward performance.

That first night, my fingers pecked madly at the typewriter as I composed a list of basic questions for *Nimble's* designer. "Was amateur construction feasible? Had any others been built? How much would it cost to have one built? What did he think it would cost if we built it ourselves?"

The creator of *Nimble* was Vere B. Crockett, of Camden, Maine. Crockett was a part-time yacht designer and maritime journalist. His main vocation was the sale of municipal bonds to customers up and down the coast of Maine. His whole design portfolio probably amounted to no more than 20 fully-developed designs. He was not the Sam Crock<u>er</u>, who had a very prolific career as a designer and builder of lovely traditional cruising boats in Manchester, Massachusetts.

Mr. Crockett was a patient and genial soul as well as a gifted designer. He replied promptly to our initial inquiry. "Yes, it would be feasible for an amateur to build the little schooner....." Although the construction was traditional, it was not unduly complicated. Several sets of plans had been sold to amateurs since the design had originally been developed in 1956. Mr. Crockett was sure that at least some of the boats had been completed. Of course, if we wished, he could make arrangements to have one built for us professionally. He had an estimate from Snow's, a boatyard in Rockland, Maine. For $15,000 he could deliver one complete.

In those days, $15,000 was like the moon. We could see perhaps $1,000 or $2,000 that we could scrape together to allocate for the project. Anything more would have to be earned or scrounged as we went along.

19

The enthusiastic obsession of the amateur boat builder sweeps aside all considerations of practicality and perspective. Here we were, living in Cambridge, Massachusetts. My wife was working as a librarian. I was in my first year of law school. We lived in a one-bedroom apartment in a big brick building. Our lifetime capital was about $2,000, most of which was earmarked to pay for the rest of my education. We had neither place nor time nor money to build a 30-foot, 7-ton cruising schooner.

All of these things must have occurred to our parents when we first confronted them with the idea a few days or maybe even a week later. They must have realized how absurd it was for us to be even considering a major boatbuilding project at this time and place in our lives. They must have realized that we just couldn't do it, that it was crazy for us to even think of it, and that surely if we tried, we would fail.

Fortunately, they did not voice these perfectly rational and understandable misgivings. Fortunately, they did not react with skepticism or scorn. Instead, my parents greeted our proposal to build our own schooner with an amiable interest and even gentle support. Their interest and support made them part of what became our most important obsession for the next three years. Anything less would have cut them off from this crucial portion of our life experience.

Another letter to Mr. Crockett and $50 transformed the tiny drawings of *How to Build Twenty Boats* into a full set of blueprints. It was the best $50 I have ever spent. How many hours we pored over those plans and the simple set of typewritten specifications that accompanied them! Fortunately, Crockett was a careful and able draftsman. Not only were the plans accurate and consistent, they also showed the lines, sail plan and accommodations of the little schooner to good advantage and further fueled our fevered imaginations.

We decided to build the dream ship in a field behind my parents' home in Wilbraham, Massachusetts. We were

20

undaunted by the facts that Wilbraham was nearly 100 miles from Cambridge and that somehow this project would have to be fit in around the continuation of my law school education. Attached to the big red barn behind my parents' home, was a small 12 x 12 shed, which at one time had been a crude workshop. More recently, my father had filled it up with books and other debris. If I built shelves in the barn to hold the books that were piled in the shed, could I use the shed as a workshop for the boat? My father good-naturedly agreed. About 150 feet in back of the barn there was a level place in the field where in years past my mother had tilled a large vegetable garden. There we would build the hull. We had a place.

But the place was only the beginning. There was a great deal that neither of us knew about building a traditional sailing craft. I was handy with tools and I had worked around small sailboats for several years. As mentioned above, at age 13, I had transformed a rotten flat-bottomed skiff into a rather bizarre "sharpy type" sailboat. *Te Amo* was rigged with a dead pine tree for a mast and had a sail from a Herreshoff 12-1/2 that had sunk in the 1938 hurricane. More recently, I had done some maintenance work around larger power and sailing craft at Prout's Neck. But all this was a far cry from building a 7-ton bent-frame conventionally-planked schooner from scratch. I turned to the books. Howard Chapelle's *Boatbuilding* became for us, like many other amateur boat-builders, the Bible. I read it several times from cover to cover, re-reading again and again the vital chapters on lofting, steam bending, and planking. We read and compared every other book on amateur boatbuilding that we could lay our hands on.

So in the winter of 1965, we established a pattern that was to last for the remainder of my law school years. From February, 1965 until I graduated from law school in June 1967, I doubt that we spent more than 2 or 3 weekends in Cambridge. In those years, my law school had classes on Saturday. I was transformed overnight from a faithful attendee to a flagrant cutter of Saturday class meetings. Weekend social invitations from student friends were ruthlessly turned down in favor of driving to Wilbraham to work on the boat.

We would leave each Friday night as soon as Anita had finished her work. Soon, we had the drive west down to a science. Our time was about an hour and a half to an hour and 45 minutes en route, depending upon the traffic. All day Saturday and all day Sunday we would work on the boat in Wilbraham. My parents provided meals, did our laundry, and generally "supervised" the new project growing in their back field. We returned to Cambridge, exhausted, after supper on Sunday night. I don't remember when I studied law. It certainly wasn't on the weekends.

The first project, as mentioned above, was the making of some kind of a space within which to build the boat. We had to have a shop in which to assemble and keep our tools, plans, and some of the materials. During our first few weekends in Wilbraham, I set about building bookshelves in the barn. Gradually, my father's books and ephemera left the workshop and were neatly shelved in the barn. At the same time, my remaining hand tools and power drill were marshaled in the dusty workshop. My father gave us a miniature wood stove. We set it up in the workshop for heat.

The available tools were discouragingly insignificant. We started with a 1/4-inch electric drill, several hand screwdrivers, brace and bits, a few old planes, handsaws, etc. We had absolutely no heavy power tools. Later, my father-in-law gave us an ancient Craftsman 6-inch disc sander of early 1950's vintage. Relatively early on, I bought (for $40) an equally ancient 8-inch table saw from the estate of a deceased neighbor. These, plus a Sears & Roebuck 3/8-inch electric drill and a 1/5 horsepower saber saw, were our only power tools for most of the project. With them we would build our ship.

At an early stage, we faced a very important question. What will be the name of the new ship? It was a momentous

22

question. Yet it did not take us long to decide. My father has always been a lover of words. He has been known for his rich and ornate vocabulary. From him, came the name of our schooner.

"Serendipity" had been a word in more or less common use within our family for many years. Back in 1964, the word had not been "discovered" by either singing groups or antique dealers. The word "serendipity" was coined by Hugh Walpole in his short story "The Three Princes of Serendip". The word describes not so much a place or a person, as a state of being. It is that happy condition in which one makes pleasant discoveries when one least expects them.

Of course, in recent years "serendipity" has become much more popular. When our *Serendipity* was first documented, there was only one other yacht with that name in *Lloyds Register of American Yachts*. There must now be dozens.

Serendipity seemed to be a particularly appropriate name for our dream ship. It sounded right. The tones rolled off the tongue in an almost musical cadence. The hidden meaning, the property of making pleasant discoveries when least expected, seemed to be the ideal association with a dream ship. It was early, even before the blueprints were lofted on the floor, that we chose the name by which our schooner would be known.

Of course, particularly in its early days, there were those who could not understand our obsession and who very properly viewed the matter from a more practical perspective. My wife's cousin, then dying of cancer in the hospital in Springfield, was an enthusiastic supporter of our venture. One of his associates, a very successful local businessman and experienced yachtsman, took the other view. "Who knows if a screw might pull out when you're out in the middle of the ocean? . . . You'd better get an older boat, perhaps one that doesn't look too good, and then fix it up."

His comments were founded on sagacity and experience. But he lacked understanding of the fire of the dream. He lacked understanding of that peculiar obsession which drives one to want to create with one's own hands. He lacked the vision of youth consumed by a single object, by a dream ship. Even the cold water of his comments could not quench our fire.

Chapter 2

Every boat builder knows that the first step in building a round-bottomed wooden boat is "lofting". The idea is to reproduce the lines and offsets of the boat "full size" to insure the accuracy of the many complex curves and provide ready access to patterns, bevels, etc. Most professionals regard lofting as a pleasant, mildly challenging exercise in large-scale drafting. To us, back in 1965, the lofting of *Serendipity* loomed as a monumental hurdle right at the beginning of our undertaking.

First of all, to a person who has never done any lofting, the whole process appears difficult, mysterious and rife with opportunity for devastating error. The explanations then available were none too clear. Even beloved Chapelle, though read repeatedly on the subject, failed to instill much confidence in us. Could we really reproduce the lines of our dream ship in life-size likeness?

And then, of course, there was the place. The books blandly referred to "the mold loft" - as if every amateur builder setting up in his backyard had a large expanse of perfectly smooth covered flooring on which to lay out lines at leisure and leave them there during the course of the construction. Neither our 12-foot x 12-foot cubbyhole of a workshop nor any part of my parents' house or barn had the space necessary to lay out the lines even half-size, let alone in full scale. The implements were another problem. The books spoke in terms of "battens" having just the right degree of flex to obtain smooth curves. The cross sections required lighter battens than the waterlines and diagonals. Sitka spruce was recommended as the proper wood. And proper mould loft weights, currently popular doorstoppers and paperweights in nautical gift shops, were in those days virtually extinct.

It is easy to imagine how the lofting stage can prove the ultimate damper for a boatbuilding dream. But we were not to be so easily daunted. The solution lay in fortuity. Spring vacation at Wilbraham Academy, a small local prep school, coincided with my spring vacation from law school. We were graciously given the use of the school gym for a week, provided that we did not mar the hardwood playing floor. Of course, there could be no thought of leaving our lines laid down on the school's basketball courts while we took two or three years to build the vessel. We would have to loft on paper or some surface which could be rolled up and taken home.

But Chapelle had warned ominously about the risks of lofting on paper. The sheet might shrink or expand, introducing incurable distorting error into the sweet design of our ship. He grudgingly allowed that if we had to draft on paper, red rosin building paper was probably the best of a bad bargain.

We had no choice. We stilled as best we could the Chapelle-inspired qualms. We cautiously rolled out on the gym floor three 35-foot strips of red rosin building paper and taped them together with heavy package tape. Thirty-foot batten stock was out of the question. We crudely spliced together several strips of spruce (not Sitka) of different thicknesses. For weights we used whatever was available. A large chunk of type metal (about 30 pounds) was the best. Smaller pieces of marble and door stoppers filled in. And there were many times when one of us just had to hold the batten in place while the vital line was struck.

There is nothing like learning as you go along. With Chapelle in one hand and Mr. Crockett's plans in the other, we labored in the cold and drafty gym to make our dream ship come alive. Lofting, it turned out, was fun. The essential geometry of locating the points by coordinates and then "fairing" the table of offsets into smooth lines is not a terribly difficult concept to grasp. But doing it a bit is indispensable to a feeling of confidence.

Fortunately, Mr. Crockett's table of offsets had been corrected once after a prior boat had been lofted and built. There were few discrepancies of any consequence. That does not mean, however, that we became veteran lofters overnight, or even over the week it took us to transform the blueprints that we had received from Crockett into a full-scale reproduction. The transom, a curved and raked affair of classic proportions, was particularly difficult. Even after we had painstakingly gone through the whole intricate procedure described by Chapelle and had reproduced the curve and contours on the plan, I was not satisfied that we had done it right.

Another sticky spot was the relationship between the wood keel, the rabbet (the groove in the wood keel for the edge of the garboard plank or "strake") and the iron keel. Offsets in that area were sparse. It was hard to visualize how all of the components would come together. We had to make assumptions with very little to go on by way of experience.

At the end of the week, the loft plan was complete. The red rosin building paper was covered with a grid-work of waterlines, buttocks, diagonals, and cross sections enlarging to full size the lines and offsets drawing furnished by Crockett. Superimposed were the proportions of some of the main timbers, the stem, the keel, the horn timber, etc., scaled up from the construction drawing. What a feeling of accomplishment we had when the vacation was over and the job was done!

Of course, our crusade was not a single-front affair. While we were lofting and drawing in the gym, we were also preparing for the next steps in the construction. Time in Wilbraham was precious. I tried to do as much groundwork as I could at odd moments during each week in Cambridge. Procurement of suitable materials at reasonable prices was a great challenge and preoccupation. In those days, there was no

Woodenboat magazine, rife with enticing ads to encourage the amateur boat builder. The mid-1960's was the nadir of wooden boat building. The old yards and nautical suppliers were going out of business. The revival was yet to come.

Fortune often favors the foolhardy, including the amateur boat builder. We certainly received our share of fortune's favors. One example was the oak for the backbone and frames of our stout and sturdy craft. White oak was what we wanted. We had read enough in Chapelle and otherwise to know that "*quercus alba*" is decidedly superior to its red, gray, or even black cousins as a material for boatbuilding. We saw in *The Rudder* magazine (then still in publication) advertisements for a yard in White Plains, New York, M.L. Condon, that offered white oak timber for boat building. But we could afford neither Condon's prices nor the shipping costs from White Plains.

We somehow got the name of a local sawyer from Hampden, Massachusetts, who, it was said, could provide white oak. Harold Koncitek was an unlikely patron saint for our project. But he was one of many, whose amiable understanding and helpful support became vital to making our dream come true.

I had prepared from the plans a long list of dimensioned white oak timber. According to the boatbuilding books, it had to be seasoned for two or three years, preferably by immersion in salt water. When I mentioned this requirement to Mr. Koncitek, he looked at me and laughed. Everything he was cutting was green. I called Mr. Crockett. Could we use green oak despite the warnings of Chapelle? Crockett acknowledged that seasoned oak was best but that boatyards in Maine had been using green oak for years. "Go ahead".

So it happened that Harold Koncitek cut for us the necessary timber for the backbones, frames and deck beams of *Serendipity* from the woods of western Massachusetts. We gave Mr. Koncitek the order in March of 1965. Chapelle warned never to use sappy oak cut in the spring, but we disregarded that one, too. While we lofted, he cut.

At that time, Mr. Koncitek was cutting oak on wood lots in the Berkshires, sawing up the largely red oak for shipping pallets. But every once in a while he would come upon an oak tree that had round leaf lobes instead of sharp. Those he set aside for us.

Mr. Koncitek must have taken some kind of interest in our project, although his gruff personality would never let him admit it. The oak he brought to us in April of 1965 was beautiful. We marveled at the heavy, sweet-sour smelling, rough-sawn timbers as we unloaded them from his old truck and stacked them, "stickered", in a corner of the yard. First of all, there were the 4-, 5- and 6-inch by 10-, 12-, and 15-inch timbers for stem, knee (yes, he even gave us a "sweep" for the knee), and horn timber. Then there was the 2-inch stock for the deck beams, sawn a little full in 6-inch wide planks to allow for the crown. There was the framing stock, sawn 1-5/8 inch by 4 inches, which would provide two frames per plank after ripping and planing. There were other miscellaneous boards, all of which had been carefully included on my list. All of it was "clear," that is without knots or serious blemishes. The heavy timbers boxed the hearts of their trees. The framing timbers were, as requested, quarter-sawn.

The most difficult, of course, was the keel. He told us he had cut down five large white oaks before he found one which would yield from its heart a straight timber 6" by 10" by 21 feet long. The price we paid for all this beautiful white oak was fifteen cents per board foot - twenty cents per foot for the keel.

Once we had the oak, however, we faced the problem of how to preserve it. "Checking", the cracking of the wood from shrinkage during drying, was the hazard we worried about. Lots of linseed oil was the answer. The books conflicted on whether "raw" or "boiled" was better. We used

29

both.   Almost immediately, all of the oak was painted and slopped with gallons of linseed oil.

We found a spot for the smaller timbers in the garage out of the sun. The keel was too long. The best we could do was to put it out on sawhorses at the building site in the field behind my parents' house and cover it up with a piece of tarpaper. There it would have to sit, for months, until the fall or even later, when we would be ready to form these raw timbers into the skeleton of our dream ship.

In April 1965, we undertook the first tangible construction of the boat itself, or at least a pattern for it. The plans called for a 4800 lb. cast iron heel running nearly full length, bolted to the wood keel with 3/4-inch galvanized bolts. The books told us that we had to construct a pattern for the keel (a little larger than the finished dimensions to allow for shrinkage), which could be used by the foundry to form the sand mold for the molten iron. Starting with our rolled up loft drawing, we "took off" a paper pattern of the ballast keel by punching little holes along the outline into a second sheet of building paper beneath and then "connecting the dots" to make the pattern. These dimensions were adjusted by the shrinkage factor.   At one point, in the bow, there appeared to be an ambiguity in the plans. Was it intended that the wood keel would taper between the rabbet and the top of the iron keel? Or was the top of the iron keel to be the same width as the rabbet with the taper in the iron? We resolved the issue in favor of the former. The sides of our iron keel pattern forward were almost parallel with very little "drag". The cross section was more trapezoidal going aft.

Apparently building a pattern, even a large one, is usually done in a "bread and butter" fashion with successive layers of solid wood laminated or screwed together to reach the desired thickness and dimension. Being ignorant of pattern making, we proceeded to make our pattern as a hollow plywood box, fortunately well reinforced. My mathematical

We are about to depart for the foundry with our keel pattern. In the background is our small workshop. The pattern is lashed to the boat trailer from my old sailboat, *Te Amo.*

ability (or inability) had all it could do to figure out the adjustments we had to make in order to get a pattern with just the right dimensions so that the iron after shrinkage would be right.

In those days, New England foundries willing to cast iron keels were few and far between. However, the Reid Foundry in Amesbury, Massachusetts, was not only willing, it solicited the business by an ad in the *National Fisherman.* So, one day in late April, Anita and I pulled up at the Reid Foundry yard in Amesbury trailing a light boat trailer bearing our plywood keel pattern.

It didn't take long for the foundry man to tell us that we had done it all wrong. The plywood pattern was probably too flimsy. There was probably not enough drag in the forward part to permit the pattern to be removed from the mold. Why hadn't we painted or varnished the pattern so the sand would not dry out on us? And where were the blocks for the core

31

boxes? "Core boxes?" At the time we had built our pattern, we had been oblivious of the need to create indentations in the sand mold (by means of small blocks on the pattern) for the foundry men to locate the sand "cores" which would form the holes for the keel bolts through the iron. I guess we had assumed that they would probably be drilled. Of course, we were wrong. And the chief of the foundry men let us know it.

Ultimately, he, like many others, took pity on us. No, we did not have to bring our beautiful new pattern all the way back home. He figured he probably could cope with the lack of drag on the pattern. Somehow he would figure out how to handle the cores. We should come back in a week. Our two-and-a-half-ton keel would be ready then.

All boat owners, and particularly amateur boat builders, know the thrill and impatience of anticipation, while some major part of the project is being done by others. Needless to say, we could scarcely wait for the week to pass. Finally, on the appointed day, I called the foundry. Was our keel ready? Yes, it was, although it had come out light. "What do you mean, 'light'?" "Well, it only weighs 4,100 pounds instead of the 4,800 pounds specified". As I spoke on the phone, I ran with cold sweat. What was wrong? It must been our pattern. Somehow, we had failed accurately to reproduce some dimension. Our new keel, the first piece of our actual boat, was wrong.

The culprit, I figured, was the bow. I had been wrong to assume that the taper was in the wood keel rather than the iron. We called Crockett. He confirmed the error. How I wished I had called him before I had made that pattern! Our bow was 600 or 700 pounds light. What should we do? Should we make a new pattern and a new iron keel? It wasn't the foundry man's fault. He was not about to try again for free.

Crockett's counsel prevailed. We were not to worry. If it was too light, we could put a few hundred pounds of inside ballast forward.

We were somewhat deflated when we went to get the keel. Instead of the little sailboat trailer, we brought a 2-1/2-ton rented stake truck. The keel was loaded at the foundry with a huge chain fall. Everything looked fine. The outside had been ground to some semblance of smoothness. The holes for the 3/4-inch bolts were all neat and clean with little square countersinks on the bottom for the heads. But I fought back the tears. The keel was too light . . .

When we arrived back in Wilbraham that May afternoon (I took the day off from classes), we found that my mother's field had been newly plowed. In one corner was a stack of a half a dozen red oak 4 x 4's, which Mr. Koncitek had

We unloaded the 2+ ton iron keel by driving out from under it. Here we have levered it up onto some oak cross timbers.

included with his last shipment. They would be the sleepers for our cradle. We unloaded the 2-plus ton monster the only way we could. I drove the rented truck out into the field, chained one end of the keel to an apple tree not far from the edge of the field, and then rapidly drove the truck out from underneath the keel. It was just like pulling a tooth. The keel almost buried itself in the soft earth of the field. But neither truck nor keel was damaged and the job was done.

With a crowbar and some timbers, we moved the keel into position on its new bed of oak sleepers. It was amazing how much we could move with an 8-foot oak timber merely by positioning the fulcrum. Archimedes was our patron saint as we puffed and heaved. By the end of the afternoon, we had the keel dug out and lined up on six oak cross-ties. A coat of red Rustoleum was our final gesture. The iron monster gleamed as we drove back to Cambridge. The 700-lb flaw was all but forgotten, at least for the moment.

The new keel, freshly painted with Rustoleum anti-corrosion paint sits on its oak sleepers in the freshly plowed garden. The tarpaper covers the newly-arrived 6" x 10" white oak keel timber from Mr. Koncitek. More fresh white oak lumber is piled in the background.

By the time we got our new gleaming red ballast keel set up on the sleepers, it was nearly summer. I was committed to work the whole summer of '65 at the yacht club in Prouts Neck. There was just enough time to set the sleepers up on skids (red oak supplied by Mr. Koncitek) and run a tight wire center line between stakes driven in fore and aft. This gave us a base line for centering the remaining timbers of the boat and establishing their altitudes. We were then ready to address the shaping of the massive wooden keel timber.

Although molded six inches its entire length, the width of the oak keel varied from a maximum of 10 inches to a minimum of approximately four inches at either end. With the help of the loft drawing, rolled out on the lawn, we were able to replicate on the glistening and linseed-soaked oak the lines we had drawn off on the gym floor a couple of months before.

We then realized the extent of our naivete and our unpreparedness. We had absolutely no tools (or ability, for that matter) to work this massive oak beam from a square timber into a delicately curved and tapered wood keel which would exactly fit along the top of the iron keel and accurately join the other members to which it would be bolted. The books, of course, blithely mentioned band-sawing and hewing with an adze or broad axe. But we could not afford a bandsaw. Those were the days before the revivals in wooden boat building and woodworking tool manufacture. Adzes and broad axes were simply not to be had. And I distrusted my ability to use such exotic edged implements without amputating fingers or toes.

Trying to shape that great oak keel was undoubtedly the most discouraging episode of the early stages of building *Serendipity*. Initially, we chewed away the excess timber by various makeshift means. The small hardware store in the center of Wilbraham was a resource for common tools, steel fasteners and other last-minute items. The store also rented less common tools, including a small electric chain saw. Maybe we could use this to taper our massive keel timber?

We first took the width measurements of the keel at various stations and transferred them to the timber. Faired together, they made an acceptable guide to cutting down the keel. The chain saw, however, was a crude and unreliable tool. Six inches of oak was probably beyond its ripping capacity. At

Trying to shape the 6" x 10" oak timber into a tapered keel with a 12" electric chainsaw was a frustrating and ultimately feckless task.

any rate, it could not cleave to a line, and would wander alarmingly as it gnawed lengthwise along the timber. It soon became clear that we could use this crude tool only to reach the roughest approximation of a keel, and that we would have to reach the pattern line in some other way.

After a day of frustrating, sweating, anxious labor, we had chewed off a corner of the bulky timber. However, our chewed line bore no resemblance to the smooth curve we had drawn on the oak from the loft plan.

Only the young have enough enthusiasm to overcome setbacks like these. At the end of our last weekend in Wilbraham, I returned the rented electric chain saw to the place from whence it came. Our keel timber was a ragged, jagged caricature of a keel. Had we ruined it beyond salvation? More seriously, how would this half-finished timber last the summer? Would it check, warp or twist beyond recognition while I was chafing away the summer at Prout's Neck? The best we could do was douse it with more linseed oil, carefully block it up, cover it, and hope . . . I would have all summer to figure out how we could try to make it into something.

At this point, May was upon us and my first-year finals at law school. We could not do much more on the boat before we would have to leave for my summer job at the Prout's Neck Yacht Club in Maine. (In those days, law students did not get legal summer jobs after their first year but had to do whatever they could. The Prout's Neck job, where I made $150 per week plus housing - more than I made per week in my first year of law practice. It was also a wonderful summer job – teaching sailing, running races and living pretty much on the water. My vision of a dream ship had been mightily nourished during the preceding summer at Prout's Neck.) Although we would have to shut down the building site in Wilbraham, we hoped to get needed supplies, fasteners and even tools at the various ship chandleries in Portland so we would be ready to go in the fall. We carefully covered the linseed-oil soaked oak lumber with tar paper, stacked the heavy timbers, similarly slathered with linseed, in the garage, and covered our new red keel with a strip of roofing paper and headed off for Maine.

The last thing that I did before leaving for Maine, was to source the heavy ¾" galvanized bolts specified to bolt the deep galvanized keel to the 6" x 10" oak keel. The yellow pages of the phone books were the first resort in those days before computers, the internet and Google would bring all products in the world to one's fingertips. The New England Bolt Company, Everett, Massachusetts seemed to be a likely spot. A phone call confirmed that they could provide ¾" galvanized machine bolts in any length. A trip to Everett with my list of bolt lengths measured from the red monster sitting in the garden resulted in a trunk-load of ¾" bolts, some as long as

24", complete with heavy nuts and big square washers. They were piled in the workshop in Wilbraham, awaiting resumption of work in the fall.

Of course, *Serendipity* was never far from my thoughts during that second summer at Prout's. We had the plans with us and showed them to anyone who was interested. I made long lists of supplies, fasteners, fittings, and various kinds of glues, compounds and gorps.

On a half-day off, I ventured into Portland to the two large ship-chandleries there, The Harris Company on Commercial Street and Sargent Lord & Company, nearby on Portland Pier. These were truly left-overs from a prior age. Sargent, Lord, in particular, evoked a feeling of 19th Century seafaring and reeked with the smell of tar. Would it be possible for me to purchase bolts, screws, fittings, glue, paint and other marine supplies needed to build *Serendipity* on a wholesale basis?

In those days, there were no marine discounters such as West Products or Defenders. Retail customers purchased their marine fittings and supplies from dealers such as James Bliss & Co. in Boston, or Inland Marine, run by my friend Len Preston, in Springfield, inevitably at hefty list prices. Professional boat builders, however, were usually able to buy directly from distributors and at discounts of up to 40% or even 50% off list prices. The ability to buy at wholesale would thus mean a lot to my ability to afford to complete this project so audaciously started.

Some amateurs tried to get on the discount schedule by using a professional looking letterhead. "So and So Boatshop", and by hinting to suppliers that they were in the business. This did not appeal to me. My approach was to go to the suppliers, tell them about my project, and simply ask if they would sell to me at wholesale prices. It did not always work – some suppliers felt constrained by their own distributorship arrangements to protect their own dealers and turned me down.

Such was the case with the Harris Company, then Portland's largest and most successful marine supplier.

Marshall Madsen, manager of the smaller Sargent Lord & Co., did not have the same compunctions. He was willing to give me the same prices as he gave to any of his other fisherman or boat builder customers. Because his inventory was smaller, frequently he would have to order himself from his suppliers in order to fill my orders. But, ultimately, over the years of the building of *Serendipity*, Sargent Lord became my default supplier of marine fasteners and supplies. During the summer of 1965, we stocked up on twelve-foot lengths of galvanized rod together with "clinch rings". From these, we would fashion "drift bolts", which function like giant spikes to pin the heaviest of backbone timbers together. We also bought boxes of various sizes of galvanized bolts to connect the smaller back-bone members, strips of canvas in which to bed the wood keel to the iron, the necessary bedding compound, and a quantity of the new-fangled two-part epoxy glue, which claimed to create the strongest and most durable wood to wood bonds then known.

Although as a young law student, I scarcely had a credit rating or history, in those days business was done in Maine on bases other than pure numbers. Mr. Madsen offered me a charge account at Sargent Lord, and I would order by phone from standard catalogs, including the thick Harris Company catalog. After we had returned to Massachusetts, the orders continued. Recycled shipping boxes tied with twine regularly showed up at my parents' door. The laboriously typed bills were itemized down to the last screw, and were immediately paid.

There was one important *Serendipity*-related project for us to accomplish while we were in Maine that summer. The design called for a small auxiliary motor, a Palmer 4-cylinder gas engine of 22 hp. Because of the danger of fire, we were hoping to be able to install a diesel, if we could afford one, but that was all far in the future. What the presence of the engine meant was that we would have to bore a "shaft log" when we fashioned the backbone. I had pored over my ever more thoroughly thumbed copy of Chapelle and carefully read up on how to bore a shaft log. It became increasingly clear that we totally lacked the tools, powerful drills and long ships-augur bits, or "boring bars", even if we could muster the ability, to drill a 1¼" hole perfectly straight lengthwise through the center of a 6" x 6" oak timber some 26" long. But maybe one of the old boatyards in Portland could do this for us?

We were referred to Story Marine Railway, on the South Portland shore of Portland Harbor. Could they make for us a 6" x 6" x 26" shaft log, bored 1¼" lengthwise out of white oak? Yes, they could, if they had the oak. Red oak they had aplenty, but white oak was no longer in use in Maine boatyards. It had pretty much been stripped from the land in the prior two centuries of wooden boatbuilding.

Was there any place we could get some white oak, we asked? We wanted to stick with white oak, because we had read of its greatly superior resistance to rot. (This decision had recompensed itself over the years – now 49 years after its build *Serendipity's* backbone remains free of rot and is hard as iron.) Well, there was someone cutting oak in Saco. Maybe he would come upon a stray white oak from which he could cut a short 6 x 6 piece for our shaft log.

One day, we found ourselves off in the back woods of Saco, where a man with a portable sawmill was sawing up red oak trees to make, guess what, pallets. (We learned that shipping pallets consume an enormous quantity of red oak.) There was little white oak to be found in Maine, even at that time. Only a stray tree here or there had escaped the notice of boat builders of prior generations. It was doubtful whether he could find one big enough for a sound shaft lot. But he was willing to try. We should come back in a week.

We came back the next week. He had tried a few trees, but had not found anything. It didn't look good. I suppose we should have gone away. But we were determined to get that shaft log done while we were in Maine. Could we help him look among his woodpiles for likely candidates?

We found three or four logs of white oak lying around his wood yard, heaved them on to the saw carriage, and then watched as they were sawn into square timber. None was quite right. Mostly it was rot, knots, too much sap wood, or some other imperfection. Finally, we found a big one. Surely this would yield a suitable shaft lot. The saw cut off first one side and then another, squaring the log into a timber. We watched anxiously for signs of rot or imperfection. There were none. Triumphantly, we bore the rough-sawn 6 x 6, hanging out of the rear of our little red Rambler, off to Story's in South Portland.

We took it to the wood shop, a dark place in a decrepit shed, filled with ancient wood planers, saws and other tools of wooden boatbuilding. At that time, these tools were seeing little use. Although Story had done a brisk business in building wood minesweepers during the Korean War, since then it had fallen into a decaying torpor with only an occasional fishing boat repair on its moldering ways. Two ancient carpenters took our timber in hand. As we watched, fascinated, they set it up in a long horizontal boring machine, which bored the center hole. They then squared up the ends and planed it to exact 6" x 6" dimensions – bingo, we had our shaft log. Although twenty - six dollars seemed like a lot of money then, we were glad to pay it. We doused our timber with linseed oil and put it away in a corner of our Prout's Neck apartment until we would be able to bring it to Wilbraham at the end of the summer.

One day during that summer at Prout's Neck, I was standing on the Yacht Club deck chatting with Richard Wolfe, one of the members of the club. Wolfe was a successful auto dealer in South Portland, Maine who showed some interest in

41

the young yacht club manager. Where was I going to practice law? he asked. "Probably in Boston," I replied. He paused for a moment, "Do you know, there are some very good lawyers in Portland?" I did not know. To me, Portland, Maine was a nearby small city where I went to get paint and boat supplies, hardly a place to make a legal career.

But the words stuck, and months later, when looking at the law school's bulletin board for summer employment, a notice by a Portland, Maine firm seeking a summer clerk caught my eye. The rest of the story, of course, is history.

Needless to say, that second summer at Prout's Neck seemed a lot longer than the first. Finally, however, September came. With our precious shaft log in the trunk and other tools and supplies crammed into every corner of our little red Rambler, we headed back to Cambridge for law school, and to Wilbraham for boatbuilding.

Among our new acquisitions was a large two inch wood chisel. Chapelle and the other books frequently mentioned a "slick" for large heavy chiseling jobs on boat timbers. A slick is a giant chisel with a long handle to shape large timbers, However, in the mid-1960s, such tools were no longer in production and virtually impossible to obtain. The two inch chisel was the closest we could get to what had been described. Maybe this tool would enable us to clean up the botched job from the electric chain saw and smoothly shape our keel . . .

Chapter 3

Anxiety was running high as we drove into the yard at Wilbraham on our first visit at the end of the summer. The plowed field had grown up weeds. Our slightly weathered iron keel was nearly invisible. Over to the side was the long black form of the covered wood keel. Would it be irreparably checked, warped and twisted? It had been a hot summer. What kind of havoc had the heat wrought on the bones of our dream ship?

A hurried inspection in the garage showed that only one of the many neatly stacked oak timbers there had suffered any serious checking. Anxiously we approached the keel timber on sawhorses in the field and peeled back the tar paper. God be praised, the ragged and misshapen keel appeared not to have suffered from the ravages of dessication. Or had it? I anxiously squinted down its irregular length, seeking to detect any slight twisting or warping. It was impossible to tell . . . it must be all right.

With renewed energy, we attacked the job of smoothing and shaping the keel. Although our new two-inch chisel was pretty puny for the job, it was all we had. With an old mallet from the barn, I laboriously chipped away at the roughly sawn timber to shape what became *Serendipity's* keel. The work was complicated by the need to form the keel timber to mate with the incorrectly-measured top of the iron keel forward. Frequently we had to test to see how the shape of the wood keel conformed to our iron ballast keel by hoisting the heavy wood keel in place on top of the iron. There was a lot of chipping, measuring, and trying over more than one weekend before we had carved what would pass for a keel from our original 6" x 10" oak timber. Finally it was close, close enough

43

so that final sanding and shaping could be done after the keels had been bolted together.

When we returned to Wilbraham to start work on *Serendipity's* backbone in the fall of 1965, we had to confront an unpleasant reality. We had undertaken the building of a serious vessel with ludicrously inadequate tools. We had no bandsaw, no thickness planer, no drill press, not even a heavy sander. How were we going to form these 4" and 6" timbers rough-cut for us by Harold Koncitek into the curved stem, stem knee, horn timber and deadwood shown on the plans? Our puny tools were clearly not up to this task. Our experience with the wood keel convinced us that we needed help in shaping the other great oak timbers that would be bolted together to form *Serendipity's* backbone.

We turned to the Roy Lumber Company in Willimantic, near Chicopee, Massachusetts. Roy's was one of the last great lumber yards in the area, and dealt not only in softwoods for houses, but also carried some hardwood and offered milling services. Would they be willing to band-saw our oak timbers if we drew patterns on them? They seemed willing, as long as we would clearly indicate on the timbers where the cuts were to be made.

So we rolled out the plans and carefully took off patterns for the main timbers, the stem, the stem knee, the horn timber, and the various pieces of shaped and tapered deadwood that built up to the angled shaft log and the horn timber that was bolted on top of it. Taking a pattern off the loft drawing involved placing a piece of building paper under the loft drawing in the area in which the pattern was to be taken. We would then prick nail holes through the loft drawing into the pattern blank to define the corners of the pattern, or the arc of curved pieces. We would then withdraw the pattern piece, "connect the dots" to duplicate the loft drawing, cut it out and fit it over the loft drawing as a check. It was a laborious

44

Here Anita is pricking through the loft plan to transfer a line of dots to a piece of building paper underneath. By connecting the dots,we could make a pattern for the piece we needed.

process, but was the only way we could figure out to replicate the information on the loft drawing in a usable pattern.

We carefully drew the patterns on the various timbers, most of which had survived the summer without any of the dreaded checking. One piece had checked badly, but we had a couple of spares. The Roy truck came by and picked up the timbers to be band-sawed in the shop at Willimantic.

A week later, our band-sawn timbers returned from Roy's. All were exactly as we hoped they would be – with one exception. On one piece of "deadwood", we had drawn a centerline when we had set up the pattern. The sawyer had taken the centerline as a line to be cut, so that we had one piece of deadwood that was cut in two halves. It was clear that it was our fault, but Roy was kind enough to re-saw the piece out of a spare bit of timber without additional charge.

Once we had a more or less shaped keel timber, we had to join it to the iron keel sitting in the late summer weeds in the garden. How were we going to line up the holes in the wood keel with the precast holes in the iron keel so that they would take the ¾" bolts? The answer was, of course, "bore from the bottom" up through the holes in the iron keel into the wood keel above. So, we dug a hole in the earth under each of the 9 holes in the cast iron ballast keel. Lying on my back, with my shoulder in the hole and my head under the iron keel, I slid a ¾" spade drill on an extender bought at the hardware store up through the hole in the iron keel, chucked on my 3/8" Sears drill and pushed upward as hard as I could as the drill laboriously bit into the oak above. Only young men driven by obsession have the strength and endurance to work in such contortions. The weak drill cut painfully slowly. It became hot in my hand. It smoked and smelled. But it cut. Gradually, one by one, the crucial holes were bored.

Here you can see me lying under the keel boring upward into the wood keel with our trusty 3/8" Craftsman wood drill - a slow hot, and uncomfortable job. But we got it done!

46

Building a boat requires that everything be done in a certain order. One has to plan for future steps as every step is being completed. For instance, before we could bolt the new keel to the cast iron ballast keel, we had to check to see what was in turn bolted to it. We would have to install the bolts for the stem knee, some of the deadwood and shaft log, and the future floor timbers that would be fastened to the keel before bolting the keel to the iron ballast keel. This step is simplified in many boatyards by fitting the ballast keel, but not bolting it to the wood superstructure until a late stage in the building process. This allows through connections in the wood to be made without interference. Our plan, however, was to build the boat from the ballast keel up, so we had to make sure that all connections were in place before we bolted the wood keel to it.

Anita is sanding the edge of the wood keel with a 1957? Craftsman 6" disc sander given us by her parents. Note the pairs of 3/8" bolts already installed in the keel to hold the floor timbers.

47

The result was more trips to the loft plan, measuring, re-measuring and checking again. I tried to visualize how each member would be connected to the next and how we would line up the new members with the bolts we were pre-installing to fasten them down. The process would make my head spin, not only weekends on the job site, but during the week as I thought through upcoming steps in the building process during my law school classes. My Constitutional Law professor was the eminent Paul Freund, one of the leading constitutional scholars of his day. My notes from his course are filled not with his pithy insights into our living Constitution, but with small sketches of upcoming boat building details and with lists of measurements or materials.

By the time we were ready to bolt the wood keel to the iron keel below, the wood keel was bristling with bolts of various sizes waiting to join additional members to the backbone. Wedge-shaped deadwood timbers filled the gap between iron and wood keel aft, where the iron keel tapered to its heel. The whole thing was very heavy.

One of the final jobs before we tied the whole business together was to rough out the rabbet on the wood keel. The rabbet is a deep groove along each side of the wood keel designed to take the edge of the garboard planks. The rabbet. How long did I agonize over that relatively inconsequential step in the building of a wooden ship? But it had to be just right. The angle of the cut in the stem along the keel had to be set so that it would accommodate the angle of the edges of planks as they met the backbone. With nothing in place but the keel itself and with the stem lying in the shop, it was pretty hard to visualize what the groove should look like and how it should be cut.

Chapelle had written something about taking the bevels off the loft plan as if that was something everyone knew how to do. I did not. Eventually, by studying the loft plan and by fiddling around with an old carpenter's T-bevel, I had some idea of the angle and depths of cuts. The cuts became grooves. Gradually, we seemed to get the hang of it. I invested a few dollars in a cheap "rabbet plane" designed to plane grooves and indentations in wood. By using it and the trusty 2" chisel, I finally made a groove that would serve. We left a little extra wood to be dressed up when the thing was all bolted together and we were ready to start planking.

Everyone knows that the curse of the wooden boat builder is rot. I anxiously read all that I could on the subject matter. Nobody seemed to know exactly what caused rot or what would stop it. The consensus seemed to recommend "Cuprinol" wood preservative and lots of it. I bought it by the gallon from Sargent, Lord. We doused everything in it, again and again. I never thought I would get the green off my skin. Although there was a clear version, I couldn't believe it was as potent as the old green stuff, with its characteristic smell. So before, during and after the installation of every piece, Cuprinol was liberally applied.

The massive timbers of *Serendipity's* backbone were bolted together with 1/2" galvanized bolts and "bedded" in epoxy glue. Epoxy was just becoming known in the boatbuilding business in the mid-'60's. I was impressed with its strength and gap-filling characteristics. By contrast, traditional oil based bedding compounds seemed very inadequate.

"Stopwaters" were specified by both the designer and Chapelle. These are small dowels driven crosswise through any joints in the backbone to prevent water from seeping in through the joints. The pine dowels specified by Chappelle, however, were impossible to procure. Ordinary birch dowels would have to do the trick.

We tried not to compromise with the best of boat building standards, because we did not know where we could compromise. We figured it was best to try to follow the book as closely as we could.

49

Here is the wood keel almost ready to be bolted to the iron keel. Anita is applying Cuprinol to prevent rot. Everything was coated with this preservative before being assembled.

It was a lot easier to fit the pre-band-sawed blocks of deadwood at the after end of the iron keel. A little triangular chunk fit in forward. There were more tries. Each time the whole assembly became heavier.

The day finally arrived when we could bolt the wood keel and attached dead wood to the iron keel. We smeared the canvas strips bought at Sargent, Lord that summer not with white lead, as recommended by Chapelle (1948), but with a more modern oil-based bedding compound. The strips were to fill the joint between wood and iron. The idea was to have a flexible joint that could accommodate the expansion and contraction of the wood keel as it soaked up and dried out on a seasonal basis.

We deepened the holes under the iron keel so that we could drive the long ¾" bolts up through the iron keel, and then through the painfully-drilled holes in the wood keel to be crowned with large square washers and nuts. Tightening the nuts until the bedding squeezed out of the joint between iron and wood, gave us a very satisfying sense of accomplishment. At last, we had joined some of the major members of the boat.

Here we admire progress to date. The keel has been bolted to the ballast keel and two pieces of "deadwood" have been added at the stern. The groove of the rabbet and the bolts for the floor timbers are visible. It is late fall, 1965.

As fall deepened into early winter, we retreated into our tiny 12' x 12' workshop attached to my parents' barn. The barn itself was not available to us – it was chock-a-block full of books. In order to gain work space in the shed, I had built many feet of bookshelves in my parents' cellar and upstairs in the barn to store the books that had been in the workshop.

In the workshop, we turned to a special challenge – building the curved and shaped transom. Transoms are some of the hardest-to-get-right features of wooden boats. Designers sometimes take pity on builders and make flat transoms that are more or less vertical. This was not the case with Mr. Crockett. The transom in his *Nimble* design was an

51

attractive curved and raked one that would look great in the water, but would cost us sleepless nights and torn hair to build.

We started, of course, with the loft plan, on which we superimposed the structures of a transom knee and a transom to be connected to the upper end of the horn timber. The transom knee had been band-sawn by Roy to the correct angle. But "developing" patterns for the transom itself was fiendishly difficult.

Although we had not yet confronted the task of sourcing the lumber to plank *Serendipity*, the specifications called for Philippine mahogany, planed to 1 1/8" in thickness. The Boston yellow pages listed two sources of mahogany lumber in Eastern Massachusetts, the Palmer and Parker Company and the Winde-McCormick Company, both then located in Charlestown, Massachusetts on the Mystic River. We got the relatively small amount of mahogany that we needed for the transom from Palmer and Parker, which specialized in the various species of wood that go by the name of "mahogany." Winde -McCormick was a larger yard and dealt in all kinds of lumber and timber.

At the time I went over to the Palmer and Parker yard, they had no Philippine mahogany (which is not a real mahogany anyway) in the requisite thickness, but were willing to sell me the more highly prized African mahogany at the Philippine price. Not knowing any better, I took the "good deal" offered, only to learn later that African mahogany is wonderful for furniture and interior woodwork, but softer and weaker than the Philippine "wannabe", and hence less suited for planking boats. Be that as it may, *Serendipity's* transom is of African mahogany and has held up well over the years.

The first job on the transom was building the oak frame. Using a pattern from the loft drawing, we sawed out and screwed together an oak frame in the dimensions we thought would work. This frame was then bolted to the small transom knee, which was bolted in turn to the horn timber.

Working from a loft drawing and trying to transfer the dimensions - "was it to the inside of the planking or to the outside of the planking?" - to patterns and then to pieces of lumber or assemblies is difficult for anyone. For us, it was mind-boggling. There was also the constant fear that we would get it wrong. And on one Sunday that fall, just after we had bolted together the horn timber and the transom frame and were driving back to Cambridge, suddenly a light went on. I had properly computed the dimensions of the transom to the inside of the planking, but then I somehow had subtracted the same factor from the horn timber. The transom was an inch and a half too low and too far forward! My stomach was in knots. Would we have to do the whole transom frame and horn timber over again?

All that week, I fussed and fumed. My notebook overflowed with drawings and calculations. Chagrin was the order of the day. By the end of the week, I had come to a tentative conclusion that if we merely unbolted the transom from the transom knee, added a spacer block and used longer bolts, it might come out right. But I would have to look at it to see. I bought the longer bolts anyway, in the hope that I was right.

I couldn't wait to measure the assembly when we got back to Wilbraham that next weekend. Had we made any irreparable mistake? Or was there a simple fix?

Fortunately for *Serendipity* and her builders there was a simple fix. A mahogany block could be inserted to make the desired change in the position of the transom without interfering with the strength and function of the members. New bolts were cheap at the cost. Half a day's work, and we were back on track again.

Snafus and re-dos are an integral part of amateur boat building. If you want to do it, you have to be prepared for many a broken plank and may repeats of defective work. It is all part and parcel of the adventure.

Transom form, steam box, and wallpaper steamer, ready to go.

Planking the transom, however, was one of those jobs that was "easier said than done." According to Chapelle, the planks comprising the transom should be joined by small pine splines glued in grooves in the edges of the planks. First of all, we cut out the four mahogany transom planks from the 1-1/8" African mahogany boards I had picked up at Palmer and Parker. Cutting the spline groove with the ancient table saw was no major task. Somewhere I found some small pine battens which would serve as splines.

The problem, though, was the bending. Following the book again, we had constructed a form for bending the transom plank. Using a radius slightly smaller than that of the transom, we cut 2" x 6" forms to which we nailed a series of 2 x 4's as cleats. However, dry planks would not bend to the curvature specified. We would have to make them more flexible by steaming them. We would clamp the transom planks hot from the steamer to the curved form. They would then cool to something resembling the proper curvature.

To the uninitiated, steam-bending sounds like an arcane and esoteric art, the preserve of the expert, a major undertaking in the course of boat construction. We read in Chapelle the various alternatives. We could use a steam box, or a boiler made from pipe, or some kind of tank contraption to make our oak frames and mahogany planks limber and soft for bending. Ultimately, our solution was simple. I constructed a rectangular steam box from cheap rough lumber. Twelve feet long and about a foot square, it had a door in one end with crude gasketing. Dowels driven through both sides served as racks for the boards.

The source of steam, however, was my ingenious contribution. Rather than rig some kind of temporary boiler or teakettle on the stove, we merely rented from the hardware store a small wallpaper steamer which we connected to the steam box. For $1.25 a day (1966 rates) plus kerosene, we had an unending source of prime steam.

Mahogany, however, does not steam like oak. Our first experiments with steaming did not go well. As I cautiously applied the clamps to the first steaming dripping piece of mahogany, we found that 2-1/2 hours of hot steam had not done much good. Resisting us every centimeter of the way, the plank broke with a loud crack after we had screwed it about half-way down. On the second attempt, we soaked the plank overnight in water and then steamed it longer. Slow application of clamps aided by hot towels during the process brought that one down on the form.

We ultimately got our four bent planks, after breaking only two. But if mahogany steaming was so difficult, how much more difficult would it be to get the oak frames limber enough to assume the rather dramatic curves of *Serendipity's* ribs?

A word is in order about the patience of the parents. During the spring and fall of '65, we had initiated a pattern of arriving in Wilbraham every Friday evening, working feverishly all day Saturday and Sunday, and driving back to Cambridge on Sunday night. Nothing, of course, could interfere with the work on the boat. By the time I arrived each Friday night, I was in a fever pitch of anticipation. Not a moment could be wasted. From early morning until late supper, the work went on. The parents, however, took it all very much in stride. Mother provided three meals a day at regular hours. Both parents stopped by from time to time to admire the work in progress. They were patient with my testiness in tough spots and were liberal in their praise when things seemed to be going well.

The transom was our first opportunity to make use of the beautiful 2" x 12 silicon bronze flat head wood screws that we had been buying from Sargent, Lord and Company to fasten the *Serendipity's* planks to her frames. Products of the Whitney Screw Works, of Nashua, New Hampshire, the bronze screws we used in *Serendipity* were examples of the best New England manufacture. They were cut from first quality silicon bronze stock, sharp, strong and durable. But they were expensive! I can still remember the price, $10.78 per hundred, a little more than 10 cents per screw. I got a few boxes to start with, but knew that we would have to find another solution for the more than 5000 fastenings we would need for the rest of the hull planking.

When we bored for screws, both in the transom and later on throughout the structure of the boat, we used tapered drill bits that had been recently devised and perfected by Warren Fuller, of the Fuller Manufacturing Company, Warren, Rhode Island. Previously, drilling pilot holes properly tapered to receive wood screws had required either expensive pilot hole bits each size and length of screw or by using a succession of straight drills of decreasing diameters to create a hole best suited to tapered wood screws. Fuller, however, manufactured wood bits that were tapered and had countersinks and counter-bores that could be set at various depths on the drill bit with small set-screws. This simplified the boring of screw holes

Here is the transom frame with the lowest transom plank clamped in place while I secure it permanently with bronze screws.

immensely. I soon became one of Warren Fuller's many satisfied customers.

The transom also gave us the opportunity to plug the counter-bored screw holes in the odoriferous African mahogany with ½" mahogany plugs, which we then sanded flush to conceal entirely the heads of the screws. This gave us a great sense of satisfaction, to be creating at least a small part of the finished skin of our dream ship.

As the weather got colder, we retreated into the little shop to fabricate the stem and the other components of the backbone. Our great keel assembly, bristling with bolts for future additions, lay in the garden on its 4 x 4 oak bearers.

Would it be spring before we were able to assemble the rest of the backbone? The limiting factor was not only cold and possible snow that would make it unpleasant to work outside. What might prevent further backbone progress until spring, was our decision to join the backbone members not only with the ½" galvanized carriage and drift bolts we had bought at Sargent, Lord during the summer, but also with the new-fangled epoxy glue. This was probably an unnecessary and possibly a counterproductive step. White lead or flexible bedding compound probably would have been just as good, maybe better, since no glue would be strong enough to resist the shrinking of the oak timbers as they dried out. But we did not know any better, and the instructions on the glue can said most definitely that the product was not to be applied at a temperature lower than 50 degrees Fahrenheit.

A few warm days in the fall enabled us to add the next layer of deadwood and the shaft log to the keel. At this stage, we learned how to drive drift bolts. Drift bolts are bolts in name only. They act more like long spikes, holding by friction in deep holes rather than with a nut. Drift bolts are used to join large and heavy wood backbone members in situations where it is impossible to through-bolt. The idea is to drill a hole through (or deep into) the members to be joined of a diameter 1/16 of an inch smaller than the size of the drift bolt, cut a piece of galvanized rod to the length of the hole, fit a galvanized clinch ring (rather like a thick, tight fitting washer) over one end, peen that end over so that the ring forms a kind of head to the bolt, grind a dull point on the other end, and then drive the drift bolt down into the hole with a sledge-hammer. The bolt has to be exactly the right length. If it is too long, then it might bottom out in the hole before the ring is driven flush. And heaven help if a glancing blow of the sledge might bend the bolt being driven! Once driven, a drift bolt cannot be extracted. We followed Chapelle's detailed instructions as we joined together the various pieces of white oak deadwood crowned by our shaft log from Maine in the stern. The joints were liberally buttered with epoxy - that did harden, despite sometimes marginal building temperatures.

In the workshop. The stem knee has been glued to the stem and bolted with half-inch galvanized bolts. It is being clamped with our newly-acquired bar clamps.

In late November and early December, we turned our efforts to fabricating *Serendipity's* stem, the sturdy oak timber that would become the bow of our dream ship and cut the waters in which she would sail. The bow of our noble craft consisted of three heavy pieces of oak. There was the stem timber itself, cut out of a slab of white oak 4" thick by 12" wide by 8 feet long. The forward edge of this piece had a graceful "S' curve – *Serendipity* was designed with a "clipper bow". The other two pieces of the stem assembly were the massive stem knee, cut from a piece of oak with a gentle curve in the grain, designed to join the stem timber to the keel, and the gammon piece, that would extend the graceful curve of the bow under the bowsprit. These had been rough-cut by the Roy Lumber Co. They now had to be carefully planed so that their "faying" or joining surfaces would fit so tightly together that from the outside they would seem like a single piece of wood.

Once the stem assembly had been bolted and glued together (there was no problem with temperature in the workshop), we had the two ends of *Serendipity's* backbone ready. For lack of space elsewhere, we stored them on my parents' side porch. What visitors must have thought when they came to the door!

Serendipity's horn timber and transom on the side porch ready for installation when weather permits.

Often during long stretches in the little shop, as I worked along, cutting, drilling, chiseling, smoothing, or gluing, Anita would keep spirits jolly by reading aloud from a corner by the stove. In that fashion, I got my second exposure to many works of Thornton Burgess, a children's writer whom I had first read as a small child 15 years or more before.

Christmas Day 1965. Bolting the stem to the keel. Everyone helped.
Here are Anita (standing on the keel), my father, me, my brother Paul, and
our dog Spicy. Mother took the picture.

Although we had expected to have to wait until spring
to bolt our backbone together, Christmas 1965 brought us an
unexpected present. Although we had had snow in early
December, there was a thaw in the latter part of the month. We
anxiously watched our thermometers. Would the temperature
possibly reach 50 degrees? On Christmas Day itself, the
mercury crossed the magic line. We observed the usual
Christmas ceremonies early, and before the morning was far
advanced, were carrying our heavy backbone members out to
the garden.

One important issue in getting the backbone bolted
together was to align everything in a perfectly straight line.
When we had earlier bored the holes for the connecting bolts,
we had used a wire stretched between stakes in the ground
running fore and aft directly under the keel to line things up.
As we erected the stem and horn timber, we dropped a plumb

bob from the timber to the wire. Much to our relief, it hit our wire, or came mighty close.

Erecting the stem was a milestone in the building of *Serendipity*. The whole family helped. We smeared the faying surfaces with epoxy glue, lifted the massive timbers aloft, fit them over the bolts and turned down the nuts. *Serendipity* suddenly began to look like a ship. The graceful prow rising in the air reminded us of Viking ships, or perhaps dragons. We stood back and admired.

One of the many boatbuilding books I read in those days, stressed the importance of taking time during the process of building a boat to admire the work that had been accomplished at every stage. We took that to heart. One of the great pleasures for us in building *Serendipity*, was stopping to admire what we had done. "To think that we did that!"

Once we had erected the stem, we braced it against possible warping in the weather, but did not wrap it up or otherwise protect it against the weather. As we installed the backbone and bolted everything together, however, we doused everything liberally with Cuprinol.

It was later in the early spring that we got another warm weekend to bolt the horn timber to the shaft log. This involved driving two long drift bolts down through the 5"-thick horn timber, through the shaft log into the deadwood beneath. This was tricky. The bolts had to pass through the shaft log on each side of the bored shaft tunnel without penetrating either the tunnel or the outside surface of the shaft log.

For boring long holes for drift bolts and the like, we used 24" "barefoot ships augurs" that I had bought at the Harris Company the summer before. These long augur bits had no screw point to draw the augur into the wood (and possibly astray from a straight path). Instead one had to drill a starter hole with another drill, and then follow with the augur, carefully turning it with a brace by hand, always watching that the long bit remained precisely lined up. We could sometimes use a line-up jig consisting of a piece of scrap with a hole in it that could be so clamped as to keep the bit in line. Other times we had to do it by eye. How we sweated, as the cutter on the augur slowly bit deep into the heart of our precious timbers. This was a one-shot proposition. There would be no way that we could repair it, if we screwed up.

We were lucky. The two crucial holes for the horn timber drift bolts drove deep and true. They neither breached the shaft tunnel nor the surface of the timber. We were ready to drive the drifts.

Of course, the mistakes are always made on the easy parts. When we relax, we lose the fierce concentration that had attended the difficult challenges. It was this way with the horn timber. The first drift drove flawlessly, deep into the timber, right to its clinch-ring head and brought the timbers together

Raising the horn timber. I am driving one of the key drift bolts with a sledge hammer while neighbor Art Taylor and his son steady the work and look on.

until the epoxy glue squeezed out the crack between them. The second, however, was another matter. Although it seemed to drive well at first, when it came to the last two inches, for some reason it bound and would go no further. Maybe it had been slightly bent. Maybe the pilot hole had not been bored deeply enough. There was no going back. There was no way we could pull that drift bolt. I stared at the protruding 2" and the useless clinch ring.

Finally we made do, since we had to make do. I slid the clinch ring down flush with the wood and hack-sawed off the drift bolt just above the ring. Several mighty blows of the sledge peened the bolt over in place. I was relieved that the wood seemed to take up – the glue squeezed out of the crack. Although clumsy and botched looking, it seemed to work. Another of my many mistakes in building *Serendipity* had been forgiven.

One of my boatbuilding books recommended, "Do not think of the project as a whole. It will be too daunting. Just think of the next task to be done. When you have finished that, think of the next." I found this to be good advice. Disciplining myself to follow this advice made it possible to go from one task to another. As if by magic, *Serendipity* began to come into being.

From the very beginning, we had determined to record and memorialize our endeavor on film. I knew nothing of photography. Nor did Anita. Our equipment consisted of an early "Instamatic" and an earlier Brownie-type box camera which shot black and white roll snaps. We diluted a few Instamatic color pictures (30 cents per print) with several black and white snaps (8 cents per print), for variety, of course. My mother had an old fashioned camera that took larger black and white photos.

Throughout the project, the cameras were never far away. Most of the moments of triumph and many tedious tasks were captured this way. At least we had something to show

64

our friends in Cambridge what we were doing each weekend. Most of the pictures were taken by me and show Anita performing various tasks

We were able to sustain the dream, even during the long winter and spring of 1965-1966. Of course, the completion of the backbone was a great step forward. There it was out in the garden, looming like a great sea serpent above the rotting weeds and patches of snow of that mild New England winter. Each weekend, as we went forward with the next step of the procedure, we would wander out at least once or twice to look at the looming graceful curves of the backbone of our ship.

Serendipity's backbone viewed from the side in the snow.

Once we had the stem and the horn timber erected, *Serendipity* really began to look like a ship. But spring was late to come in 1966. We did not take too much time to admire what we had done before we launched into the next stage of the project, the cutting and setting of the moulds, around which our dream ship would take form.

Chapter 4

A conventionally built round-bilged vessel is given its shape by a series of temporary transverse frames called "moulds." Longitudinal battens, called "ribbands", are screwed to the moulds to create a kind of open, basket-like framework, inside which the wood frames are bent. As the vessel is planked, the ribbands are removed one by one. The planks are screwed to the bent frames, not the moulds. When the vessel is finally planked, all of the ribbands are gone. The moulds are then removed. And presto, you have a ship!

We were a long way from "presto!" In the late winter of 1966, there was still deep snow on the ground that

Here is one of our freshly cut out mould patterns - lying in in a cleared place in the snow in front of the garage.

practically covered our strong and noble keel, with the stem and horn timber protruding like the head and tail of some kind of sea serpent. But we could use this time to make the moulds and get them ready to be put in place when the weather would allow.

According to the books, the moulds are laid out from the full sized plans on the mould loft floor. Our workshop was too small even to unroll a small part of the giant rosin paper sheet. And outside, the snow had finally come - to the tune of about 6 inches. The basement meeting room of a local church provided the solution this time. I managed to secure some very cheap sheathing plywood, crummy on both sides. But it was good enough for patterns of the half cross-sections from the mould loft plan. We used the same technique, punching a

Anita marks the center line on the cross spall of one of the simpler moulds near the bow. It takes up most of the space in the workshop. Behind the mould, the stove-pipe for our tiny shop stove is visible. Fed with scraps, it kept the shop warm enough for us to work in.

series of holes along the pattern line and then "connecting the dots" with a light batten. The saber saw made short work of cutting out the thin plywood. We ended up with a half a cross section at each of the 10 mould stations.

Dragging the plywood patterns one at a time into the tiny workshop, we cut out the moulds themselves from some rough 1 1/4" #4 pine that I had seen at Roy's Lumber Yard when I had been there earlier about the band sawing. At about 12 cents a foot, the price was right. We avoided the knots as best we could.

Here I screw on gussets that join the two "futtocks" that constitute each half of a mould. They are being constructed on top of each other so that they will be exactly symmetrical.

Most of the moulds were too big to be assembled in the tiny shop. Were we going to wait until spring to put them

68

together? Of course not! Out came the snow shovel. A large square area was shoveled in front of the garage. On a couple of cold, clear weekend days, we screwed the mould- halves together and installed the cross spalls. One by one, the rough bulky moulds were finished.

It is a cold winter day, but work goes on. A large "midships" mould has been completed. Behind several boards of mould stock dry leaning against the shed. Spicy seems to approve of progress.

We lugged them up onto my parents' side porch to keep them out of the weather. It was cold as we worked. We wore gloves. Our breath congealed in the crisp winter air. The dog looked on quizzically.

The porch seemed cluttered now. A good part of it was occupied by the horn timber and the transom, which were awaiting another warm day so the epoxy glue would harden. The moulds took up the rest of the space. Neighbors and visitors had to thread their way through these odd and awkward looking pieces of furniture to get to the front door.

The transom assembly is to the left, several moulds too large for our limited storage space in the shop and garage are to the right. Visitors to my parents' home had to thread their way between boat assemblies waiting for installation.

But the sight made us proud. For here were the pieces of our dream ship, the actual backbone and curves of the form of the hull actually coming into shape. They fueled our fire.

In the meantime, on the materials procurement front, I was trying to figure out the problem of fastenings. After considering the virtues and drawbacks of the then available marine fasteners, I decided on silicon bronze screws. Galvanized screws or nails would have been cheaper. But we were building a dream ship for an eternity, not for short working life of a few years. Monel "Anchorfast" ring nails were also highly touted in the publications. But I didn't have enough faith in my ability to drive something perfectly the first time. And Anchorfast nails are awful hard to get out . . . The drawback, of course, to bronze screws is that they were expensive. And we needed about 4,500 2-inch #12 screws to hold the yet-to-be-purchased mahogany plank to the yet-to-be-bent white oak frames.

My friends at Sargent Lord in Maine were unable to be of much help. They themselves bought from a distributor and were unable to give me much of a discount. Of course, discount marine suppliers such as "Defender" and "E&B" were nonexistent in those days. I was ultimately able to convince an industrial supply company in Boston to sell me 4,000 2" x 12 Whitney bronze screws for a reasonable price. Seven cents apiece was what they ultimately cost, a large sum in those days.

Vere Crockett's specifications called for galvanized carriage bolts for bolting together the main members of the backbone, fastening the floor timbers to the frames, splicing the sheer clamp and bilge stringer, bolting down the toe rail, and eventual bolting of the sheer clamp and deck beams. But galvanized bolts would rust. Bronze bolts would not rust, but were much more expensive.

We ultimately compromised. Bolts of a diameter of

On a sunny day, Anita brushes the last of the snow off the transom. We are getting ready to set the moulds!

5/16" and greater would be galvanized. Bronze was simply too expensive in these larger sizes. It would also take some time for these larger bolts to rust away. However, for the many 1/4" bolts to fasten floor timbers and sheer clamp to the frames and the deck beams to the clamp, we dug deep to pay for a respectable stack of bronze carriage bolts of different lengths, all carefully figured out in my law school notes.

It gave us a good feeling to start accumulating these treasures. We had a special corner of the workshop for the growing stack of bronze fasteners, galvanized and bronze fittings, and the like. Every once in a while, I would look at them, turn the gleaming, machined copper-colored screws and bolts over in my fingers, and think of how strongly they would hold our dream ship together against the onslaught of the seas.

There is still snow on the ground as we set up the first mould - starting amidships - on the keel between the stem and the horn timber.

By March of 1966, our project had been underway for a year. To the uninitiated, we had not accomplished very much. All that there was to see was the keel stretched like some weird snake out in the field and a few odd-shaped parts on the porch. I am sure the nay-sayers felt confident that spring. But we knew better. In a few short weeks, as spring gradually came to southern New England, our awkward odd-shaped parts became a ship!

As soon as the deep winter began to yield to slushy cold pre-spring, we were out in the garden again. *Serendipity's* backbone was waiting for us. We stripped the tar paper off the keel and got ready to set the moulds on the backbone. We started in the middle. With level and plumb bob, we set the largest mould in place.

The rest of the moulds followed, lined up as best we could between our soaring stem and the center of the top of the transom. We secured each mould by screwing it to the keel

With the fitting of the last mould in the bow, one can really sense the shape of our ship!

and to a strong-back running along the tops of the cross spalls fore and aft from the tip of the stem to the top of the transom.

It took a single weekend to set the moulds. What a sight! Now we really could see what the hull of *Serendipity* would look like. We examined the skeleton from every angle. We concluded that Vere B. Crockett had designed a sweet, sweet hull. Somewhat more tentatively, we reassured ourselves that so far we had not fouled it up too much. Bursting with excitement, I clambered up on top of the strong-back and stood astride my vessel. What a shot in the arm that was . . . We were nearly buoyant as we drove back to Cambridge after that weekend.

We did not dare tarry too long to admire the shape of the moulds. After all, the moulds were only the temporary framework. We had to get to work on building the real ship! So we went to work on installing the ribbands.

The sheer ribbands describe a graceful line from bow to stern after a light spring snow.

The boatbuilding books all recommend that one use straight-grained softwood such as spruce or fir, which bends in smooth curves, to make ribbands. The problem was that we did not have any straight-grained softwood, and when we priced it at Roy, it seemed more expensive than we wanted to afford. What were we to do? Mr. Koncitek came through. *Serendipity* is undoubtedly one of the very few boats which was ribbanded with oak. He was happy to provide long, thin 16 and 18 foot 1 x 2 battens of green red oak at a price which can only be described as nominal - 10 cents a foot. Undoubtedly they were heavier and harder to handle than their soft wood cousins, but that was all we had. We spliced and screwed them together with the cheapest zinc chromate screws we could find. They would have to do the job.

Ribbanding *Serendipity* was a one - or two -weekend job. Mr. Koncitek, bless his heart, never missed a promised delivery date. We never were disappointed when we came home on a weekend expecting to find our oak shipment. If the

We are finishing up the ribbands as Bill Hawthorne comes by to admire the work and give us some encouragement.

75

moulds were exciting, the ribbanded hull form was positively intoxicating. And spring was coming to boot!

We started with the sheer batten, which would define the upper line of the hull of our vessel. *Serendipity* was designed with a graceful sheer, rising markedly forward to the clipper bow, dipping amidships, and rising less markedly aft to that hard-to-build curved and raked transom. As we screwed the sheer ribband to the moulds, we could see the shape of our ship materialize before our eyes!

After the sheer ribband was attached, the rest followed rapidly, spaced about 8" to10" apart from sheer to keel. Now we really had a vessel before us. We stood back and admired, conscious that what we saw was all temporary, to be replaced by a real ship of white oak ribs and mahogany planks.

Of course, this temporary construction does go very fast. But the sudden blossoming of the "pattern-boat" did not totally obscure the fact that there was a great deal of really hard work to do in building the real boat ahead. We had in our back yard, a convincing representation of what the hull of *Serendipity* would look like. But all of the woodwork, the

Ribbanding is nearly done. Doesn't *Serendipity* look like a real ship?

moulds and the ribbands, on which we had labored so diligently over the last several months, were not part of the actual ship. They would be destroyed. The real *Serendipity* was yet to be built.

This fact was hard to understand for the onlookers and sightseers who began to stop by in increasing numbers as winter became spring that year. Wilbraham was then a small town. Word of the boatbuilding project on Main Street naturally spread. My mother was an enthusiastic tour guide. Whenever anyone would come by to see the boat, she would take the visitor in hand, pointing out the various parts of the boat and relating anecdotes of how the project had gone so far.

We thanked her for this, for it left us free to work, pausing only briefly to acknowledge our visitors and to grunt in different tones in answer to their questions.

As March became April, we were faced with what we thought would be one of the big challenges of the entire project – bending the white oak frames. The most commonly asked question to date had been "How are you going to bend the ribs?"

Everyone has heard that oak frames of yachts and small ships are somehow mysteriously "bent", apparently with the aid of steam to form rather complex curves. It's hard to imagine how this can be possible. Indeed, for us, particularly after our poor experience at bending mahogany, the prospect of bending the oak frames was more than a little intimidating.

To be sure, the books said it could be done. However, the recommended means varied. Some suggested that boiling the frames in a tank full of water with glycerin added was the only way to get bent frames that would not break. Other authorities suggested that a steam box would do the job. We had already constructed the steam box. And the wallpaper steamer appeared to provide a reliable source of steam. Maybe oak would bend better than the mahogany. We turned our attention to our frame stock. All of the authorities had recommended that green oak would bend much better than seasoned stock.

For several months now, the 1-5/8" by 4" rough-sawn oak boards had lain stacked and "stickered" in the back yard. They had checked but little. However, they were not as green as they had been. After all, they had been sawn nearly a year before. Would they be too dry to bend successfully? The amateur builder is always haunted by a multitude of worries and concerns. Boatbuilding books are full of foreboding prescriptions. It must be done one way, or dire consequences will occur. Chapelle, in particular, set a high standard. What would happen if we failed to meet it?

We started with the oak stock. The white oak frame stock that Mr. Koncitek had cut for us was a number of 1 5/8" by 4" clear oak planks which we would have to rip and plane to the requisite dimensions. Although we could patiently rip each plank into two 1 5/8" x 2" sticks with the ancient table saw, juiced up with a new 1 hp motor and an 8" carbide -tipped blade, we had no way to plane the rough stock to the exact dimensions called for.

Enter Charles Merrick, farmer, local politician and Wilbraham town historian. Charlie had heard of our project and taken an interest in what we were doing. He stopped a couple of times at the building site to check on progress. On one of his visits, he mentioned that he had a big thickness planer and would be glad to help us out with some planing if we needed it. Now was the time we needed it. We loaded the rough stock into the Red Rambler and drove the mile down Main Street to Mr. Merrick's farm. There, in one of the outbuildings, he had a splendid large "cabinet planer" that would handle boards up to 15" wide. Planing our rib stock was child's play for this machine.

As we ran each piece of the rough stock through the planer, we inspected it carefully for the "run" of the grain. According to the boat building books, we wanted the annular rings in the wood to run more or less parallel with the surface of the hull to facilitate bending and to reduce possible splitting when the plank fasteners were driven. We were able to get most of the rings lined up properly and after several hours work with Mr. Merrick, we had about 80 pieces of rib stock, most about 10-12 feet long by 1 3/8" x 1 ½" as called for in the specs.

But were they too dry? Some books said that it might be advisable to soak rib stock for several days before trying to steam bend. We tried some overnight in the bathtub. However, there was not room enough for the larger ones. And we could not really believe it would make a difference. We would bend what we had as best we could.

There was one other pre-requisite for frame bending with which we were only marginally equipped. As the frames are bent in place inside the ribbands, they must be clamped in place. A major frame bending project requires a vast number of C-clamps. We had started the project with a couple that were left over from *Te Amo*, plus some that my father found in the cellar. Over the months we had been working, I had tried to accumulate clamps and had looked for them wherever I could find them. New clamps, we found, were expensive. For months we had been looking for sales at hardware stores, close-outs and flea markets. These yielded about a half dozen more. At Christmas, clamps had been nominated as preferred Christmas presents. A few more had come in that way. The best were the 4" malleable iron C-clamps from Sears Roebuck. But they cost money, and I tried to get as many as I could second-hand. Despite my best efforts, when we undertook to bend *Serendipity's* ribs, we had only perhaps 20 or so usable clamps instead of the 60 or more recommended by Chapelle. Somehow, we would have to recycle what we had in order to keep the job going.

Easter weekend 1966 was cool and overcast, definitely not ideal weather for boat building. But nothing would stop us

79

then. Peter Plumb, my oldest and dearest friend from my youth, came from New York, where he was at Columbia Law School, with his fiancée, Pam Pelton, to help us with the rib bending. Peter had followed our progress with great interest and encouragement and was glad to help when he could. We did not know how many frames we would be able to do in a three day weekend, but we wanted to do them all.

When we started on Saturday morning, there was still a bit of damp chill in the air, but the sun seemed to mellow the day out in pretty good shape by noon. The air was taut with anticipation. Would it work or wouldn't it?

We put the first batch of ribs into the steamer. Some came from the bathtub, some from the pile. We would see which ones bent better. While the wallpaper boiler did its work, we breakfasted nervously. We planned to start in the waist of the boat, where the frames made long, gentle curves and there was plenty of room to work. The tougher bends aft toward the quarter would come later after we got the hang of it. And we would leave the bow until the end, to use up the bits and pieces.

From a diagram in Chapelle, I had made an implement which would fit over the square frame heads. With this, I could twist them to lie fair against the curving sides. After some soul-searching, I had also resolved another point disputed among the written authorities. Despite dire warnings of "rot pockets", I had laboriously chiseled small recesses into the wood keel into which the frame ends would be screwed. Concerns of rot I partially allayed, by dousing the whole business repeatedly with Cuprinol.

The books said about an hour an inch for bending oak, so we left the stock in the steamer for about an hour and a half. This coincided with how long a charge of water in the boiler lasted. We opened the steam box door. With gloved hands we pulled out the first rib. "Quick, shut the door before the steam escapes!" I was standing inside the mould while Peter, Pam

80

By noon, a good crowd had gathered. Mark Rollins and Mr. Randolph look on as I grasp a 'midships frame and force it down against the ribbands. Peter Plumb is clamping as I go.

and Anita clustered around the outside, clamps in hand. My eyes bulged as the hot frame was carried from the box. The ends were actually drooping! Then it was in my hands. Clumsily, I jammed the foot of the frame down into the box-recess in the keel. The heat from the wet wood penetrated the thin cotton gloves. But I was oblivious to all of this. Would the frame bend? It did. We had to work very fast. The effect of the steam would last for less than a minute, after which the wood would become hard and intractable once more. We took the future frames from the box one by one. I was inside the ribbands, standing on the keel. Peter, Pam or Anita would pass me the hot and steaming frame. (Yes, we all wore gloves).

81

I grabbed it, stuck one end into the socket already chiseled for it in the side of the keel just above the garboard rabbet, and, with my foot, pressed the frame against the ribbands, drawing the top toward me as I worked upward. The others were busy with the clamps, drawing the frame hard against the ribbands before it cooled and stiffened. It turned out to be surprisingly easy, if somewhat tense. The first batch, which went amidships, was bent in place in a few minutes. Boy, did those ribs look great!

We went ahead, batch after batch, refilling the wallpaper steamer with water and the steam box with frames. As we waited for the steam box to do its thing, we carefully liberated clamps and replaced them with toe-nails through the ribbands into the damp frames. These held the ribs in place more or less satisfactorily, so we were able to make do with our inadequate supply of clamps.

The frames near the stern took a bit of a twist. I am twisting the frame with the home-made frame as I force it against the ribbands with my foot, while Anita and Peter Plumb clamp.

Now and then, we broke a rib. It was particularly difficult to get the ribs to take the relatively sharp bend at the stern near the transom. Another tough spot was where the ribs had to take S-curves about two-thirds of the way aft in the way of the future engine and shaft log. My heart would drop to my feet, each time we heard a cracking sound as I tried to walk a rib into place. Ultimately our 80 pieces of rib stock were not enough. At the bow, where the ribs were nearly straight, and at the stern, where they were severely curved, we had to use a few pieces of previously broken ribs, to be cut off later.

Believe it or not, we bent every one of *Serendipity's* 72 oak frames in that single weekend. No, we did not go to church that Easter. Our time was too precious. Having four hard workers going continuously was what it took. Peter and Pam were towers of strength. It is scarcely conceivable how we

The frame-bending crew on Sunday afternoon - 72 frames bent and in place. Whew!

could have done it without them. There was simply so much to be done all at once, every time a hot rib came out of the steam box.

83

What a feeling of tired satisfaction we all had as we gazed up at the skeleton of *Serendipity* rising from within its nest of ribbands! In a single weekend, our vessel had become transformed from a keel with some temporary forms and ribbands into the backbone and ribs of our actual boat! That

Fitting and securing the floor timbers to the keel inside the frames and among the moulds to fit the floor timbers was fussy work in confined spaces.

Sunday night as the Murrays headed for Cambridge and the future Plumbs to New York, the general feeling in both cars was elation.

Once the ribs had been bent, our next tasks were to secure the foot of each rib to its socket in the keel and then to fit the floor timbers. The first was easy – a single hole and a 2 1/2" x 12 bronze screw.

The main structural fasteners of the frames to the keel were not the single screws in the frame foots, but were transverse "floor timbers" of 2" x 6" oak bolted to both frame and keel. It was for these floor timbers, that we had installed a procession of protruding 3/8" galvanized bolts before we bolted the wood keel to the iron. The specs called for a floor timber to span every other frame pair, with more in the way of the future engine beds.

It was at this point that we had to devise a way of getting in and out of the boat fairly efficiently. When we were bending the frames, we scrambled in and out over the transom with the aid of a crude ladder. We reinforced and improved this so that we could go in and out of the framework to fit the floors. Crawling around inside *Serendipity's* skeleton, still encumbered by the moulds every three feet was not easy. Nor was it easy to measure for the trapezoidal floor timbers, some with curved ends and bevels where the hull shape changed.

The books blithely said "take the bevels off the loft plan" and cut them out. That was easier said than done. With only ribbands to represent *Serendipity's* skin, we had to estimate where the end of a floor timber would meet the future planking and make sure that it would not interfere with the lie of the planks against the frames.

Making and fitting the floors was frustrating work. How many times did I climb in and out of the framework, crawl in and among the moulds, measure, mark, take the piece outside and cut, and repeat the whole process again? At the end, we had to fix the locations of the existing bolts in the keel on the floor timber and bore the floor timber edgewise to accommodate them. This was also tricky, and we made mistakes. Sometimes, the mistakes required us to discard the piece. In other cases, we could ream out a hole or re-bore it in part to make the bolt fit. A right-angled attachment on the 3/8" drill was necessary to bore the holes for the gleaming 1/4" bronze carriage bolts which connected frames to floors. Progress was slow in those weekends following that exhilarating Easter experience. Bending the 72 frames took us one weekend.   Fitting the 20 or so floors took three or four more.

As the sun rose higher and the days grew longer, as the fields became brown with plowing and then green with vegetation, we finished up a number of odds and ends.   We discovered how cramped it can be to work around the hull of a

Some of the bolts securing floor timbers to frames could be best tightened from outside.

boat in mould. Often our bodies became sore and our tempers became frayed from the contortions to which we were put in order to seat a nut or drive a screw.   There was an air of expectancy about the project as we finished these odds and ends and secured and consolidated our gains of Easter weekend. For we all knew that an even greater challenge was coming.   During the summer of 1966, *Serendipity* had to be planked.

The thickness of *Serendipity's* planking was specified to be 1 1/8" finished. This meant that we had to start with rough lumber of at least 1¼" thick that would plane to 1 1/8". With hardwoods, such as oak or mahogany, 1/8" is usually enough difference between the rough and the finished.   With softwoods, however, it can be as much as 3/8" or even more.

The plans and specifications called for the planks to be made of a wood called "Philippine mahogany." I knew from my boatbuilding books that Philippine mahogany was not real mahogany (which comes from Honduras, in Central America), but is a trade name for a couple of species, known as okoume

A view from the strong-back showing several of the floor timbers under where the engine will be located.

and tangile, that have long been harvested in the Philippine Islands.   It is moderately strong, clear and straight grained, moderate in weight, and moderate in resistance to rot, and was

87

"moderate" in cost at the time we were building *Serendipity.* There were, of course, other options. We could have used cedar that was at the time still used to plank Maine lobster boats. We could have used teak, which was known as the "eternal wood" because of its exceptional durability. Pine and other species commonly sold in lumber yards, however, were either not strong enough or not rot resistant enough to qualify.

After weighing the pros and cons, I ultimately decided to stick with Crockett's choice. But where could we get such an exotic material at a price that we could afford? Those were the days when money was expensive and time was cheap. Although law school is supposed to be a demanding and challenging undertaking, I had sufficient time to make it worthwhile to go to a great deal of trouble to save even a little money. Our original small savings for this project had been badly depleted by keel, screws and bolts, and cost of the oak. My wife's grandmother generously added $1,000 to the project treasury which gave us a new lease on life. But even in those days, mahogany was going for upwards of $.50 a foot. How could we get the 750+ board feet which we needed to plank the hull as specified?

When we had gone to get the wood for the transom, we had ended up with African mahogany, also not a true mahogany. It had a beautiful deep brown color and a clear grain. Our books told us that it was not quite as strong or rot resistant as the Philippine version, but it would be worthy of consideration. One disadvantage of African mahogany was the peculiar sour smell that it gave off when cut or sanded – not at all the smell one associates with wood, but more like rotting vegetables.

We started our search with the mahogany specialists, The Palmer and Parker Company, Charlestown, Massachusetts. However, when I visited their yard, they advised me that they did not have any 5/4" Philippine mahogany in stock at the time. They did have some 1" African mahogany that they

88

would be willing to sell us for the same price as Philippine, quite a good deal as a matter of money. They explained that the wood was cut robustly, so that 1" rough stock would likely plane out at 15/16" smooth. We were tempted by the idea of getting wood that usually sold for 60 cents per board foot or more for a discount. However, would planks that were only 15/16" instead of 1 1/8" thick be too thin? The boatbuilding books were equivocal. It seemed that boats of 30 feet in length can be built with planking of less than an inch, but a full inch or a bit more was more common.

Ultimately, we called Mr. Crockett. What did he think? Would it be OK to substitute 15/16" African mahogany for the 1 1/8" Philippine mahogany originally specified? Mr. Crockett was not enthusiastic. Lighter planking than specified might not give *Serendipity* the strength and stiffness required to take the stress of the seas. We had better stick with 1 1/8" stock, be it African or Philippine.

Since Palmer and Parker were not offering any deal on 5/4" African mahogany, we had to look elsewhere for our planking. Palmer and Parker suggested their nearby competitor Winde-McCormick, just down the street in Charlestown. Although Winde-McCormick did not advertise itself as a mahogany specialist, when I called they told me that they had plenty of Philippine mahogany, and in the 5/4" thickness that we needed. The problem was that Winde-McCormick was strictly a wholesale yard. They sold to other lumber yards, and occasionally to professional boat yards, not to the retail public. I went over there and spoke with the manager. I told him about what we were doing and how far we had come on our dream. Somehow he came around. "OK…" - they would sell us our planking lumber – 750 board feet of Philippine mahogany. The price - 38 ½ cents per board foot.

The next challenge was to get the lumber from the Winde-McCormick yard in Charlestown to our building site almost 100 miles away. Wilbraham was far outside the area in which the yard would deliver. We could have, and as events transpired, should have, had it shipped by common carrier. At the time, however, that sounded too expensive. So I decided to haul the lumber out there myself.

Of course, I should have rented the 2-1/2 ton stake truck that I had used for the keel. It would have done the job with ease. But it would have cost me $50 or so. And $50 would have bought quite a lot of screws. A good rugged trailer should do the job, and at a quarter of the price.

I should have given more thought to the mass and weight of what we proposed to haul. Philippine mahogany weighs approximately 20 pounds per board foot. So our future planking would weigh in at over 1500 pounds. Our little red Rambler American was an early compact car, weighing not much more than a ton itself. The largest trailer we could find to rent had a load capacity of 1000 pounds. These calculations, so easy to make in hindsight, did not take place when I decided to haul our lumber in a rented trailer.

So it was on a pleasant weekday in May, during reading period before my exams, that I headed over to a discount trailer rental place in.l, Brookline to pick up the trailer. On the way, I picked up Arthur Thomas, one of my roommates during my junior year at college and a dear friend. During my senior year, Arthur had taken a year off. He had returned to finish his last year at the same time I was doing my second year of law school. We took up where we had left off. Arthur was interested in our project and was glad to help when he could, as on this pleasant day in May hauling a bunch of boards from Charlestown to Wilbraham.

With trailer in tow, we then drove to the Winde-McCormick yard in Charlestown. We were in luck. The wood was gorgeous. The bundle on top of the pile was composed of 22 footers. My "random lengths and widths" definitely favored the long side, at least until the tallyman noticed and insisted

90

that we take some "8's" and "10's" as well. Some of the planks hung for nearly half their length outside the trailer.

I was thus able to get a large proportion of long lengths, 16', 18' even 22' long. Longer planks would mean fewer "butts" or joints, and a stronger more watertight hull. As we neared 700 board feet, the trailer seemed to be quite full. The load was definitely bigger and heavier than I had imagined that it would be. We put the last of the boards on, strapped them down, and hung a red flag on one of the protruding 22-footers to warn following vehicles of the protrusion. Then we were off. . . slowly and laboriously. The little red Rambler strained to get the trailer and its load under way. Going around corners, one could feel the momentum of the load behind, almost like the tail wagging the dog. We should have stopped there.

But youth and inexperience blunders on despite the murmurs of caution. If we could get the car up to speed, undoubtedly things would smooth out and we could just tool along the Turnpike. And so we slewed and swayed our way through Cambridge, trying to still the feelings of apprehension. Everything would smooth out once we "got up to speed" . . .

At the Cambridge entrance to the Massachusetts Turnpike, the little red Rambler strained as we struggled to accelerate the massive load. As we crossed 40 miles an hour, I felt the trailer to the rear of us begin to sway. "My heavens!! . . ." but we continued on. By 50 mph, the trailer felt as if it had taken charge. I scarcely knew whether we could control it. Perhaps, we better look for an exit....

Too late! "Screee . . . !" As if grabbed by a giant fist, the little Rambler was spun in circles as the trailer disgorged its load upon the pavement. We careened madly from side to side and around and around as planks flew in every direction over the highway. We could hear brakes shrieking behind us as drivers saved themselves from the spinning car and spewing planks. Arthur's face, normally a deep chocolate, grew pale. Neither of us said anything.

There is a God that looks out for fools. And ours was on duty that day. The car came to a stop at the side of the highway, the trailer protruding out into the roadway. We looked around. The trailer was still attached to the car, but the axle had broken and two of the tandem wheels had come off. Our precious mahogany lumber was scattered all over the highway. Traffic was slowed to a crawl as cars and trucks tried to thread their way around us and go on their way.

Moments later, we heard a siren and a state police cruiser pulled up. We were still dazed. We got out of the car. We were trembling. How we were not hit by following traffic, how we avoided causing a major accident, how our car remained on the road at all and how we escaped with our lives, must have been a matter of Divine Providence.

The trooper took charge and directed the traffic around the accident scene, as Arthur and I collected the boards from the traffic lanes and piled them beside the road. We disconnected the car, which miraculously did not seem to be damaged. We manhandled the empty trailer onto the grass, found the missing wheels some distance away and put them in the trailer. Finally, we were more or less cleaned up.

The trooper took a report of the mishap, but said nothing about traffic charges. We told him that we would get a truck to fetch the wood and would somehow get the trailer off the highway. Off we went again in the red Rambler, this time to a Luby Truck Rental place, where we rented the kind of vehicle that we should have had in the first place - a 1½ ton stake truck. It was nearly noon when we returned to the site of the accident. We had alerted the state police, and the trooper was there once again to keep the traffic away, as we loaded our lumber from the side of the turnpike into the back of the truck.

With some trepidation I also called the trailer rental place and told them what happened. "How much weight did you have in that trailer?" "I don't know, but it was certainly not full." My $100 deposit on the trailer was forfeited, but the man at the trailer rental place left it at that. I suppose that he was relieved that the broken axle had not resulted in worse damage than it did, regardless of the cause of the failure. Leaving the trailer to be picked up by its owner, we were off again headed west with the priceless goods aboard. That planking had nearly cost us our lives. But nothing could stop us from pressing forward.

The rest of the trip to Wilbraham was a comparative piece of cake. We backed the truck into my parents' yard and unloaded the mahogany planks under the old apple tree. Some had been scuffed or splintered at the edges by being flung around the highway, but they were basically unscathed. We stacked them carefully with stickers (small wood sticks) between each layer to keep them straight and allow them to continue to dry. Late in the afternoon, Arthur and I drove the truck back to the Luby Truck Rental in Cambridge and exchanged it for the red Rambler. I drove Arthur back to Adams House, where he lived, and then went back to our apartment to study for exams.

What a day! We had loaded and unloaded that 750 board feet of mahogany lumber 4 times, had been in a terrible accident, had switched vehicles mid-stream, and had delivered the goods some 100 miles away – all in a day's work. Clearly someone or something had been looking out for me, and saved us both from a foolish and careless miscalculation and poor judgment.

Chapter 5

Although we did not have a precise time schedule for the completion of *Serendipity*, as the project went forward it became clear that we would have to aim to have the hull, at least, finished by the time I finished law school in June of 1967, or by the end of that summer in any event. After all, presumably I would get a job after graduation and we would be moving somewhere for this job. We had more or less ruled out staying in the Springfield, Massachusetts, area. Why build a cruising sailboat and then settle 100 miles from the sea?

In order to have a chance of finishing *Serendipity's* hull by the summer of 1967, we would have to get the biggest single job, the planking, done during the summer of 1966. Law School was out in early June and did not resume until after Labor Day. This left potentially three whole months of time to work on the boat.

There was one problem. In that day, as in this, law students ordinarily used the summer between their second and third years for "summer clerkships" in law firms. This summer employment gave a firm an opportunity to preview a potential future hire before having to extend an offer. It gave a law student the chance to try out a particular firm to see if it was the kind of place where he or she would want to work.

When I started law school in the fall of 1964, I had a vague expectation of perhaps going to work in Boston, Massachusetts. But my conversation with Richard Wolfe on the deck of the Prout's Neck Yacht club during the summer after my first year in law school had planted a new seed in my consciousness. How about Portland, Maine?

Up until that time, I had not thought of Portland as a venue in which to ply my legal profession. But the idea of actually living there on the shore of beautiful Casco Bay and practicing law there was intriguing....

Back in Cambridge for the fall of my second year, I looked up the local legal talent in legal directories. According to the usual credentials of academic training and distinction in practice, there were indeed some very good lawyers in Portland. Should I consider the possibility of going to Portland to start my legal career? The idea was tantalizing. Boston I knew from four years of college and two of law school. But Portland was unknown.

That fall, one Maine law firm advertised at Harvard Law School for a summer associate. When I saw the little 3 x 5 card on the wall outside the placement office, I signed up for an interview. The interview impressed me. I went up to Portland to see the firm in its locale. When the offer of a summer clerkship at Pierce, Atwood, Scribner, Allen & McKusick in Portland, Maine came, I accepted it - with one condition. "I would love to come, but would like to come for just 5 weeks." This surprised them, as usually summer associates want to maximize their summer earnings by working as many weeks in the summer as possible. But they assented. So it was that the summer of 1966, our summer for planking the boat, would be compromised only to the extent of 5 weeks. We would be in Maine for the month of July and the first week of August. The rest of the summer we would be in Wilbraham hard at work on *Serendipity.*

Planking a conventionally built boat is probably the single most difficult and time-consuming single phase of construction of the hull. Boat planks, unlike house planks, are neither either straight nor parallel sided. Every plank must be cut and shaped to an individual pattern, and planed to fit against its neighbor tightly enough to keep out the water with only a little caulking to help.

I had never planked a ship, or even a boat, before. *Te Amo* was a flat-bottomed skiff with a bottom cross-planked

95

with common boards. I merely covered the rotten spots with fiberglass. The Crockett schooner was traditional in every respect. I had considered, and quickly discarded, the idea of strip planking. It was too hard to fix and there was too much sanding involved. We would do it the old way.

So ultimately I had to learn how to cut and fit traditional "carvel" planks from my boatbuilding books. Every boatbuilding book devotes a good deal of time and space to planking. There seemed to be general agreement on how it should be done. We had to start with the "garboard," then the "sheer strake," and then work up and down in between. Each plank had to be "spiled". The planks had to be "lined off" in advance, and then there were "shutters", "stealers" and "butts". Everything had to fit just right for the caulking. After reading and rereading the relevant sections in Chapelle, Seward and Rabl, I took a deep breath and we started in.

Step one in turning the pile of rough Philippine mahogany into the skin of *Serendipity* was to get the 5/4" rough-sawn lumber planed to 1 1/8" thick. This was too big a job for Charlie Merrick. After some phoning around, we decided to send the planks to Roy's who had done the band-sawing of our oak and had supplied the rough stock for the moulds. While I was finishing my exams in Cambridge, Roy's truck came, picked up the planks in Wilbraham, planed them, and brought them back. At the end of the month, when we moved to Wilbraham for the bulk of the summer, the planed planks were waiting for us. I think Roy charged us $.02 a board foot. The finished planks were beautiful, planed on two sides to finish exactly 1-1/8" thick. The pink hues of the freshly planed wood gave promise of rich coloration when sanded and varnished. Of course, there were no knots. This was the stuff which would be the skin of our ship.

The prospect of spending the entire summer in the tiny upstairs bedroom at my parents' home was somewhat daunting not only to Anita and me, but also to my parents. Thus, we were happy to accept the offer of Dudley and Jeannette Cloud, from across the street, to house-sit their small house while they spent the summer at their farm in Vermont.

On a bright sunny day in early June 1966, we finally started. According to the book, the first plank to go on each side of the hull was the bottom plank that butts up against the keel. It is called the "garboard strake," or "garboard" for short. But before we started even with that, we had to lay out, or "line off" the planks on each side of the hull. This involved measuring along one of the frames nearest to each mould station, and dividing the total distance along the frame by the number of planks we anticipated having, and then marking the respective frames with a mark representing where we thought the edge of each plank would come. This gave us a rough guide to the widths of the respective planks. A pattern would ultimately have to be made for each plank, but the marks from the lining off gave a reference point from which to start.

As indicated before, our power tool supply was sadly wanting. We were one notch better off than old time boat builders who sawed out planks by hand. We had our trusty Craftsman saber saw which could, with some difficulty, slowly cut curved lines in our 1 1/8' mahogany stock. The only tool we had to dress the edges of the planks, bevel them for the caulking, and match each plank edge to the meeting edge of the previous plank, was a Sears 18" fore plane, which we bought for this job.

Although we left the caulking of the seams between the planks for later, we needed to bed the plank-ends at stem and horn timber in some kind of goop that would keep them watertight. Traditionally, this was a simple oil-based seam putty with little adhesive ability and a limited service life. At some early point in the build, we had become aware of the remarkable products invented by Mr. Ralph Travers of Travaco Laboratories in Chelsea, Massachusetts. Mr. Travers was a polymer chemist by training and had made important

97

contributions to the development of polymer chemical products, including early epoxy resins, for use in the Second World War. In the 1950's, he had continued to build on his wartime experience to invent and manufacture a line of marine adhesives, sealants and caulking compounds based on two-part epoxy resins. One of his earliest products, Marine-Tex, was a thick epoxy putty that could be used for repairs of broken or deteriorated wood. This was well known to us before we even started on *Serendipity*.

In the mid 1960's, Mr. Travers came out with "Caulk-Tex", an epoxy-based flexible caulking compound with great strength, durability and adhesive quality. Mr. Travers claimed that boats caulked with his new product would be watertight and would never need re-caulking. This was a tall claim at a time when wood boats generally needed re-caulking every 5-7 years, and re-puttying every couple of years. Somehow, we became convinced that we should use Caulk-Tex for *Serendipity*, both for bedding the plank ends and eventually for caulking the seams. There are few decisions that I have rued less. In fact, the original Caulk-tex has held up so well that *Serendipity* has not needed re-caulking in the first 50 years of her life, and did not need re-puttying for the first 30 years.

The drawback to Caulk-Tex (other than the need to mix it in batches each time we used it) was its cost. It cost $50.00 per gallon (in 1966 dollars), about 4-5 times what conventional seam putty cost in those days. Because we would ultimately need several gallons, I decided to go to the source in hopes of getting a better price. One afternoon in the late spring before we were going to start planking, I drove over to Chelsea, Massachusetts in hopes of convincing Mr. Travers to sell us his remarkable products at wholesale prices.

Travaco Labs and its small workforce were housed in a small brick building in industrial Chelsea. Mr. Travers, a large, tall man in evident poor health, explained to me that he had developed the best epoxies known to date based originally on his military work and that Caulk-Tex would indeed do what was represented on the can, provide a high strength, flexible, waterproof bond for an indefinite period of time. When asked whether he had patented his discoveries, he solemnly assured me that he had no faith in patents, which only give possible free-loaders the information they need to get around them. His compounds were protected by the secrecy of his recipes and a number of false clues that he implanted in each product to deter reverse engineering. So far, no-one had been able to copy his products or to develop a worthy competitive product to Marine-Tex or Caulk-Tex.

Ultimately, Mr. Travers graciously agreed to sell me all of his products, including Caulk-Tex and "Liquid Marine-Tex", a very strong liquid epoxy resin, at his distributor price, list less 50% less 10%, which amounted to a total discount of 55%. Even $23.00 per gallon was more than conventional seam and bedding compound, but the superior qualities of the Travers products were convincing. We have never regretted this decision.

Caulk-Tex came in two parts, a bright pink "goo", and a brown pasty catalyst. It only took a little catalyst to cause the pink goo to set overnight into a rubbery mass that could be sanded. When we needed some Caulk-Tex to bed a plank end or, later on, to caulk a stretch of seam, I would scoop out a big glob of the pink glue onto a small scrap of smooth wood or plywood, add a smidgen of the brown catalyst, and then mix it all together with a putty knife until it was a uniform tan color. After mixing, it could be worked for a half an hour or 45 minutes before it would start to set up and become too stiff to spread. Although we tried not to waste it, there were many times when I had made a little too much, or when the spreading became interrupted, and we had to throw away a rubbery glob of cured Caulk-Tex with the mixing board.

Sad to say, Caulk-Tex is no longer being made. Mr. Travers died at some point after *Serendipity* was launched, and

Anita is starting to "mix the gorp" to bed the end of a plank where it met the stem or transom. A glob of the pink base is spread on a piece of scrap wood, then a small dab of the dark brown hardener is added and mixed in with a putty knife.

his business was sold to a larger manufacturer of marine compounds. Although Marine-Tex is still available today, Caulk-Tex was discontinued some years after we used it to build *Serendipity*. The reason apparently was that it contained too many toxic chemicals.

In order to have a way to hold the planks as we cut them out and then planed them, we built a "planking bench" in the garden next to the hull. This consisted of some posts driven into the ground supporting a long single plank top, with an old turn-screw wood vise screwed to a heavier post near one end. It ended up about 10" wide and 16' long. We would lay each board on top of the bench for measuring and then cutting with the saber saw. The vise was for holding the plank on edge for the endless planing and re-planing needed to make it fit.

The garboards were particularly difficult for us for two reasons. First of all, they were our first efforts, and we had to learn everything as we went along. Second, each one was nearly 22 feet long, all in one piece, with a difficult twist in the after third to accommodate *Serendipity's* wineglass after-quarters.

Planking has several defined steps, each of which must follow the other. First of all, we had to remove the ribband that was in the location where we were going to fit the plank. We backed off the screws and toe-nails that we had driven to hold the fresh-steamed frames to the ribband we were removing. The ribbands were what had given the frames their shapes. Now the ribbands would be removed one by one as they were replaced with real planks that would give *Serendipity* her skin.

The next step was to "spile" the hull to get the curve of the edge of the plank that is to be butted to the existing structure, whether that is the keel in the way of the garboards, or the last preceding strake in the case of the other planks.

The first step in cutting out a new planks to clamp the spiling batten next to the last plank in place.

Ships planks, unlike house planks, are not straight or parallel sided. The planks of a ship's hull, which appear parallel in place, are actually squiggly, snake-like tapered pieces, each of which has to be made to a pattern. In many cases, it takes an 8" board to make a 4" plank. Fortunately, we had boards as wide as 20" among our carefully selected "random lengths and widths" from Winde-McCormick.

Spiling involves using a light, flat board called a "spiling batten," to record the curve of the edge of the last plank in place and transfer it to the stock to be cut, using a carpenter's circular compass. Mr. Merrick kindly planed down a couple of scrap pine planks to 5/16" thick for use as our spiling battens. A small school pencil compass would be our scriber. With these crude tools, we set to work.

Using a compass to mark the spiling batten a uniform distance from the edge of the last plank at every frame.

We would first clamp our spiling batten to the frames in the approximate location of the future plank and as near as convenient to the last one.

Then we would take our circular drawing-compass and set the points at the maximum distance from the edge of the spiling batten and the edge of the preceding plank (or the keel

Transferring the marks from the spiling batten to the stock from which the plank will be cut.

rabbet in the case of the garboards). The next step was to use the compass to make a mark on the spiling batten reflecting the compass separation from the edge of the preceding plank at each frame. We then removed the spiling batten and clamped it to the lumber stock from which we would cut the new plank. We next reversed the previous process and used the compass to transfer the marks on the spiling batten to the new stock.

Finally, we took a thin "drawing batten" and used it to draw a smooth curve through all of the spiled reference points. The result is a replication on the flat planking stock of the curve in the plank edge needed to fit the new plank to the hull. This process gave us one edge of our new plank.

103

.   But we had to get the other edge as well. This we did by referring to our marks on the frames from lining off. We then clamped a long batten, which we called the "planking batten," on the frames, following more or less the marks from the lining off. We measured the distance from the edge of the last strake to the planking batten at each frame and listed the measurements in order. Finally, we transferred these distances

Anita clamps on the drawing batten that will define the outside edge of the next plank to be hung.

to the new stock, measuring from the spiled line on the board at the location of each of the spiled marks in the same order as the measurements were taken off.   Fairing the curve with a drawing batten, we thus got the other side of the future plank.

More custom and exotic measurements were made for planks which intersected the bow rabbet. It was a laborious process, with a high potential for error. Fortunately, most minor errors could be fixed with a little extra planing.

After we had laid out the shape of the plank on the 1 1/8" mahogany board, we had to cut it out with our little Craftsman saber saw. How we cursed that little saw! Even with a new blade, it seemed to creep at a snail's pace, especially when cutting with the grain. We swapped off on the sawing job. Neither of us liked to do it.

Anita strains as she cuts along the curved line on the plank with the underpowered saber saw.

Once sawn, the edges of the planks had to be planed smooth in the planing bench. I did all the planing by hand with the 18" fore plane. The grain of our 1-1/8" mahogany was just dense enough to require some real physical effort for this work. Once the plank had been planed to our spiled lines, it would be clamped in position so we could see how close we had come to a proper seam with the next plank. The planks were supposed to meet at their inside edges but leave a gap of about 1/8" at the outer edges to permit the introduction of cotton caulking and later putty in the seam.

Almost always the seam was uneven, with high and low spots. I would mark the high spots with chalk, then take the plank off and plane the high spots again. The planks themselves were not light. Each one had to be fit and clamped several times. Then it would be fit again, chalked again, and so forth.

Planing the edges of every plank by hand was a laborious task. Concave edges could be planed by holding the plan at a 45-degree angle to the work.

Finally, after several clampings-on, chalkings, un-clampings, and planings we were satisfied. Our planks were by no means perfect. Here and there, we could see cracks of light. And the width of the seams did vary. But Caulk-Tex was beginning to build our confidence. This gorp would cover our mistakes. Each can had a picture of a cartoon character attempting to pry loose a board which apparently had been fastened with "Caulk-Tex". A little balloon said "This *@!# stuff won't leggo!". The picture of that little man gave us hope. If our seams were puttied with this miracle stuff, they would stay tight.

As said before, the garboard was the hardest. First, was spiling the keel rabbet. The groove in the oak keel that would take the edge of the garboard looked straight to a casual observer. In fact, the varying angles at which the frames met

106

Anita is using our old 1/4" drill to bore pilot holes for the screws to secure the starboard sheer strake to the frames.

the keel meant that that first plank was anything but straight. It turned out to be a sinuous serpent that we had to cut from one of our wider boards. It was relatively wide (for some reason the garboard is prescribed as one of the wider planks), and 22 feet long (one piece).

The hardest part was getting the garboard to twist from where it lay at a 45 degree angle to the keel amidships to nearly vertical at the deadwood in the stern. We tried everything. We rented the wallpaper steamer again and jammed the garboard into the steam box as far as it would go. Rags were stuffed around the opening to try to keep all the steam from leaking out. We steamed and we steamed.

The truth of the matter is that Philippine mahogany is much less receptive to steaming than the still-green oak of the frames. When we took our plank out to test, it remained stiff and hard with only a trace of suppleness from a lot of steaming. We finally decided to go for it and dragged the hot and moist plank over to the boat. We would force it into place with clamps and baulks of timber jammed into the ground.

107

It had taken almost an entire day of planning and fitting (roughly, because we could not get the plank twisted into place when we were trying it) to come up with the first garboard. It took us about 15 minutes of screwing down clamps and hammering down braces to destroy it. With a loud crack, the plank split in two.

I am planing the edges of the garboard strake in our improvised "planking bench". The edges of the plank are neither straight nor parallel.

The next day we did it all again, spiling, marking and drawing the edges, saber-sawing, planing, fitting and steaming. Somehow, it seemed to go better. Perhaps the plank absorbed more steam. Or maybe we had learned something the first time around. At any rate, by the end of the day we had *Serendipity's* port garboard strake clamped and screwed into place.

We fastened the garboard (and all the rest of the planks) to the frames and the backbone with our 2" #12 silicon bronze screws from the Whitney Screw Works, Nashua, New Hampshire. Driving the thousands of bronze #12 screws, through mahogany and into oak, even semi-green oak is no easy task. Here's how we did it.

The first, and probably most important thing was boring the right size and shape hole. A traditional wood screw is tapered. To generate its maximum holding capacity, ideally it should be driven into a hole a little smaller than the screw's diameter, but having the same taper.

In the old days, one had two choices. One could drill several successive holes, each a little deeper and a little smaller in diameter to approximate a tapered recess. The alternative was to buy a very expensive and clumsy screw hole drill that had a sleeve for the bit that would enlarge the upper part of the hole to give a crude taper.

Right about the time we were starting on *Serendipity*, Warren Fuller of Fuller Machine Co.in Warwick, Rhode Island, began marketing tapered screw-hole bits equipped with countersink bits attached right to the drill bits. There were different sizes for the different screw sizes, and one could set the countersink at the correct depth with set screws on each side of the countersink and a tiny Allen wrench. I don't remember how we found out about these remarkable tools. For a long time before they were generally distributed, I ordered them by telephone directly from Warren Fuller. The Fuller tapered bits and countersinks were lifesavers. We had several in each size, some pre-set to a given length of hole. We broke several and wore out some more, but they were not expensive and we reordered several times. Thanks to Warren Fuller, the vital task of boring the pilot hole and countersinking for the screw head was a relative piece of cake.

Once a pilot hole had been drilled and countersunk deep enough to take the head of the screw and a 1/2" mahogany plug, we would drag the screw through a bar of soap to make it easier to drive. Not all soaps are good for soaping screws. Many are too hard and crumbly, or for some reason do not adhere to the threads of a screw. Ivory, however, seemed to be ideal. It was soft enough that the screw would fill its threads with soap and drive easily through mahogany and into oak.

In 1966, power screwdrivers and hammer drills with screwdriver bits were still to be invented. We started out by turning the screws by hand using a large aluminum screwdriver that had an arm that folded out to the side for greater leverage. This was laborious in the extreme, and we sought a better way.

Here I am driving screws to secure the port side sheer strake to the frames using a speed reducer on the electric drill. Most of the time it was easier to do it with the brace and bit.

The "better way" was also low-tech - a simple hand brace with a 3/8" screwdriver bit gave plenty of leverage to drive in the most recalcitrant screw, without twisting it off in the process. Round and round I went with the brace and screwdriver bit, as we drove two or three bronze screws into each frame crossed by each plank.

The final step in the planking was plugging or "bunging" the countersunk screw heads with ½" plugs of the same wood as the planking. These we could and did buy by the thousand from Sargent, Lord. The bungs were dipped in epoxy glue and then tapped into the counterbores with a mallet.

The planks were hung alternately up from the garboard and down from the sheer on both sides of the boat.

A few times, when we got behind in this somewhat laborious process, my father took up the mallet and drove bungs. The driven bungs stood proud of the planks, but would be sanded flush when we faired the hull.

We started on the planking in earnest when law school let out in late May, and by the end of June had cut, fitted and screwed on several courses of planks on both sides of *Serendipity's* strong oak frame. We started with the garboard on each side, then went to the top plank, or "strake", called the "sheer strake", again adding this plank to each side before going to the next in line. The sheer strake was the largest and longest in the boat. We made it in two pieces on each side, with the butt block amidships. It had a terrific curve in it

111

When we really needed help, my parents were glad to do whatever they could. Here is my father sitting on the cradle, a pail of bungs next to him about to tap a few of them in place after dipping them in epoxy glue.

because of the flare of the bow. We had to make sure that the top of the plank would take just the right curve that would define the sheer of our lovely dream ship. Ultimately we had faith in our spiling batten and cut it out. Hanging it in place was a lot easier than the garboard, because we did not have to fit it to an adjacent plank or rabbet.

At first, our progress was barely noticeable. We were lucky to get one full length strake on one side done in a day. It seemed like it took a million cuttings and fittings before the thing fit - more or less. Our arms were tired from the sawing, tired from the planing and tired from the turning of screws.

With all tasks, even the longest and most tedious ones, eventually you can look back and realize accomplishment. As the planks began to creep down from the sheer and up from the garboard, the skin of our ship became real. As June became July and my summer clerkship in Maine loomed nearer, we gradually became better at planking. After a while, we found that we could do a whole strake on both sides using two or three pieces per side. I remember that one day we did a whole strake on both sides and a half on another. That was about our maximum efficiency. Of course, special tasks such as fitting a "stealer" in the tuck of the reverse curve of the quarter took a lot of time and slowed our progress.

Although we had picked out the planks at the lumber yard to get the best and longest ones we could, none of them, except for the garboards, ran full length. For all the other planks, we had to use either two or three boards, fastened at the ends, or "butts", to small squares of 1 1/8" white oak called "butt blocks" inserted between the frames. The books warned ominously about problems to be encountered. Butt blocks had to be carefully fitted. On the one hand, it was necessary that the space between the frames be filled completely. On the other hand, there was the danger that butt blocks too tightly fitted would collect water and rot. The butts had to be carefully spaced. No two butt blocks were to be within the same pair of frames, at least not unless five or six planks intervened. We studied diagrams showing the proper spacing. We were worried. Although we had switched to Caulk-Tex for bedding the plank ends, we continued to use epoxy glue for the butts. We had also found out that Anita was allergic to the epoxy glue. The Caulk-Tex was all right. But if she touched the epoxy glue or even got close to its vapors, her face and any exposed skin would break out in a nasty, itchy rash. So when it was time to glue butts, she had to steer clear. She was probably glad to get a respite from our frenzied, intense labors in the summer heat.

Because of Anita's allergy, and in the interest of efficiency in our totally inefficient operation, at first we fit the planks without butt blocks, planning to fit the blocks *en masse* later on. This meant that we needed to use bolts to draw the plank ends to the blocks. After several planks were on, there was no way we could use a clamp to secure a butt two or three

113

strakes in from the edge of the work. The bolts were also expensive. So it went . . .

Amateur boat builders, like many species of birds, tend to flock together. By admiring and commenting on each other's projects, they support and encourage each other to overcome the many hurdles and difficulties in such an undertaking. Publications such as *Woodenboat* and *Practical Boatbuilder* are now available as secondary sources of advice, help and inspiration. In 1965, of course, we had none of these resources. Wilbraham was 100 miles from the sea. There were no local boatyards, where one could find similarly-inclined souls with whom one could swap stories or compare projects. The magazines of those days, *Rudder*, and *Yachting* were giving little attention to amateur building of wooden boats. We were pretty much on our own.

To be sure, there was the legend in Wilbraham of Phil Edson, who had built a 32-foot Friendship-style sloop on a lot near the top of Wilbraham Mountain. The project had taken 10 years or more. Phil was a fastidious cabinet maker and took his time. There was a rumor that the boat had actually been launched. There was also another rumor that by the time it was launched, its owner had lost interest and sold it soon afterwards. Years before, as a teenager, I had seen this boat as it was being built. But by the time we were started on our own, it had disappeared. Its mountain building site was empty.

Somehow, by chance, that summer we actually met another amateur boat builder who was working on his own boat nearby. Harold Walker of West Springfield, Massachusetts, had heard about what we were doing and came over to take a look. Maybe he had read about it in the Springfield newspaper. The local Wilbraham correspondent had sent in a rather wordy article earlier that spring. Of course, the article was completely inaccurate so far as boat building terminology was concerned. But it gave an air of glamour and notoriety to the project.

114

At any rate, we were happy to meet Harold and to receive his approving comments on our undertaking. He was, however, worried about the butts. Harold patiently explained that if I installed each butt block right after its two planks were hung, it would be possible to pull the planks and butt block together with clamps and they could be then held together with ordinary screws. The two-inch #12 bronze screws that we had bought at Sargent Lord were a little too long for this. Walker came to the rescue. He had bought a large quantity of $1\frac{3}{4}$" x 12 bronze screws for planking his boat (his planking was a little thinner than mine) and was willing to sell me as many as I would need at 1955 prices - something like 2 or 3 cents each.

So one summer evening, after fitting several planks, we knocked off a little early and drove over to West Springfield to see Harold's boat while it was still light. He received us warmly and showed us around his back yard boat shop on the banks of the Connecticut River. There was his beautiful 18" band saw sitting in the garage with elaborate home-made roller stands. He explained how these enabled him to single-handedly saw out the keel and other the large timbers for his 34' power boat. Then there was the cellar shop. He brought out special drift bolts that he had made for securing his engine beds to the floor timbers. He had taken pieces of galvanized rod, carefully ground rounded points, welded on "heads" from "clinch rings", and then had the whole things re-galvanized. I couldn't help but to make a mental comparison to our drift bolts from raw 1/2" galvanized rod with hammered points and clinch rings crudely peened on. Of course, all of the hammering, peening and pointing had destroyed the galvanizing in many points, but we had used them anyway. Were our standards too low?

When we went out to the back yard to see his boat, we were confronted by the sad truth. In the back yard was the partly planked frame of Harold's dream ship. The frames and timbers of the boat were weathered and aged. The butt blocks, carefully fitted with slanted tops to shed the down-flowing waters, had been clamped and screwed in place years before. Although the project had been started eight or nine years ago, he was barely at the point we had reached in a mere 13 months of part-time commuting from Cambridge. There was a kind of rueful tone in his voice as he explained that he really "hadn't had much chance" to work on the boat in the last three or four years . . .

The workmanship on the weathered partly-planked frame was flawless, particularly in comparison with the many crude solutions that we had resorted to on *Serendipity* (thank God for Caulk-Tex!). But it was clear that this dream ship would never be finished. Mr. Walker had lost the spark, the energy, the driving obsession that had led to the successful completion of his first boat and that we hoped would lead us to the completion of ours.

We were a little alarmed. Is this what would happen to our project? Would the flame that burned so brightly flicker and die? Would the weeds grow up around the half-finished hull of *Serendipity* in Wilbraham's field? Would our bronze fittings, nuts and screws gather dust? Would we someday show our never-to-be-finished project to some young boat builder and explain to him that we hadn't "had a chance" to work on our boat in the last few years?

We picked up 500 of the bronze screws that Harold had bought wholesale nearly 12 years before. It was depressing to be long in the presence of a dying dream. We shook ourselves. We must not let it happen to us! The next morning, we sawed and planed, fit and gorped, bored and screwed with renewed vigor. With Mr. Walker's counsel and the 1¾" screws, we fastened the butt blocks as we completed each strake. The process became a cinch.

By mid-July, we had come four or five strakes down from the sheer and four or five up from the garboard. We could really see the skin of our boat filling in. But our time was up. I would have to put aside my plane and saw. Somehow we would have to get the ingrained gorp off my hands and out from under my fingernails. The old work clothes, encrusted with every kind of compound and glue and reeking of Cuprinol, would have to be exchanged for a white shirt and tie. My summer clerkship in Maine was about to begin. We packed up the Red Rambler and headed north, but not without many regretful glances at our half-finished beauty in the field amid the growing weeds.

When we arrived in Portland, we found that temporary summer housing was virtually unobtainable. Decent apartments were very scarce. One had to get on waiting lists with Portland's larger landlords, J. B. Brown & Co, Dartmouth Realty, and Forest Park. A five-week furnished rental was out of the question.

My father mentioned to us that family friends, the Fergusons, had a summer cottage on Great Diamond Island in Portland harbor. He suggested that they might rent it to us for the 5 weeks. At first, we rejected the idea – I was not in Portland to hang out on some island, but to work every day in the city. In addition, summer rental rates were a little more than we could afford on the $100 per week I was being paid.

After several days of fruitless searching, we agreed to give the island cottage a try. My father had said that many Portland families live on the Casco Bay islands during the summer while commuting to work in town. The price (perhaps reduced by a secret subsidy deal between my parents and the Fergusons) was only $50 per week – more than we expected to pay for an apartment, but do-able. So it was that we anxiously took the 10:30 am Casco Bay Lines steamer from Custom House Wharf to Great Diamond Island, where we found a funky turn-of the century wood cottage with a westerly view of Casco Bay, the City, the mountains of western Maine, and, on clear days, Mount Washington. The boat ride had taken about 15 minutes. There were several boats a day, including a return

117

trip to the island at 5:30. The cottage was simple but comfortable. We took it.

That was one of the key decisions of our lives. Although I hurried back to Portland and the Pierce Atwood law office after we saw the cottage, at the end of that first day of work I was on the 5:30 boat back to Great Diamond. As we sat on the veranda watching the sun set that evening, the possibility of settling in Maine then and there became a bit more probable. How could this be beat? To come home every summer evening to an island – and with *Serendipity* moored nearby – would be a life that I had not dared dream of up to then.

At any rate, the 5 weeks in Portland went fast. Work at the law firm was interesting, and I grew to have great respect for the "good lawyers" in the City of Portland. I found myself imagining our future more and more in terms of life and practice in Maine.

This does not mean that I totally forgot the project that we had left in the field behind 477 Main Street in Wilbraham. Of course, we had a long list of things to be picked up at Sargent Lord - galvanized bolts of different sizes for bolting together bilge stringers and clamps, bronze boat ring-nails for nailing down the plywood deck, odd boxes of screws of different sizes, and even a few fittings for when we would be ready for the "final touches". All were purchased after careful evaluation and a determination that we had found, in fact, the cheapest source. Carrying them back to Wilbraham in the red Rambler would save freight.

The most important contribution to the building of *Serendipity* from this Portland interlude was a matter of luck. I had heard that Royal Lowell, a well-known local boatbuilder, was building a large power boat on Long Wharf for Richard Waltz, a local plumbing contractor. So the first chance I got, I went to the Portland waterfront and to the half-ruined Long Wharf at its center. Sure enough, there was a plastic shelter on a corner of the wharf next to an old electrical generator building. Inside was under construction a beautiful oak and mahogany 54' cabin cruiser based on enlarged lobster boat lines. I met Royal Lowell, the yacht's designer and chief builder. The work was behind schedule and way over budget. But I could not help admire the beauty of the workmanship, the complex fits of the mahogany interior and the sweeping lines of the planks. I wondered if the planks that we were laboriously fitting on *Serendipity* would look half as good when primed for finish painting.

The more important discovery on Long Wharf for us, however, was an old lobster boat hauled out and blocked up on the wharf not far from the Lowell building project. Next to the lobster boat, sitting on an upended wooden crate, was a very old man – caulking.

"Caulking!", that magic art by which a hull transitions from a collection of planks fastened to frames to a watertight and sturdy vessel, capable of floating and keeping out the seas. As we had been applying the planks to *Serendipity's* frames that summer, I had become acutely aware that someday the seams between these planks would have to be caulked. Indeed, the water-tight integrity of *Serendipity* would depend upon how well and truly we caulked those seams. And caulking was something which I certainly had never done before. In fact, I had never even seen anyone caulk a boat.

Of course, I had read Chapelle (and any other source I could lay my hands on) over and over again. It sounded esoteric. There were little pictures of the indispensable "caulking mallet", a clumsy-looking affair with an elongated, banded head and an excessively short handle. There were the caulking irons, a "dumb" iron to wedge open hairline seams to accept the caulking, and the "making" irons ranging in size from 0 to 3. The caulker somehow knew how to select the right size making iron to drive the cotton or oakum between the planks with just the right degree of firmness.

The books warned about the pitfalls of inept caulking. The caulking must be driven into the seams "just right" - firmly enough so it would hold and not "crawl", and yet not so firmly that it would crack the swelling planks or separate them from the frames.

How was I to determine what was "just right" from reading in a book? I got the acute feeling that somehow book-learning alone was not going to make me into a good enough caulker to do the job. I needed a little hands-on experience. Of course, there were no boats being caulked in either Wilbraham or Cambridge. But here was an opportunity for me to learn by watching it being done.

I wasted no time in meeting 'Mac', the caulker. He had spent most of his adult life as an itinerant caulker. When there was work to be done, he went around to boatyards and would caulk, or re-caulk wooden boats that needed it - mainly fishing boats and lobster boats, but over the years also yachts. Mac had no objection to my coming down to the wharf during my lunch hour to watch him caulk as I munched my lunch sandwich. As he worked, I could see how he looped the strands of caulking cotton over his left index finger, held the loops up along the open seam, and deftly forced the loops into the seam by tapping with a "caulking mallet" on a "caulking iron". After the first pass, he would go back and drive the overflowing loops into the seam so that the cotton became hard and firm. You could hear a satisfying "thud" when the mallet hit the iron. Aha! Now, I could see what Chappelle was writing about in his famous *Boatbuilding* tome.

During my 5-week stint at the law firm that summer, a number of my lunch hours were spent on Long Wharf beside old Mac watching him caulk and committing the process to my visual memory. When he learned why I was interested, he invited me to try it for myself. The seams of the lobster boat he was caulking were old and "tired". It was hard to get the caulking in tight without driving it right through the seam and out the other side. Joe explained that caulking *Serendipity* with new and hopefully tighter seams, should be easier.

By the end of the summer, thanks to Mac, I had at least a rudimentary idea of what caulking was all about. The cotton, he confided, came in long hanks. But it wasn't fit to use that way. The hanks had to be unrolled and rolled up again in convenient balls. If one kept the ball in a can or pail, it would not get contaminated with dirt, bark or twigs which could cause trouble in the seam. There was a funny way in which one held the iron, kind of underhanded, so that the fingers would be free to clutch the cotton and kind of "wriggle" it into the seam in little loops.

Although Mac used a traditional caulking mallet, he allowed that really any mallet would do. This was a great relief to me. For in those days, before the revival of traditional tools, a caulking mallet was simply impossible to obtain. The old wooden mallet which I had inherited from my father would have to do the job. When we loaded the red Rambler to return to Wilbraham at the end of the summer, the big pile of gear and gunk from Sargent Lord included several hanks of caulking cotton and two caulking irons.

By August 16, our island sojourn in Maine was just a memory, and we were back at work in Wilbraham, bound and determined to get *Serendipity* planked before the fall. During our absence, the weeds had indeed grown higher around *Serendipity*. Our planing bench was almost invisible in the vegetation. We had a little more than two weeks of unremitting toil ahead of us to finish the planking before the start of my third year of law school in early September.

The summer of 1966 was a hot summer in New England. It seemed that cutting out each single plank with our tiny saber saw took forever. Sweat poured down our foreheads and dropped on the smooth surface of the planks. There were also the innumerable fittings, chalking of high spots, and planing – all by hand.

121

Securing the planks for fastening required two kinds of clamps. Conventional "C" clamps held the future plank to the frames. However, we frequently had to force a plank to lie more tightly against its neighbor. Professional boat builders had special "planking dogs" which provided a purchase so that one could use wedges to force the plank up or down along the frames. Although in recent years these traditional wooden

The inside of the planks at the turn of the bilge had to be hollowed a little where they met the frames so that they would lie fair against the curved frames.

boatbuilding tools are being manufactured again, in the 1960s, during the trough in wooden boatbuilding that we experienced then, such tools were unobtainable. We had to do the best we could with makeshift solutions. On more or less flat surfaces, we could use bar clamps made from pipe to draw a plank up to its neighbor. Where the frames curved, or where there was no room for a bar clamp, we had to use blocks clamped or

122

screwed to the frames and wedges to force the planks together so that seams would be tight.

On a good day, we could do a single strake (composed of either two or three parts) on both sides. Most days were less. As we added strakes, we alternated between building up from the keel and coming down from the sheer. The gap began ever so slowly to narrow. As we approached the "turn of the bilge" where the frames were very curved, each plank had to be hollowed from the inside to lie fairly on the curved frame. We did this with the old Craftsman 6" disc sander that my father in law had given us when he saw how meagerly we were

Here is Arthur Thomas helping clamp on a plank as we pushed to finish the planking in late summer of 1966.

equipped with tools. Over the course of the project, that sander did mighty work, until it finally burned out. Near the end of the job, we replaced it with a new Craftsman 7" disc sander and grinder.

Friends were always welcome, either to watch, or preferably to help. My college room-mate, Arthur Thomas, who had shared with me the harrowing hauling fiasco with the

123

mahogany planking stock in May, returned for a day or two in August and got right to work helping to fit and fasten planks.

Later that month, another college classmate, John Harmon and his wife Gail came by to admire *Serendipity* and to give a hand with a tricky strake.

John Harmon, friend from college and before, and his wife, Gail, stopped by to check on progress and were put to work. Here John drills for a strake that is clamped up against its neighbor by a pair of our pipe bar clamps.

Anita's sister Priscilla, then entering college, came to visit and found herself holding a wrench on a through-bolt for a particularly difficult butt-block, and then helping make the pattern for the "shutter".

As the ribbands were gradually replaced with solid planks, *Serendipity* began really to "take shape." One of my boatbuilding books had stressed the importance of taking enough time during a boatbuilding project to admire the progress of the work. We took this advice to heart and paused frequently – how remarkable it was that this thing of beauty was taking form under our very eyes!

As August because September, our massive pile of 1 1/8" Philippine mahogany had melted away. We would have barely enough stock to finish – which was just right.

Anita's younger sister, Priscilla, came to visit - and to help. Here, we can see a trial fit of the pattern for the last "shutter plank" in the bow.

The last plank is called the "shutter", which shuts in the last gap in the hull and makes it complete. This one is particularly tricky to fit. One has to get both sides just right so that both seams are tight. There is no way to clamp the shutter while it is being screwed to the frames. It was a real puzzler for a young amateur boat builder building his first planked vessel.

We ended up by making a plywood pattern for each of the three sections of this last strake. That was laborious, but if the pattern fit, then we could be pretty sure that the plank would. The 3/8" stock for the pattern was tacked over the gap that that plank would fill, then the contours of the plank were traced on it from the inside. The pattern stock was then removed, and the outlined pattern was cut out with the saber saw. Pushed in place, it fit. We then traced around the pattern

Boring for the screws to secure the "shutter plank" to the stem. Note the improvised clamping device to hold the plank in place.

on the last of our plank stock. Once more with the saber saw – we were sure tired of this. A quick dress with the plane, and, "Hooray", the shutter was in place.

It was really exciting to have a completed hull, even though without fairing and caulking, it would not float. We drank deep draughts of admiration of the beauty of the hull. We looked at it from every angle. Wasn't that a graceful curve where the bilge curved in and then reversed again under the counter! And didn't the bow have a dainty flare? That bow certainly would beat down the savage seas and keep us dry and safe.

On the other hand, the temporary moulds were still in place secured by the strong-back and a single ribband running lengthwise above the sheer on each side. We had never cut off the ends of the ribs since they had been originally bent that memorable Easter Weekend. Although the planks all faired gracefully into the stem rabbet at the bow, at the stern they

126

protruded past the transom, giving an untidy impression. Many of the nearly 5000 screw counter-bores were yet to be bunged. The cradle that had grown with the boat needed strengthening to eventually carry *Serendipity* off to be launched in the sea. But having that planking done gave us a tremendous boost. Indeed, we felt that we had completed the largest single job in building our dream ship. Little did we appreciate, how many hours of work still lay ahead.

Here we are admiring our fully-planked hull. We had made it - finished planking before the start of school in the fall. But it is obvious that we have a long way to go. . . .

Most of all, I had to go back to school. What a luxury it had been to have day after day with nothing to do but to get up and work on the boat as long as strength and light would last. Once more we were relegated to weekends. How would we possibly be able to have this boat completed and ready for launching by next summer? Or would we end up like Mr. Walker, with a semi-completed boat that would never see the sea?   We did not allow ourselves to consider this last possibility.

Chapter 6

Our first project on weekends after my return to law school in the fall of 1966, was to sand and fair the recently planked hull. Conventionally planked hulls do not achieve their smooth convex curves until the angular planks have been "faired" into smooth continuous surfaces. In the old days, this was done with large "fore planes" wielded by muscular shipwrights working from temporary scaffolds erected around the hull. Lacking both the planes and the skill to use them, we resorted to a new acquisition, a Craftsman four-inch electric belt sander, to fair and smooth the planks. We thought long and hard before we gave out the nearly $80 which it cost. The belts

Here is Mark Rollins "bunging" on *Serendipity's* starboard side.   There seemed to be a million screw-holes.   For each one we had insert a glue-dipped bung and drive it (gently) home with a mallet, then cut off the gross protrusion with a chisel, then, finally sand it smooth.

were over $1 apiece! Heavy and clumsy, it seemed to do the job. In the last days of summer, I stood for long hours on plank staging at various heights pressing the grinding, roaring machine against the planks and trying to dodge the sawdust coming out from every side.

Then we had to glue in the remaining wood bungs. Every one of over 4,000 silicon bronze screws had been deeply counter-sunk. A wooden bung had to be driven into each of the counter-sinks to cover the screw head. They were held by epoxy glue. Since Anita was disqualified from doing this work by allergy, my father stepped in to help out with this semi-skilled task as I pressed ahead with more difficult undertakings. "Thunk, thunk" went the mallet as he drove the soggy bungs home. As soon as the glue had dried overnight, I came along with first a chisel to cut off the worst of the protrusion and then the belt sander to sand them off flush.

We enlisted anyone who came by, including my friend Mark Rollins, and Mrs. Randolph, wife of my high school

Cutting off the ends of the planks at the stern.

physics teacher. They were good sports and glad to help for an hour or two on an otherwise boring monotonous job. We cut off the protruding plank ends at the stern, trying to make sure that we got the right angle so that they would blend in with the surface of the transom.

The fairing was an interminable job that seriously tried both us and our Craftsman sander. We had to pause frequently to give ourselves a rest and to let the overheated tool cool down. In an era before vacuum powered dust collectors, fine Philippine mahogany sawdust was everywhere, filling our nostrils, choking our lungs and coating our clothes, arms and legs. We also had to be careful that the sander followed the smoothcurves of the hull and did not create flat spots or divots.

Fairing the side of the hull with the new belt sander. It did a better job than the old disc sander, but it was very heavy to hold up against the work.

From time to time we checked by bending a light wood batten along the faired hull and looking for humps or gaps in the surface. My shoulders and arms ached after a few days of sanding and grinding away.

At this point, we also cut off most of the ribs that had protruded jaggedly above our sheer plank. We left only a few

131

sticking up on each side. The next step would be to remove the temporary moulds that had given *Serendipity* her shape. We were concerned that without the moulds, and without a deck, the newly planked hull might splay outward at the middle or change shape in some other way. We attached cross-spalls made from retired ribband stock across the protruding frame-ends at 3-foot intervals before we dismantled the moulds.

Here we have just cut off most of the frame ends and fitted temporary cross spalls on the remaining ones. We are about to remove the moulds.

There are many points in the boat building process where one's skill is tested. There are times when the builder sort of "holds his breath". The ultimate of these, of course, is the launching. But there are others along the way. "Drawing the moulds" was one of these points. The large, sturdy moulds had been the principal formers of the ship now for almost a year. What would happen when we pulled them out of our new hull? Would the graceful curved sides flatten out? Would the hull become lopsided? Would the stiff, rugged sides sag or become floppy? There was a certain tightness of the chest as we clamored inside the hull and unscrewed the galvanized screws which connected the bases of the moulds to our oak keel. Off came the strong-back, on which I had so triumphantly strutted almost a year before when the moulds had been first set in place on the naked keel.

Here Anita is handing one of the moulds down to me. They came out so easily!

With a little nudging and hauling, out came first one, then another, of the great clumsy cross-sections. The hull held! Quickly, then jubilantly, first one, then all of the 10 moulds were dragged out and tossed over the side. We were soon in a vast open expanse, the inside of our ship. There was no change in the form of the skin. The sweet curves were all still there. As we trundled and tramped around inside, the hull was firm beneath our feet. Luxuriating in the sheer volume of our creation, we stood inside as we sawed off the jagged and uneven frame ends. Almost miraculously the sheer line of

133

Serendipity, graceful and rising in the bow, crystalized into view.

We could not spend too much time admiring our newly-revealed handiwork. The moment of truth had finally arrived. It was time to caulk our planked hull. Had I learned enough from old Mac, the caulker, on the wharf in Portland last summer to be able to make sure that the seams of our dream ship would be tight and keep the water out?

The first step was to unravel the hanks of caulking cotton purchased the preceding summer at Sargent Lord and to roll the loose strands into balls. That was easy. Then, with the caulking iron in my left hand and my old wood mallet in the

Driving the bunched cotton into the seams with mallet and caulking iron.

right, I hooked a couple of strands of cotton over my left index finger and, using the iron, nudged it into a seam. A gentle tap with the mallet drove it in far enough to catch. I moved my finger along, gathering a loose loop of cotton as I went. Another nudge, a tap, and the cotton was hanging in a loose loop along the seam. I did this several times until I had covered about three feet. Then it was back to the beginning to gather smaller bites of the loop on the iron and nudge and tap them in place. I stood back. The seam was filled with cotton now. As I wiggled and tapped, my little loops were scarcely as regular and neat as Mac's. But somehow the cotton got into the seam. As I tapped it home, I listened for the same kind of sound I had heard on the pier in Portland. "Ponk, ponk". It sounded all right.

Anita is forcing Caulk-Tex into the freshly caulked seams. This was slow and patient work. The moulds are lying under the apple tree in the background.

At first, of course, it went slowly, tentatively and diffidently. But later I saw the little loops getting more and more regular. The right "ponks" came quicker and more authoritatively. The task advanced. Only at one place, high under the sheer strake near the bow, did the cotton come through. Otherwise, our seams held.

At this point, the cotton was a tight roll driven far enough into the seam so that there was about ¼" of seam exposed. This part of the seam would be filled with the seam putty. As indicated before, although traditional oil-based seam putties were available and cheap, we elected to go with the relatively new, high-tech and expensive "Caulk-Tex" two-part epoxy-based caulking putty from Travaco Labs. We had been able to buy this in gallons at an attractive discount. However, the downside was that each batch of Caulk-Tex had to be mixed on the spot and had a very limited work-life.

Anita did most of the puttying, following me along as I finished driving in the cotton. She mixed the Caulk Tex on scraps of plywood with a putty knife. We estimated the proportions of compound and hardener by eye and were satisfied if the resulting mixture was more or less the right color tan. She would then force as much compound into the seam as it would hold, scraping off any excess, and going along once more to make sure that the seam was full. We would ultimately sand off any scraps of Caulk Tex that protruded above the level of the planks.

We quickly found that temperature made a great deal of difference. On a warm day, it was easy to force the gooey, sticky compound into the seams. However, as it became colder, the Caulk-Tex became stiffer until it was virtually impossible to work. Caulking was a slow job, at best. Although Anita could do the puttying, she had never been on the dock in Portland. I had to drive home all of the cotton by myself.

Caulking was time consuming and took the good days for the remainder of the fall of 1966. As the weather became cooler, the compound became stiffer and harder to mix and work into the seams. It also took longer to harden. We were lucky to be able to finish caulking the hull before it became simply too cold to work. The last caulking took place after Thanksgiving.

When we removed the moulds we fastened temporary cross-spalls to every fourth frame, which we left long for that purpose.

By now we had a hard deadline to finish *Serendipity* and get her launched. During our relatively brief Maine sojourn, I had met Judge Edward T. Gignoux, the sole United States District Court Judge for the District of Maine. On Columbus Day weekend, Judge Gignoux offered me his clerkship for the following year. I was thrilled to accept. But I would have to start work with him in Portland, Maine on the day after Labor Day, the following September. We had less than a year to finish *Serendipity* far enough so that she could be launched and accompany us to Maine. We had no work plan, and no real idea of how long each of the remaining tasks would take us. We just figured that we would have to work, and work hard, every available moment to make it!

We were acutely aware that we were building outside, and that fall rains and winter snows would soon fill the open hull and make all soggy – even rotten. We needed some kind of temporary roof under which we could continue work throughout the winter, if possible.

137

Our solution to the shelter problem was to erect our own roof over the boat using the remaining extended frame tops as uprights. To each one of them we screwed simple trusses composed of single "rafters" cut from plank scraps tied together with plywood gussets at the peak. To these, we screwed thin longitudinal battens also of plank stock, re-sawn to half-inch thickness spaced about 6" apart. This gave us enough structure to support a "roof" of heavy transparent plastic sheeting. The last was supplied by my brother, Paul and his friend Jim Severin, from some source or other. The

Our temporary "roof" was made of rafters screwed to some extended frame heads with longitudinal purlins of scrap covered by a huge plastic sheet that we cut to size.

transparent sheeting was secured by thin battens running up and down the outside of each rafter above the sheeting.

When we say "screwed", we mean screwed using old-fashioned wood screws. We used expensive bronze screws for all work on the boat itself. However, the various patterns, jigs, cradles, ribbands, moulds, shelters and the like were all constructed using flathead steel zinc-plated wood screws, screwed in by hand or with a brace and bit.

This was before the advent of drill-driven sheet metal screws, or, for that matter, square or star drive screws that could be driven with power drivers. Midway in the job, we acquired a geared-down screwdriver attachment for our ¼" electric drill. That was far from perfect. One had to hold it carefully lest it slip and gouge the work. For this reason, we used it mainly on temporary work that was more or less "in the clear" where we could easily hold the drill in one hand and the attachment in the other to keep the bit in the slot. When complete, this shelter was remarkably weather tight and cozy. We could enter or leave the boat from the rear via a ladder set up against the transom. A flap in the plastic panel over the stern served as the "door".

In bad weather and as the caulking was finally completed, we went to work inside our now seemingly roomy hull with its green-house roof. The first task was to install the "sheer clamp", a long timber running lengthwise along the inside of each side of the boat just below the sheer line. The clamp not only provides strength and support for the hull in general. It also serves to support the ends of the deck beams.

We turned to the pile of white oak from Mr. Koncitek. We had specified four 18' 1½ x 3½ " timbers to be scarfed together to make two continuous timbers each over 30' long. Sure enough, there they were, none the worse for several months of sitting in our carefully "stickered" lumber pile. We took them to Mr. Merrick, who planed the sides of each timber so that they were smooth and exactly 1½" thick. However, we did not have any means of planing the edges, so we left them rough-sawn, which they are to this day.

The clamps, and later the bilge stringers, were scarfed together by crude lengthwise scarfs secured with epoxy glue and 3/8" galvanized carriage bolts. They were long, heavy and ungainly to hoist up under our plastic roof and into the hull using only person-power. Bolting the sheer clamp to 36 frame heads on each side was not easy. The curve and flare of *Serendipity's* bow meant that the clamp had to twist a good deal in two directions at once as we forced it down in position. We probably should have steamed it. But by then the wallpaper steamer had been returned and our steam box put away, hopefully for the duration.

With clamps, cussing, swearing, and persistence, we managed to wiggle and sweat the long timbers into place, from butting up against the stem forward to brushing the transom aft. We clamped them in place with our numerous c-clamps left over from the frame bending exercise and secured them to the frame-heads about 2" below the sheer strakes on each side with ¼" bronze carriage bolts. They were expensive, but we

Here the sheer clamp is clamped in place and ready for bolting to the frame heads. The structure of our "greenhouse" roof is clearly visible.

had decided that any fastening smaller than 5/16" in diameter should be bronze.

In most vessels the sheer clamps are secured to the transom by "transom knees". Traditionally, these were cut from natural "crooks" from tree stumps. At the time *Serendipity* was built, however, there was no source for exotic wood products of this kind, so we had to make do with knees laminated from strips of oak that had been re-sawn from rib stock and then re-planed on (guess!), Mr. Merrick's planer. I made a crude jig around which we bent successive 3/8" strips of oak, drew them down with clamps and glued them with epoxy glue. When they were dry, I sanded off the unevenness on the sides and we cut the bevel of the transom in one side of each knee. It was a laborious and time consuming process that took place in our 12 x 12 mini-shop in the shed next to my father's book barn. It is fair to say that my knees looked a lot

In my hand is a completed laminated stern knee while the other one is still in clamps.

141

rougher and less artistic than the knees that we saw in the pictures in our boatbuilding books. But they would have to serve the purpose of holding the sheer clamp and the transom together.

The two "bilge stringers" were specified as 1½" x 6" white oak timbers scarfed into single lengths. Bilge stringers run from bow to stern along the inside of a boat at the "turn of the bilge", where the bottom of the boat gives way to the sides. Their function is to stiffen and strengthen the hull both generally and at this crucial location.

Here I try to smooth a crudely cut scarf in one of the bilge stringers. The two halves were edge-bolted together with 3/8" galvanized carriage bolts.

Yes, we had the necessary planks in the lumber pile. They were a lot heavier and clumsier than the clamp timbers. After planing the sides, we fashioned scarfs, then glued and bolted the two stringer scarfs together edgewise with epoxy glue and 3/8" galvanized bolts.

142

Although it was getting cool out, we sweated as we hauled the bilge stringers up into the hull and bent them in place. With the bilge stringers, there was no way for us to clamp them in place while we bored the necessary holes and secured the necessary fastenings. We marked the frames with the approximate location of the upper edge of each bilge stringer. Then one of us had to stand on the timber while the other nudged it in place, bored a hole through the frame and out through the planking, countersunk the hole on the outside,

I hold the starboard bilge stringer in place while Anita bores a hole for a bolt from the outside.

drove home a ¼" x 6" bronze carriage bolt from outside to inside, and got a washer and nut on the bolt in the inside. Once we got a couple done on each side, the stringers were secure enough so that it was not necessary to stand on them. Each bilge stringer was bolted to each frame on its side of the boat – 36 bronze bolts per bilge stringer. After we had the bilge stringers in, we plugged the counterbores in the planking for the 72 bolt heads with 5/8" mahogany plugs.

Here I lay out a deck beam by tracing our pattern on a 2 x 6 oak plank. Mr.
Boland helps (or watches?).

Of course, as we performed the various tasks, we had to
be continuously thinking ahead about the next task, and what
we needed to do to prepare for it, so that the work could go
forward without delay or disruption. The 36 deck beams were
specified to be cut to a particular "crown" out of 2" white oak.
Although we had a stack of 2" x 6" white oak timbers in the
wood pile, cutting 36 of them to the curve of the deck with our
Craftsman saber saw was a daunting prospect. The saber saw
had been barely able to get through the 1 1/8" mahogany. How
could we expect to cut through 2" white oak?

As was the case with the heavy oak backbone timbers,
in the absence of access to a band saw, we called in our friends
at the Roy Lumber Company. Could they bandsaw our deck-
beams? Yes, they could, if we could clearly draw the shapes of
the beams on the rough timbers.

Returning to the loft plan for the "camber" of the deck
beams, we used a flexible batten to lay out a pattern beam on a

piece of ordinary ¾" pine stock. This we could easily cut out with the saber saw and clean up with the plane. We then took our pattern and a large pencil and drew the shapes of all 36 deck beams on our white oak deck beam stock. We were careful to avoid knots or "sapwood", which is more prone to rot and deterioration than wood nearer the heart of the tree. The Roy Lumber Co. truck came by to pick them up in due course, and in due course, they were delivered back to us. I do not have any record of what Roy charged us to do this crucial work, but my recollection is that it was extremely reasonable under the circumstances.

Chapter 7

While we were thus engaged struggling with the structures of *Serendipity's* hull, we had to plan ahead for such items as *Serendipity's* spars, her sails and her auxiliary engine. Much of this sourcing work was carried out from Cambridge during the week. Fortunately, a Law School class schedule leaves abundant time during regular working hours to call various potential suppliers. Letters can be written, read and answered in the evenings.

Most amateur boat building projects, especially in small towns, generate a good deal of local interest. Ours was no exception. From the beginning, there had been onlookers, critiquers, and skeptics. But there had also been enthusiastic supporters, who frequently came around to view the progress of the boat and to urge us on.

One of my high school teachers, Mr. Spottiswoode (Bim) Randolph, lived across the street. When he heard about this crazy new venture, his own imagination was ignited. He pored over our plans with us. He, too, became enamored of the simple, sweet lines of Crockett's design. How could he get one of these vessels built? Soon he was calling Crockett. It happened that one of the "Nimble" schooners had just come on the market. Before I knew it, my neighbor across the street owned my dream ship!

The *Elise,* renamed after Mrs. Randolph, had been built about 1960 in Rockland, Maine. A little rough around the corners, nonetheless she represented a quantum leap over our poor efforts in boatbuilding skill. We went down to see her in Cape Cod. She had been bastardized a bit with a Genoa jib and some other "compromises". But she was beautiful, she sailed well, and the reaffirmation of our faith stifled our jealousy.

Mr. Merrick, our planing saint, stopped by occasionally to check on progress. And then there was Mr. Boland. As the vessel progressed from frame to ship, he became a Sunday regular. Every Sunday morning, we could count on him stopping in on his way to the center of town to pick up his newspaper. He usually stayed for an hour to an hour and a half. He was early-retired, and had little to do. I half listened as he rambled on, telling us the story of his own unfinished dreams. I soon learned that it didn't really matter how I answered his questions . . . But he was company of a sort and his good wishes were sincere.

Sourcing the various materials to construct a traditional schooner yacht in the mid-1960's was a continual challenge. The 1950s had been the last great hey-day of wooden yacht building for those yards such as Graves, Luke, Hinckley, Snow and Newbert and Wallace that had survived the Depression. These were the days when Concordia was importing wood yawls from Abeking & Rasmussen in Germany, and American Marine was importing wood Samurai sloops from Japan. The traditional suppliers of yacht fittings such as Wilcox-Crittenden, Perko and Merriman were still in business providing everything from wood blocks to marine toilets out of bronze for a respectable community of professional wood boat builders.

The advent of fiberglass boatbuilding in the late 1950s changed all of this almost overnight. Wood boatbuilding came to a more or less screeching halt over just a few years. The new boats being built had a little wood trim and plywood interiors. Hardware on most fiberglass boats was stainless steel or at least chrome plated.

Many of the old sources of lumber, fittings, fastenings and the like went out of business or drastically reduced their lines. Some items, such as wood shell blocks and galvanized rigging hardware became entirely unobtainable. For example, Wilcox-Crittenden, of Middletown, Connecticut, which for nearly a century had made everything from galvanized cleats to galvanized anchors and many things in bronze as well, was sold to "The North and Judd Manufacturing Company", and its

147

line of products was greatly shortened to correspond to current demand. Perko Marine Lamp and Manufacturing Company, which also manufactured a full line of traditional brass and bronze hardware in Brooklyn, New York, moved its operations to Miami, Florida, discontinuing most of its traditional products. Merriman Brothers, which had made bronze hardware for the Herreshoffs, both Nathaniel and L. Francis, in Bristol, RI, had also been bought up, had moved to Hingham, MA, and had cut its formerly complete line of hardware to only a few items. While it still made the wood shell blocks that had made it famous, the choice of fittings had shrunk to a few options of front and side shackle, and the price had climbed far out of reach for a young amateur boatbuilder.

By the mid-1960s it had become very difficult to source fittings and materials to build traditional boats out of wood. This changed with the revival of interest in wooden boatbuilding under the leadership of *Woodenboat* magazine in the late 1970s. Since then many items that were unobtainable in the 1960s have been manufactured again – in most cases by new firms focused on the traditional boat market. But at the time we were building *Serendipity*, everything was hard to find.

Another issue was that of price. Marine paraphernalia is notoriously high-priced. Retailers get healthy markups to compensate them for handling seasonal and special use merchandise. This was known to me from my days at the Prout's Neck Yacht Club, where we could buy wholesale from the Harris Company in Portland. When we started *Serendipity*, we did all we could to find sources that would provide our needs of glue, paint, screws, fittings and the myriad of other "stuff" we needed on a wholesale basis.

Already mentioned is Sargent, Lord & Company, an old-line ship chandler on Portland Pier in Portland. Marshall Madsen, its owner, and his staff, were most understanding of the plight of the young boatbuilder and were willing to extend

148

their wholesale price schedule to cover our purchases. That was a great help, and we ordered a great deal from Sargent, Lord. Much of it was shipped directly to 477 Main Street, Wilbraham in crude recycled cartons bound up with heavy twine. Other items, I would pick up on my trips to Portland.

In those days, most marine gear, boatbuilding supplies and yacht fittings were sold through large distributors who published annual catalogs. The catalogs pretty much consisted of reprints of pages from the manufacturers such as WC or Perko with line drawings (not photos) of the various fittings and items offered. Although wooden yacht building had pretty much died out, a few yards were still building wooden fishing boats and lobster boats, which resulted in a limited and shrinking demand for traditional boatbuilding paraphernalia. In Portland, there was the Harris Company and Sargent & Lord. Although the Harris Company was much bigger and had a bigger selection in their thick catalog, they were not inclined to put me on their discount schedule.

In Boston, James Bliss & Company had been in business since the 19th century. In recent years they had been gradually phasing out of ship chandlery and into yacht gear and model boats and supplies. Atlantic Marine Hardware was another old Boston chandlery, barely hanging in there on the Boston Waterfront. They did not publish a catalog, but their dusty warehouse was worth exploring. In New York, Manhattan Marine published a thick catalog. Much of their gear consisted of Italian or Taiwanese knockoffs of WC or Perko fittings. Their prices were high and there was no discount. In the mid - 1960s all of these were more or less on their last legs. Fifteen years later, they were all gone. Of course, such enterprises as West Marine and Hamilton Marine, which rose to take their places, were some years in the future.

Throughout the project, sourcing and scheduling of needed fittings, materials and supplies consumed many hours during each week that otherwise might have been spent studying the law.   Sometimes the "Yellow Pages" yielded helpful results.   There I found a small old Boston chandlery, "Al Pendleton Supply".   Al dealt largely in rope, wire rope as well as all forms of cordage. He had a small storefront office a street or two off the Boston waterfront. He had no catalog, just a small listing in the Yellow Pages of the Boston phone book. I called him, and then went to see him. Yes, he would be glad to supply us, and at an attractive discount price.   We ultimately ordered our stainless steel rigging, our nylon anchor lines, and our manila running rigging from him. More on that later.

By a fluke that I now cannot remember, we learned of the existence of the Rostand Brass Manufacturing Company in Milford, Connecticut. This was an old line bronze foundry that had manufactured a large line of traditional bronze deck fittings for boat and yacht builders in New England for many years. They were still publishing a catalog that looked as if it came out of the 1940's with line drawings and descriptions of their various products. What a gold mine! When we found out about Rostand in late 1966, the company was on its last legs. But what a great catalog! All of the old fittings I had been looking for were there.   They had bronze stanchions, bronze ports, bronze blocks, bronze cleats - everything.

With the virtual drying up of the market for traditional bronze yacht and boat fittings, Rostand had turned to government contracting for much of its business. But they still had the patterns for their line of bronze fittings, and their aging workforce still knew how to make them.

The problem with Rostand, though, was the delivery. My contact there, sales manager Frank Cameron, was always harassed. Apparently he tended to promise more than he could make. He complained to me about the "expediters" on military contracts.   They came and sat in his waiting room inquiring hourly about their orders for day after day until they were delivered.   By comparison, my plaintive telephone calls and letters could be of little effect.

The Rostand catalog featured their bronze marine windows and port-lights. This was important to us. We had decided that all of the windows in *Serendipity's* cabin should be opening. In the summer of 1965, I had helped Mr. Mortimer Pratt bring his 43' sloop, *Meddler VI,* overnight from Prout's Neck to Annisquam to escape an approaching hurricane. The trip was made unpleasant by the smell of diesel fuel that permeated the closed and stuffy cabin. I remembered that. We did not want the cabin of our dream ship to be stuffy.

Although WC and Perko were still making a few windows, the selection was limited and those offered were very expensive. Rostand had a much larger selection. Best of all were Rostand's prices – if not right out of the 1940s, they were very attractive by mid-1960s standards. It was not long before I was on the phone to Mr. Cameron, asking about ordering windows and other items for *Serendipity.* When the orders arrived at our little apartment in Cambridge, it was like Christmas. The cartons were packed with real excelsior. We turned the gleaming bronze fittings over and over again in our hands, marveling at the workmanship, the machining, the intricate casting, the sturdy quality . . .

Serendipity represents the compromise outcome of the battle between the practical and the nostalgic, between the hard-headed and the sentimental, between the doer and the dreamer. As a cruising sailboat, she is sturdy and tough, but also inefficient and slow. Her lines are beautiful and nostalgic, a reminder of past eras, but she was not simple to build. She was a blending. My romantic traditionalist soul yearned for traditional materials and methods, hemp rigging, cotton sails, and pitch for the seams. My practical hard-headed doer insisted upon modern materials, a diesel engine, fiberglass on deck, and Caulk-Tex. The tension between the beautiful and the romantic on the one hand, and the practical and the feasible on the other, ran like a theme throughout the project.

151

In the fall of 1966, we were beginning to focus on two major items that we would need to finish and use our vessel, the sails and the auxiliary engine. The problem, of course, was "which we could afford". Our pocketbook had been strained beyond our anticipation by even the careful scrounging purchases that we had made. Despite the most vigorous efforts at economization, the costs already had risen beyond our estimates. There were just so many unexpected needs. Caulk-Tex, although purchased wholesale, had been over $20 per gallon. There had been tools, C-clamps, temporary timbers and framing. There had been many items for which we had simply not budgeted back in those days of bedazzlement when we had first caught fire with the dream. We approached the matter of sails and engine soberly, and sent out letters of inquiry far and wide in search of economical sources.

The original 1950's specifications for Crockett's *Nimble* called for sails of "Egyptian cotton". By 1967, traditional sail making and the materials from which traditional sails were made were but a memory on the U. S. sailing scene. Yacht sails were uniformly made of Dacron - hard, crinkly, stark white – in a word, artificial. For *Serendipity* we wanted traditional sails from long-staple Egyptian cotton – like the 1938 Herreshoff sail that I had been given for my first boat, *Te Amo*. The trouble, of course, was that we couldn't find a sailmaker who could provide it. The closest they could come was "Vivatex" or "Duck", canvas from American cotton of shorter fiber and coarser quality.

There was one sailmaker in Portland, Fortune Yacht Sails, run by Richard Fortune, Jr.. He remembered how they had made cotton sails in days of yore, but he had not made any in a long time. If we wanted, he could make us a suit from common canvas, but he did not recommend it. We ought to bite the bullet and get some modern Dacron sails.

There were other sailmakers who advertised in yachting publications. Armed with several copies of our sail plan, I

152

typed up and mailed out requests for their quotations for a suit of sails, jib, foresail, mainsail and gaff topsail, as specified and dimensioned on the sail plan, in both Egyptian cotton and in Dacron. In all, we must have corresponded with about 10 sailmakers in search of white wings for our dream ship – at an affordable price.

We received quotes from most of the sources solicited. None of the American sailmakers could offer sails in Egyptian cotton, although several offered Wamsutta canvas as an inadequate alternative to Dacron. Prices varied, from around $650 to $900 dollars for the suit. Canvas sails were usually only fifty to one hundred dollars per set cheaper than Dacron. The best bid in terms of cost was for 6.5 ounce Dacron from Thurston Sails in Rhode Island.

A small ad in *Rudder* magazine led us to "the source". A gentleman in New Jersey, whose name has become lost in my memory, advertised in the classified sections of that venerable publication. He was an agent for Jeckells' Sails of Wroxham, England. Jeckells could supply sails of "Egyptian Cotton, Terylene, etc." We sent him our plans. He sent back a beautiful, cuddly, soft sample of the Egyptian cotton fabric from which they would craft our sails. They would be all hand-roped with hemp, and the price was amazingly affordable.

Hallelujah! This was right out of the 19th Century! The old ways and materials were still alive and well in the Old Country! We rubbed the sail swatches against our cheeks. Just as soft and supple as the skin of a baby! The small stubs of hemp had an authentic tarry smell and feel.

Jeckells' price was right. They wanted $480 for the entire suit of four sails in fine spun Egyptian cotton, hand finished in hemp, traditional pattern. Even adding shipping and customs, that was by far the best price. Could we count on this foreign supplier with which we had no experience? We figured that we would take our chances and sent them a

The two swatches of Egyptian long staple cotton sail cloth that arrived in the mail were as soft as bedsheets and sealed the deal for Jeckells Sails, in Wroxham, UK.

deposit. The finished sails would come sometime after the first of the year 1967.

Amateur boat building truly is like a continuous Christmas. We would open each arriving package with expectation and glee. The sails were among the best "presents". Jeckells was then and probably still is one of England's fine old-line sailmakers. Situated in Wroxham, at the head of the Norfolk Broads, they had made sails for gaff-rigged boats continuously and probably longer than most sailmakers this side of the Atlantic. Their product reflected the best in British craftsmanship and tradition. The bundle smelled faintly of hemp. The Egyptian cotton was beautiful, as smooth and soft as bed sheets, although naturally of heavier weight. The hand-roping, seaming, hand-sewn cringles, grommets, and what-not, were a delight to the nostalgist's eye. We unfolded the beautiful sails in our tiny living room in Cambridge. They covered the entire floor and some of the furniture to boot. We gazed at them rapturously, fantasizing about how they would spread, like white wings, against the sky . . .

Finding the right auxiliary engine was a major challenge. The boat had originally been specced for a 22 HP Palmer gasoline marine engine. This was an engine of early post-war design that had been made by the Palmer Engine Company, Cos Cob, Connecticut. Many New England sailboats in the 30' range were outfitted with these engines, which performed reliably according to the standards of that day.

By 1965, Palmer was more or less on its last legs. Like many marine manufacturers, the company had been sold to a larger entity, which regarded the furnishing of marine engines as more or less of a sideline.

A more popular alternative was the 18 HP Universal Atomic Four manufactured by the Universal Engines Company of Oshkosh, Wisconsin. Atomic Fours were more common than Palmers in auxiliaries of the size of *Serendipity*, they were cheaper, and they were still being manufactured by their original maker. We could easily adapt the engine bed configuration in the plans to fit an Atomic Four.

A more quixotic possibility was an Acadia "make and break" engine manufactured by the Acadia Engines Company, Bridgewater, Nova Scotia. These engines were of a design from the earliest days of the 20th century. In the 1960s, they were still being manufactured to power the open cod-fishing boats in Nova Scotia and Newfoundland. They were manufactured in several sizes, 4 HP, 8 HP, 12 HP, 16 HP. There were two or three cylinder sizes. Higher horsepower was obtained by linking two or at most three cylinders together. Ignition was by a spark coil from a dry cell, "make and break". There was no transmission. When one wanted to go forward, one started the engine going forward. To change to reverse the operator had to change the timing via a cam lever just at the right time, so that the engine would run in the opposite direction. Starting was by a crank.

In the 1960's, Acadia Gas Engines had a glimmer of a renaissance in building and sales of their historic gas engines. Their U. S. distributor, Walter Hadley, West Redding, Connecticut, extensively publicized and advertised these practical curiosities.

I say "practical" because in the usage to which they had been put for six decades, powering the open "trap boats" and dories of Newfoundland and Labrador, these engines had been supremely practical. Ultimately simple, slow turning, fixable with a pair of pliers and a screwdriver, these engines were sold as "complete kits". A Newfoundland fisherman who had built a "trap boat" on the beach could order from Acadia everything he needed to power his craft. It would arrive on the steamer in a big wooden crate. After a couple of days of installation work, he would be chugging off to jig for cod.

Could these unusual and rare creatures be adapted for sailboat auxiliary use? They certainly had been in the early decades of the century. I corresponded voluminously and eagerly with Mr. Hadley. There were several advantages. First of all they were cheap - $800 for the complete kit, including a small galvanized tank, propeller and shaft. They were sturdy, simple and practical. They turned slowly - 700-800 RPM. An 8 horsepower twin could easily push our ship. Most appealing, however, was the nostalgia. Their individually-cast cylinders were painted traditional greens and blues. They gleamed with brass and bronze fittings. I could virtually hear the "pocka-chunka-chunk" of the little two lung engine pushing *Serendipity* through the coves and inlets of the Maine coast.

Of course, there were drawbacks. The first was the gas. We would be sailing on a time bomb. The second was that there was no electric starting. Starting the engine meant priming the cylinders with raw gas, backing down the timing, and turning over the flywheel by hand. Hopefully, it would "catch" on the first try. If it didn't, the process had to be repeated. I was a little concerned about having to do this

156

maneuver in some untoward strait with *Serendipity* twenty or thirty feet from the rocks. Other disadvantages included the lack of any neutral gear and the rather tricky procedure to make the engine go in reverse. One had to change the timing just at the right instant so that the connecting rod would reverse its travel and drive the crankshaft in the opposite direction.

A serious problem with all three of these engines was that they ran on gasoline. Although gasoline auxiliary engines were the norm on both wood and fiberglass sailboats built at that time, they posed serious dangers. Gasoline vapor is both explosive and heavier than air. A gasoline leak could fill the boat with explosive vapors that could be ignited by the merest of sparks, blowing boat and crew to oblivion. Yachting news and the rumor factory regularly included stories of yachts blowing up when their owners unwittingly lit their cigarettes or their stoves, or from a chance spark from two metal objects striking each other.

The rational alternative was a diesel auxiliary engine. Unlike gasoline, leaked diesel fuel does not vaporize. It will not ignite unless mechanically vaporized and pressurized as in a diesel engine. So diesel auxiliaries are very safe in the confined quarters of a sailboat. Diesels had become pretty much standard on yachts as well as commercial boats larger than 50 feet. Although L. Francis Herreshoff inveighed against diesel engines for small yachts ("heavy oil engines") in his 1949 publication, the *Common Sense of Yacht Design* as heavy, bulky, and above all, smelly, by the mid-1960s the trend was in the direction of smaller and lighter diesels that could be adapted to marine use.

J. H. Westerbeke, now a leading "marinizer" and distributor of small marine diesels, was founded in the mid-1960s. But at the time we were building *Serendipity*, the smallest sailboat engine that they offered was the 4-107, a 40 HP marinized version of a British Perkins diesel that was much too heavy, bulky and expensive to be considered for

157

Serendipity. The small 10-25 HP, 1-3 cylinder, Yanmars, Universals, Betas, and whatever were still a decade away.

To be sure, I had had some experience with a small diesel sailboat auxiliary when we sailed on Vincent McKusick's 28-foot wooden Kings Cruiser in the summer of 1966. This was one of a class of small wooden cruising sloops built elegantly and economically in Sweden during the 1950s. They were equipped with one-cylinder Volvo MD-1 diesel auxiliary engines (about 8 HP) that had a great record of simple reliability, without the danger of gas engines. I was able to ascertain that Volvo also made a 2-cylinder version (the MD-2) of approximately 15 HP that could well do the job for *Serendipity.*

The versions of the MD-1 and -2 manufactured in the 1960s were more or less unchanged from the time the engine was introduced right after World War II. They were relatively heavy, well over 400 pounds for the MD-2, with massive individual cast iron cylinders and a husky cast iron flywheel. A double belt running in a slot around the perimeter of the flywheel drove a 12-volt starter-generator. When starting the engine, this marvelous device acted as a starter. Once the engine was running, it automatically became a generator and provided a relative trickle of charging power to the battery. Starter-generators were relatively common in many engines built right after the War. By the 1960s, they had become relative antiques.

Another somewhat outmoded feature of the Volvo was that it was sea-water cooled. That is, salt water drawn from the surrounding ocean was pumped through the cylinder cooling jacket to keep it cool. By the 1960s, most marine diesels were fresh water cooled. The fresh water (or antifreeze) coolant was in turn kept cool by salt water circulated through a corrosion-resistant heat exchanger. The drawbacks to salt water cooling were that in a place like Maine the cold salt water kept the engine too cold at startup, and that over a long period of use,

158

salt would likely build up in the water passages of the engine block and ultimately block the circulation, causing the engine to chronically overheat.

But the main problem with the Volvo auxiliary engines was that when I first began the engine search, Volvo was not exporting these engines to the United States. I, therefore, reluctantly dropped them from consideration. Instead, we focused on two possibilities. Osco Engine Company of Souderton, Pennsylvania, had marinized larger Ford diesels and sold them for many nautical applications for some years. At the time we were looking for a diesel auxiliary for *Serendipity*, Osco had just started to import a small two-cylinder Italian diesel of 14 HP to marinize for use in small launches and auxiliary sailboats.

"Marinizing" an engine developed for some other terrestrial use (such as for a tractor or for a refrigeration unit on a truck) includes replacing key parts of the engine with corrosion resistant parts, converting the cooling from the kind of radiator found on vehicles to a heat exchanger that uses sea water for cooling, adding a pump to circulate the sea water, installing a marine transmission (forward and reverse) and shaft coupling, and adding some way to manage the exhaust. The Volvo MD series of engines was an example of the relatively few marine diesels that were originally developed for marine propulsion use. Most marine diesels, from the smallest to the largest, were originally developed for use in land-based applications, whether in vehicles or stationary service, and then adapted in this way to propel boats.

The drawback of the Osco was that it was expensive (about $1600) and relatively long – which would make it difficult for us to fit it in the relatively small space that had been designed for the compact Palmer. Osco seemed a little tentative about its commitment to this engine. We would be the first installation of this engine as a sailboat auxiliary. So we hesitated.....

159

Fairly early in the building process, Westerbeke announced its plans to marinize and distribute the "Pilot 50", a 15 HP, two-cylinder diesel that looked almost ideal. The problem was that when we contacted Westerbeke, it seemed like their announcement was premature. They did not know when, or actually if, the diesels would really become available. There were apparently glitches in the import process (also from Italy), or engineering the marinizing, or somewhere. A bright hope for a while, the Pilot 50 gradually faded from our horizon of engine options.

We had started the engine quest relatively early in the building process, searching for ads, brochures and catalogs, following up tips and suggestions from others, endlessly corresponding with potential sources. It was a slow and frustrating process. By the fall of 1966, I was beginning to get a bit anxious. We had installed extra floor timbers in the way of the engine location, but had not yet installed the engine beds to line up with the shaft hole bored so long ago in South Portland, Maine. And we could not build in those beds until we knew the specifications of the engine that we would be using. Would we have to settle for a Palmer or Atomic Four? Should we try the Acadia? Should we go with the Osco as the only real diesel alternative, despite the less than ideal dimensions and lack of a track record?

And then, out of the blue, we got a break. I saw a an announcement in a yachting magazine that Westerbeke would be importing the Volvo MD-1 and MD-2 line of sailboat auxiliaries. Apparently the Pilot 50 had been quietly dropped, and Westerbeke had turned to Volvo as a source of supply for what it sensed was a growing market for the smallest marine diesels as auxiliaries in sailboats of the 25-35-foot range. I hurried down to Westerbeke's warehouse in Dorcester. Yes, they had one on display. The new ones would be arriving in a few weeks on the boat. Although they usually sold only through dealers, they were willing to sell me one at the dealer price - 25% off.

Although the MD-2 would cost a bit more than the Palmer or the Atomic 4, at about $1400 it was a little less

Above: The Volvo Penta direct injection marine diesel with an output of 15.5 h.p. which weighs 420 lb. Light and compact it is an ideal auxiliary on sailing craft up to 50ft.

An announcement in a yachting magazine alerted me to the impending availability of Volvo diesels in the US.

expensive than the Osco. The MD-2 was rated at 15.5 horsepower and weighed about 420 pounds. It came with its own throttle control assembly, but we would have to fashion a linkage for the gear shift. This was before the time of "one lever" sailboat auxiliary engine cable controls. The motor would just fit within the space allotted to it under the cockpit. It would turn a 16" propeller, which was the proper size to drive *Serendipity's* anticipated 14,000+ pounds through the ocean swells at 5+ knots. It was a true marine diesel designed for small craft like *Serendipity*.

It was an easy decision. The Volvo MD-2 was tried and true, if somewhat obsolete technology, the engine would fit the space available, and the weight, although more than the gas alternatives, was not too excessive. We ordered an engine from the first shipment.

By this point, we were beginning to become a little concerned about costs. We had started this project with a few thousand dollars of savings from summer jobs. Although we scrimped and saved at every juncture as we went along, everything seemed to cost a bit more than we had hoped when we sized up this project from the beginning. By the fall of 1966, it was very clear that it would have been more economical for us to follow Curt Blake's advice and buy an older cruising sailboat, perhaps "one that did not look so good" for a few thousand dollars rather than try to build our own new boat with new materials and equipment. When I was in touch with the designer, Vere Crockett, at the very beginning of the project, he offered to have one built for us at Snow's Boatyard in Rockland, Maine, for about $15,000. At that time, $15,000 seemed to be a high price for a relatively simple 30' wood schooner. However, by the fall of 66 we realized that we would probably end up spending that kind of money and more just for materials and equipment to build the boat ourselves.

At this point, my parents stepped in to cut the Gordian knot of how to afford the Volvo diesel. They would give us the engine as a present. Although they had supported our project by providing building space, both indoor and outdoor, and by feeding and housing us during innumerable weekends and vacations while we toiled, so far we had bought all materials and services ourselves. We were most appreciative of their timely assistance.

Westerbeke promised to notify us when the shipment arrived from Sweden. In the meantime, they provided us with an installation diagram with all dimensions so that we could go ahead and fashion and install the engine beds while we were waiting for the engine to arrive.

In early December 1966 we got word that our engine had arrived. We picked it up "right off the boat" at Westerbeke's warehouse in Quincy, Massachusetts and hauled it in its shipping crate to Wilbraham on a U-haul trailer. It was stowed in the garage pending installation. It was a great relief to have the engine, and the kind we really wanted from the beginning, on hand and ready.

Here we are ready to unload the crated engine from the U-haul trailer into my parents' garage. Spicy watches. The Red Rambler, that hauled many a load of materials to the building site, is behind the trailer.

163

Chapter 8

Our last major sourcing challenge of the fall of 1966 were the masts and spars. The specifications called for two solid round wood masts, a 5" fore mast and a 6" main mast. There were two booms, a fore boom and a main boom, plus a jib-boom for the large self-tending jib. Both the mainsail and the foresail sported wood gaffs. The mainmast was crowned with an overlapping "fidded" topmast from which we could fly a gaff topsail. All of these were supposed to be made from Sitka spruce, a very light and strong wood that had been used for more than a century not only for spars of sailing vessels, but also for the wing struts and skeletons of early cloth-covered aircraft.

By the mid-1960s, sailboat spars were not being made from wood, but from aluminum extrusions. Persons with the skill to make wooden spars, either from solid stock or glued-up hollow boxes, were scarce. Spar lathes on which tapered wood spars had traditionally been turned, had disappeared from even large boatyards. Sitka spruce was also getting scarce, and had become very expensive.

It would have been theoretically possible for us to make all of the spars ourselves, out of whatever softwood stock we could obtain and afford. Chapelle had given detailed instructions on spar-making. There was even a formula whereby one could "lay out" a square timber and cut it to an octagon with a circular saw.

When I built *Te Amo* back in 1956 we had taken a dead pine tree of the correct diameter, planed and sanded off innumerable branch knots, and thus had made a satisfactory mast. The top end became the gaff. Another smaller pine tree was fashioned into the boom. All of this cost nothing other than the time to find the trees in the woods, cut them down, take the bark off, and plane the already rounded surface more or less smooth for varnishing.

But for *Serendipity* we wanted something better than dead pine trees from the forest. We wanted proper spars, made from Sitka spruce if we could afford it, or at least a plausible substitute.

This time the *National Fisherman* came to our rescue. An issue in the late fall of 1966 featured the Pigeon Hollow Spar Company of East Boston, Massachusetts. Pigeon Hollow Spar was a legendary name in wooden yacht building. They had furnished solid and hollow spars for practically all the major sailing yachts built in New England since the latter days of the 19th Century. Many New England fishing schooners had sported solid masts and spars made by Pigeon. Indeed, many a flag pole outside a New England yacht club or in a public park had been turned on Pigeon's massive mast lathes. In the mid-'60's, most of their business was in flagpoles.

Although I had read about Pigeon in L. Francis Herreshoff's *Common Sense of Yacht Design*, my assumption was that the firm had gone out of business back in the 1950's when so many of the great wood boat manufacturing companies had gone under in the face of the rush to fiberglass hulls and aluminum spars. It was, therefore, a real surprise to learn that the firm was still alive at its traditional location in East Boston. Of course, I went there to see them. It was a cold day in November.

My memory still preserves an image of the Pigeon spar factory in East Boston. It was an ancient rambling building, or set of linked buildings – more like sheds really, right on the waterfront. There was a large decrepit pier out to a handful of floats. Next to the pier was the "spar pool", where a number of long logs, or poles rather, floated chained to the pier. Those were future masts and spars that were gradually seasoning in salt water, the best way to prepare green lumber for use in maritime applications.

165

I was shown the mast lathes, massive devices on which masts as long as 120 feet and as thick as 36" could be turned perfectly round. The mast lathes were ancient and dusty from disuse. There were a few, pitifully few, wooden masts and spars in various stages of construction. There were hollow spars being glued up and clamped together on long jigs as well as a couple of solid spars (I think they were for a catboat) standing up against a wall waiting to be picked up by the customer.

The place certainly gave the impression that it had seen better days, much better days. There were only a handful of employees working in the cavernous building. In one corner, there was an operation assembling aluminum masts from extrusions – apparently Pigeon was trying to adapt to the current market. But the overall impression was on of marginal viability – Pigeon looked like it might be on its last legs.

The Pigeons themselves corresponded somewhat to the appearance of their facility. Guy Pigeon, a contemporary of L. Francis Herreshoff, was the old man. He must have been well over 80. In his day, he must have been at the top of the heap in the spar making business. By the time I met him, this was all memories, and he was coping with a dismal present in his final years.

Standish Pigeon, his son, was the person with whom I mainly dealt. At that time, he appeared to be in his 60's. He looked worn down by too many years of trying to keep the family business going under increasingly hostile business conditions. But he knew "the old ways" and he tried to keep this great old business alive.

Donald Pigeon, grandson to Guy and nephew of Standish, represented the future. He was a man in his 30's who had recently joined the family business with the aim of bringing it into the last third of the 20th Century. Clearly the effort to get into the aluminum spar business was his initiative. Guy and Standish were spar-makers and clearly loved what

166

they had done their entire working lives. Donald was a businessman who was trying to rescue a dying business before it expired.

Standish looked over our sail plan, which also contained the dimensions and tapers of the various spars. Yes, they could make these spars for us. Did we really want Sitka spruce? That was expensive. Perhaps he should price the spars in Douglas fir as an alternative? Douglas fir, also from the Northwest, is a strong, straight softwood that makes wonderful spars. Its only disadvantages are that it is quite a bit heavier than Sitka spruce and that it splinters easily when being worked. But our money was getting low. We would have to consider Douglas Fir as a matter of cost.

Did we want them to varnish or paint the spars as well? That would also affect the cost. No, we would do that ourselves at our hourly rate of $0.

A week or so after my visit, we received a letter with Pigeon's quotes on our masts and spars. It was typed by a manual typewriter with many mistakes. Ouch! The price for all Sitka spruce spars, two masts plus booms, gaffs and topmast, was over $800. That seems like a small sum these days. At that time, it was a major investment. If we went to Douglas fir, we could save about $100 or so.

Most of the money was in the masts. They would cost about $600 in Sitka spruce and about $500 in Douglas fir. The smaller spars would cost between $30 and $50 apiece. All of these prices were based on spars that would be sanded but not painted or varnished.

I went back to the drawing board and studied the chapter on spar making in Chapelle's *Boatbuilding* for the nth time. The masts were pretty straightforward, straight and with little taper – just a bit at the top of the foremast. There was a square tapered section for about 5 feet at the top of the main where it overlapped the fidded topmast. Chapelle's instructions on how to make a round solid mast were straightforward.

167

We stored the two 32-foot 6" x 6" timbers for *Serendipity's* masts on a pair of sawhorses covered with plastic, under the apple tree. Spicy is standing next to *Serendipity* with her plastic construction roof. Everything is covered by a light snow.

Maybe we could make the masts ourselves and leave the trickier booms, gaffs and topmast to Pigeon. . . .

I got on the phone with Standish Pigeon. Could we order just the booms, gaffs and topmast, unvarnished, in Douglas fir? According to his quote, that should cost $180. He hesitated. Well, really this had been quoted as a package. It would be scarcely worthwhile for them to make the small spars without doing the masts as well. He thought for a bit and finally agreed to do it. It was early winter and they (rather obviously) did not have that much to do. . . They would call me when the spars were ready for pickup.

So that left us with the masts. The foremast was specified to be 5 inches in diameter by 29 feet long. It was straight and parallel-sided up to the last 6 feet, where it tapered to a diameter of 3" at the very top. The main was brawnier, 6" in diameter by 31 feet long. It was also parallel-sided, but had a tapered and squared section at the top for the cross trees and the fidded topmast. The challenging parts would be to make them both perfectly round and to get the tapers right.

But first we had to find the timber. My first call was to the Winde-McCormick Lumber Company in Charlestown, where we had purchased the mahogany planking stock. Did they have two Douglas fir timbers that would meet our needs? What would they cost?

We were in luck. They had a good stock of 6" x 6" Douglas fir timbers in 32-foot lengths. The stock did not come 5 x 5. We would have to somehow cut down a 6 x 6 into a 5 x 5 for the smaller mast. The price – 32 cents per board foot – came out to a little less than $30 per mast timber.

I went over to the yard to pick them out of an impressive stack. This time, instead of trying to transport these long, heavy and clumsy timbers back to Wilbraham myself, we had them shipped by common carrier at a cost of around $20. The timbers arrived in due course. We stored them on sawhorses in the back yard under the apple tree and covered them with plastic against the winter weather.

We had read a great deal about the dangers of dry rot in wooden boats. Therefore, from the beginning, we had determined to combat it at all stages of the construction. Our weapon of choice was Cuprinol, a copper-sulfate based anti-rot preservative that we bought by the gallon from the local hardware store. We sloshed this on generously whenever we installed wood structure that was going to be permanent. As we formed *Serendipity's* backbone on top of our cast iron keel, our last step was to paint the oak timbers with green Cuprinol. After we pulled out the moulds, we doused the entire interior

Here Anita is applying Cuprinol to one of our first deck beams right up in the bow. This one has already been fitted. After she is finished, I will turn it over, bore holes in the clamp and frame head, and bolt the beam in place.

of the hull, and continued to apply it to interior timbers, deck beams, etc. as we went forward.

As fall became winter, we worked alternately under the plastic cover of the boat and in the shop. When the sun was out, it would be like a greenhouse inside the boat. It reeked strongly of Cuprinol.

The next major job was fitting the crowned deck beams. We made a pattern out of pine and drew them out on the rugged oak 2 x 6's which had been furnished by Harold Koncitek. Roy did the bandsaw work, so that we had a good supply of "blanks", sawed to the proper curve for the crown of the deck. The stock had not been planed. We simply installed them rough-sided and as they came off the bandsaw.

170

Starting at the bow, we had to cut the deck beams to size, notch and bevel them to fit down over the clamp and against the frames, and bolt them securely in place. There was a small notch for an oak strong-back down the center line of the ship. While this work was slow, and cold, we could really see the progress of the ship. There is something about the repetitive rhythm of frames and deck beams which one associates with nautical construction. It was immensely satisfying. It was also uncomfortable. Squeezed up under the edge of the plastic cover, inhaling Cuprinol, I tapped and chiseled as best I could.

It was slow work, about one or two beams per morning. Gradually, a framework for a deck grew in the bow, eventually reaching as far back as the fore mast step. As we worked our way aft, the first major challenge was the mast partner structure for the fore-mast. We cut semi circles 5" in diameter in two pieces of 2" oak stock and ran ½" threaded rod fore and aft to tie this structure to deck beams at either end. A stub beam on either side ended at the mast partners. It looked good and rugged.

Here one can see the foredeck and the stub deck beams along the port side. Progress was slow, but tangible.

171

Things like mast partners are very nerve-wracking. They have to be in just the right position. After all, we didn't want to have our mast "raked" forward or tilt to the side. Everything had to be plumbed up and set at just the right location so that the masts would be almost, but not quite, vertical. Out came the tapes, the measures, the plumb bob, and the loft plan. But we never knew whether we had got it exactly right. A tip from one of my books relieved us a little. We could make the mast step itself in the form of a slot so that the foot of the mast could be blocked forward or aft a bit to get exactly the right angle.

A couple of weeks after meeting with the Pigeons and giving them our order, they called. Our spars were ready. We rigged the car-top carriers on our 1967 Red Rambler American and drove over to East Boston. There, leaning up against the wall of the Pigeon shed were our booms, gaffs and topmast, all neatly sanded and ready for varnish.

I immediately noticed that the booms and gaffs did not seem to be the same color as the topmast. They were lighter and looked more like spruce or pine than the Douglas fir specified. Donald Pigeon explained. They had been concerned that if they delivered Douglas fir spars to us unfinished, the unprotected spars would likely "check" unless we applied the finish right away. Not knowing how long it would take us to get around to finishing these spars, they elected to use Sitka spruce, which does not tend to check the way the fir does, for all the spars, except the topmast. They would absorb the extra cost. Thanks to the conscientiousness of the Pigeons, *Serendipity* got beautiful Sitka spruce spars for the price of Douglas fir. This was another example of how various suppliers extended themselves to help us on our way to realizing our dream.

172

Fresh from Pigeon's the spars are stored on the picnic table on the porch. The long one is the main boom. The one with the squared end is the topmast.

Thankfully we loaded the spars on the roof-rack and carefully drove them out to Wilbraham. We put them on my parents' side porch for storage.

Slowly, our skills were increasing. Anita's role as I worked on the deck beams was largely encouragement, handing things, boring holes and turning down nuts. It was sporadic, and for long moments she had nothing to do but watch me and keep me company. This she did patiently and well. It was time to get going on the deck structure.

It was often cold as we worked up under the plastic roof inside the hull, and there were innumerable trips up and down the stern ladder bringing each deck beam back and forth from the shop for cutting, beveling and minor adjustments. Each beam was notched over the sheer clamp and was secured to the head of the adjacent frame with a ¼" bronze carriage bolt.

It started to get even colder, and then there was the first snowfall. It was too cold to work outside. So, we transferred activities to the small shop next to the barn. It was outfitted with a long low workbench under the windows. There were two ancient wood vices bolted to the floor. These were operated with massive screws turned by wood dowel handles and could hold pieces of wood of almost any thickness. For years, my father had used this space for storage of parts of his burgeoning book collection. When we started the boatbuilding project, the small shed was literally full of books – cartons stacked on every side so that one could not even see the workbench and had difficulty moving among them. In order to be able to use this space, we had to build shelves in the barn and cellar of the house for the hundreds, or perhaps thousands of books that we then moved there from the workshop.

Although the shed had electricity from an underground wire running from the house, it was unheated and without any form of insulation. We needed heat in order to work there – not only to keep ourselves warm, but also to permit the glues and compounds we were working with to set and harden. Fortunately, my father had a miniature cast iron wood stove called a Tyson Furnace. We positioned the stove toward the back of the workshop and ran a 4" stove pipe from the stove out through the wall and up alongside the shed high enough to get a good draft. It worked perfectly. There was abundant scrap wood to feed it. We could kindle a fire in the stove and in a few minutes could feel the workshop becoming warm.

The first big project in the shop that winter was to make *Serendipity's* rudder. The plans called for a large ear-shaped rudder with a generous aperture for the auxiliary engine propeller. The question was, how would this be connected to the hull, and to the tiller, so that it would function as intended and be strong enough to withstand tremendous forces from waves and sea? The literature offered various "solutions" to this problem. The simplest would be to extend the rudder shaft partly around the propeller aperture and to secure the rudder to it by straps or by long drift bolts through the shaft and rudder alike. A more elaborate solution would require a custom casting for the rudder shaft and curved aperture joined to a straight shaft where it went up through the deck. There were various methods of securing the shaft to the stern deadwood from simple bent straps to custom cast fittings.

Boring the horn timber at just the right angle for the rudder-post, was one of those tasks in which the strain of the actual physical labor was compounded by the fear of misstep. Suppose we did it wrong and got the rudder-port bored at the wrong angle? Would the rudder bind, or would we fatally weaken the horn timber? We stretched lines, took bevels, and tried to line up our crude tools as best we could by eye. A cheap Irwin expansion bit was all we had to bore the 2" hole through the seasoned oak. By the time we had driven it through about 6" of oak, the hole looked as if it had been gnawed by a mouse or pecked by a woodpecker. However, to my anxiously squinting eye, the ragged hole appeared to be aimed more or less in the right direction, so that our rudder post would line up with the slanted trailing edge of the deadwood.

Another challenge would be fitting the rudder to the boat. If we made the rudder shaft an integral part of the rudder, how would we be able to get it up into position without being able to hoist the boat several feet in the air so that we could push the shaft up in its tube from the bottom? This whole business caused me a lot of puzzlement. I looked at books and at boats hauled out for the winter at boatyards. The final decision was to make a custom casting for the edge of the rudder itself. The rudder shaft would be joined to this at the top with a keyway. We would thus be able to install the rudder and then insert the shaft down the shaft tube from the top into the keyway in the rudder casting. It should be strong enough.

The rudder itself was specified as 1½" thick, of oak. We had plenty of semi-seasoned white oak two by fours, which we planed to 1½" thick in Mr. Merrick's planer. We could glue these and edge-drift them together with ½" galvanized drift bolts.

The rudder casting was another matter. That had to be bronze. I had read a bit about casting bronze in *Boatbuilding*, and was under the impression that a pattern had to be in two parts so that it could separate when being removed from the "drag" and the "cope", the two halves of the sand moulds into which the molten metal would be poured. Working from the loft drawing, I made two long patterns of the leading edge of the rudder out of ¾" plywood and then joined them together with wood pegs so that they could be taken apart. Sanded and painted, they constituted my pattern. The hole for the rudder shaft in the top end and the keyway would be machine work.

Patterns in hand, we had to find a foundry to cast the fittings. This turned out to be difficult. The rudder casting was nearly 5 feet long, much longer than the capabilities of most bronze foundries, which concentrated on smaller items. After many phone calls, I finally found the Massachusetts Foundry, right in Cambridge, not far from Central Square. Their main work was making sophisticated castings for government defense work. But they did cast in bronze, and could cast a fitting 5' long. I went to them, patterns in hand and full of hope.

As often stated before, many people had pity on me and extended themselves, a little or a lot, to help us make our dream come true. The people at the Massachusetts Foundry were a bit contemptuous of my pattern. It did not need to be in two parts. The only requirement was that each half have enough "drag" (taper) so that it could be removed from the moulding sand in the "drag" (bottom) or "cope" (top) of the casting box. The pattern needed to be painted with special silver paint – the naked wood would draw the moisture from the moulding sand and make it stick to the pattern. The gudgeon pattern needed to have some drag on the straps so that

176

The rudder is being built here in the tiny shop. On the left is the new bronze rudder casting. The oak planks that make up the rudder itself are being laid out on the plywood pattern that we took from the loft drawing.

it could be pulled out of the sand. In short, what I present them was scarcely ready to use in a pour.

Rather than send me away to try to make things right, however, the Massachusetts Foundry bronze founders agreed to do what was necessary so that they could work with my patterns. They would cast the parts in manganese bronze, which is harder and stronger than the silicon bronze I had suggested, without charging me extra for the more valuable metal. A couple of weeks later, I came back to the foundry to pick up the rudder edge fitting and the two gudgeons in gleaming yellow bronze. The cost was about $150, not a small sum for me, but very likely a break-even proposition at best for the Massachusetts Foundry.

Everything is related in the construction of a boat. When planning and making the rudder, we also had to take into account the rudder shaft and the tube that would contain the rudder shaft. The key-joint by which the rudder would be attached to the shaft had to be machined before the casting was

177

installed in the rudder. Everything had to be done in the right order, lest we find ourselves in an impossible box.

The rudder shaft was a piece of 1½" bronze shafting, probably more robust than necessary for a boat of this size, but it fit the piece of 1½ " brass pipe that we had purchased for the rudder tube. Somewhere we got the rudder fitting machined for the shaft. The shaft was reduced to 1" and fit snugly down into a 1" blind hole bored in the top of the rudder casting. It was held fast from turning by a ¼" bronze key. We left the shaft a bit long so that we could cut it off at the right length at the top after the rudder tube was installed and the deck was in.

With these steps completed, making the rudder itself, turned out to be a piece of cake. Working with a large scrap plywood pattern cut from the loft pattern, we clamped the rudder casting along one side and then laid our 4" oak boards side by side on the pattern, so we could mark the ends for cutting (laboriously) with the saber saw. Oh, for a band saw at so many points in this process!

Holding the pieces of rudder together with pipe clamps, we bored down edgewise with our ½" ships augur and Craftsman 3/8" power drill. (This was the most powerful power drill we had on the job. We also has a ¼" electric drill left over from my first boatbuilding project in 1956-57). We used a jig for this, a 1 ½" block of wood with a ½" hole in it that was attached to two long legs. We would clamp the jig to the work with the block a few inches away from the spot to be bored. This would keep the drill aligned as it went deep in the stock. We used this kind of jig at various points whenever we had to bore a long hole in the edge of a plank or thin piece of stock.

We erred on the generous side in putting the rudder together. First of all, every piece was glued to the next with epoxy glue. Second, we had several ½" threaded rod bolts running edgewise through the entire structure and into the rudder casting.

178

Here I am holding the roughed-out rudder in position to see if it is the right size and shape to fit on *Serendipity's* stern.

After we had laid out the various planks, cut them to the shape of the rudder, spread the edges with glue and then bolted them edgewise with the threaded rod, we took the rough and unfinished rudder outside to see if it fit where it was supposed to under the transom of the boat. We held it more or less in its final position under the slanted hole we had bored in the horn timber. It seemed to be about right.

Finally, we had thin bronze straps that were let into the casting and the rudder pieces and screwed to the oak so that they would be flush with the rudder surface and not contribute to turbulence at this crucial location. Work on the rudder went forward when the weather did not permit work outside.

Once the rudder was assembled, there was the sanding of the rudder and tapering its trailing edge. The little 6" sander had a hard time sanding the white oak, which by now had

Here we have drift-bolted and glued the planks that make up the rudder and I am now driving screws for the bronze straps on either side. In the background, is the rudder pattern up against the wall.

seasoned a bit and was harder than when we had bought it nearly a year before. Following the sanding, came the inevitable coat of Cuprinol.

In those days, traditional bronze fittings were virtually unobtainable. Contemporary sailboats were being rigged with stainless steel and "Marinium", some kind of alloy involving aluminum. Each edition of the "W/C" and "Perko" catalogs held fewer bronze items. Finding the bronze fittings, which were nostalgia-required for our dream ship, became something of a challenge for us. Luck often played a part. By luck, for instance, I happened to be in Marblehead one day and looked in at the Graves Yacht Yard. In those days, I looked in at all yacht yards just to see "what was going on". Who knows, maybe they were building wooden boats. I was usually disappointed. But my visit to Graves that day was worth my

With snow on the ground, we try out the completed rudder. The Plumbs and Mark Rollins were there to help. We have horsed the heavy rudder into position and temporarily secured the gudgeons in place while we check the lineup of the shaft. Will it line up so that the rudder turns smoothly on a straight axis?

while. They were then building "Constellations", 30-foot fiberglass sailboats with wood decks and interiors. I happened to see one of the tiller fittings which connected the bronze rudder post with the wood tiller. It was just what we needed. I had to ask Mr. Graves himself. Would he sell us one of his bronze tiller fittings? He was a friendly man and was interested in our project. He was glad to sell us the fitting.

I was emboldened to raise with him the possibility of his launching *Serendipity* in Marblehead - when we were ready. His eyes twinkled. When we were ready, he would be also.

Finally, we were ready to fit the rudder to the boat and try the rudder shaft. I laboriously chiseled out the deadwood at

181

The rudder shaft is in place, at least temporarily, Peter Plumb tries out the helm. To the left is a deck beam ready for installation. The clamp for the cockpit floor is visible between the sheer clamp and the bilge stringer to the right.

the stern to accept our case bronze rudder gudgeons. Final sanding and trimming we left for later.

Peter and Pam Plumb came for the weekend. We lugged the rudder, the new bronze shaft, and our new bronze rudder head fitting out to the building site. With a few last minute adjustments, we were able to get the gudgeons to slide into their chiseled slots in the deadwood.

As best we could see, the whole business lined up. We climbed up into the boat and slid the heavy 1 1/2" bronze shaft down through the hole diagonally drilled into the horn timber. With a bit of jiggling, the machined end slid down into the long blind hole in the rudder casting.

The front porch is getting crowded. Visible are the newly primed rudder with its bronze rudder stock fitting and gudgeons as well as the spars and several small planks of precious teak that we had bought for the cockpit floor.

We attached our newly-acquired rudder head fitting and tried out the helm. The rudder swung freely, indicating that our shaft was at least fairly well aligned with the leading edge of the rudder casting. Whew! Another nagging worry eased. The last step was coating the rudder with red lead primer and stashing it on my parents' side porch to await installation sometime in the spring.

And so the winter of 1966 went on. Our work pattern established over a year before continued. During each week at law school, I planned and procured. Each phase of the construction posed its challenges. My spare time and some of my time in class was devoted to thinking out these challenges, making lists and sometimes small drawings, poring over my growing library of boatbuilding books and supplier catalogs, telephoning and writing to suppliers, buying tools, materials and supplies from sources in the Boston area, and doing all that I could from a location 85 miles from the construction site to keep the project going forward smoothly.

Each Friday, we left Cambridge right after Anita finished her work at the Park School and drove to Wilbraham. The 1967 Red Rambler was often loaded down with new tools, materials or supplies purchased during the week. We could make the trip generally in under 1½ hours, but generally arrived too late on Friday to get any work done. On Saturday morning, bright and early, work would start. Depending on the weather, we would work under the plastic roof covering *Serendipity's* hull, or in the little shop. Work would continue until dark.

Sunday was the same. On Sundays, if the weather was good, we would frequently have visitors to the work site such as Mr. Boland. It was nice to be noticed by someone!

Following the completion of the rudder, our next bad-weather task was fitting jaws to our new spars, fore and main booms and gaffs. We had found that the usual practice was to fashion galvanized goose-necks for the booms and fabricate curved wood jaws for the gaffs. The plans, however, called for simple straight jaws on both booms and gaffs, a lower-tech solution for which we were grateful. We had abundant bits of oak scrap from which to cut the twin halves of the jaw pairs. With some chisel work and a lot of sanding, they became plausible. We secured the jaws to the respective spars with long 3/8" galvanized carriage bolts from Sargent Lord. Boring the long holes edge-wise through one jaw-half, then the spar, and then the other jaw-half, keeping more or less on center of all three, was a trick, but by then we had become accustomed to working with our "ship's augur" drill bits, both in hand brace and in our relatively puny electric drills. Each pair of jaws was outfitted with a "tongue" between the jaws that would bear on the mast and reduce the chafe from the rubbing spar.

Jaws finished, we gave each spar a coat of sealer and returned them to their storage locations on my parents' side porch. It turned out later that we were a little cavalier about protecting the spars during storage. The sealer with which we

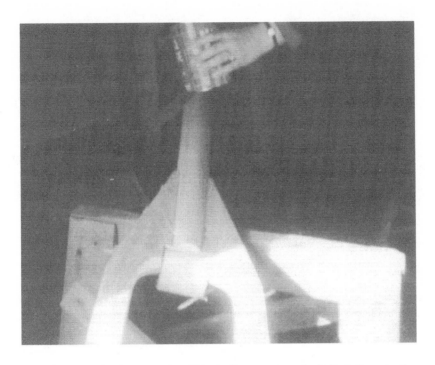

We fabricated the boom and gaff jaws from scrap oak, bolted them to the spars, and gave them a coat of clear sealer.

had coated the spars was not a hard or impervious coating, and during the ensuing months the spars got dirty and grimy. This dirt and grime got embedded in the sealer and had to be laboriously sanded off when we were ready to apply the final finish.

And so it went that winter of 1966-1967. When the weather permitted, we worked our way aft from the bow with deck beams and carlins in the way of the main cabin and cockpit. Our stack of pre-cut deck beams and 2 x 2 square oak stock steadily decreased as we cut, fitted, trimmed, fitted again, bored, and bolted the deck structure together. The framework of green Cuprinol-soaked deck beams slowly spread aft, widening as it left the narrow confines of the bow. Each day after we had finished our chiselings and fittings of the day, had

Here is Peter Plumb drilling for one of the drift bolts that will secure the starboard engine bed. The port engine bed is already in place.

bored the holes and tightened up the bolts, we splashed the whole business with green Cuprinol. The smell will remain with me forever. But we had read so often of the Risk of Rot, especially at the deck where rainwater might seep in and fatally taint our oaken timbers.

Our strokes were, by now, getting surer. Our joints were better (although still crude by Royal Lowell standards). We felt more confidence in the strength of the framework we were creating. On a warm day in the winter, we fitted an extra floor timber under the engine beds, driving home the half-inch galvanized drift bolts with sure, deft strokes of the sledge.

The actual engine bed timbers themselves came to us as the aftermath of another abandoned boatbuilding project. Phil Shaw, beloved chemistry teacher and coach at Wilbraham Academy, had long nurtured the notion of someday building a dream ship of his own. When his new house on Faculty Street was being built, back in the early '60's, a large white oak tree had been felled to clear the lot. This ancient tree had been

186

sawn into timber which he carefully put away for seasoning in his basement.

Nearly 10 years later, Phil knew that he would never build a dream ship of his own. The pile of oak lumber was taking up valuable room for storage. Would I like to use it in *Serendipity*? I went to look at Phil Shaw's oak. After eight years of drying out in a hot cellar the oak was dry as a bone and iron hard. It had twisted, bent, and checked. There were few pieces which could be used. We brought home those which looked salvageable, and piled them with the other lumber in the back yard. What could be better and sturdier to support our new Volvo engine than some 2 x 8 timbers from Phil Shaw's oak?

After working with green oak, the seasoned stock seemed as hard as flint. This only increased my confidence.

Much of the winter of 1966 *Serendipity* was covered in snow. That did not stop us. We worked on under the plastic roof whenever we could.

We had the right stuff to bear the throbbing, pulsing, churning engine that would be bolted to it.

Christmas, 1966, came and went. By now, we had brought the deck framing as far back as the cabin. Long 2" x 2" oak carlins had been fastened in place along the cabin cavity, with short oak beams for the deck along both sides of the large opening that marked the location for the cabin trunk.

It was fun to be doing "finish work" and to be bolting together the final finished wood parts which would serve our ship at sea. But we also knew that we only had a few months more to finish the tremendous tasks ahead, to build the cabin, the deck, the cockpit, to shape the masts, to do the rigging, to install the engine . . .

Chapter 9

By February 1967, we had completed fitting beams in the forward half of the hull back to the "bridge deck" between the cabin and cockpit. It was high time that we install the engine,. Otherwise the task would be made immensely harder by intervening structure. There was snow on the ground, and the conditions were not great for working outside, but we could not wait for good weather. We had to go for it.

We were driven. There was so much to do, and so little time left before we were due in Portland, Maine. Back when we started the project, I had had no real idea of how long it would take to build *Serendipity*. We had chosen the most difficult kind of boat to build – a conventionally planked wooden boat with steam bent frames. There were so many steps, and our lack of proper training and experience as well as adequate tools and equipment made everything take longer. Our guiding principle was to push ahead as fast as we could and somehow we would get the boat done enough so that we could take it with us to Maine, hopefully on its own bottom.

Yes, for most of my three years of law school, the boat was my obsession. Although the boat consumed all of our weekends, vacations and other spare time, it did not dominate Anita's waking thoughts the way it did mine. While actual work took place mainly at the building site in Wilbraham, materials procurement, scheduling, research, designing and figuring out how to overcome hurdles took every minute that could be pried from my school schedule during each week. As mentioned before, class notes are liberally besprinkled with lists and dimensions of materials and supplies as well as detailed drawings of various parts of the project as it developed.

189

By early spring of 1967, the pressure was really beginning to build. Here we had only a bare hull and some deck framing. How on earth were we going to be able to complete the myriad tasks to transform this into a seagoing schooner in the few months remaining before the end of August? Under the circumstances, we had no choice but to push the weather and ourselves. Hence, our operation to install the engine in February while snow was still on the ground.

Before we could actually lift the engine into the boat, we had to make sure that the structure, including the propeller shaft and the engine beds, would be in readiness. We had added another floor timber in the way of the engine beds just to make sure that there was enough support. This we drifted down to the backbone with 3/8" galvanized drift bolts.

Getting the precise location and configuration of the engine beds was a bit tricky. The Volvo engine, like most marine engines, was designed to be bolted to two longitudinal oak "engine beds", the tops of which would precisely line up with the propeller shaft, at the same height and same angle. In order to get these right, we had to run a tight string up through the center of the shaft log to establish the height of the center of the propeller shaft over the floor timbers and its angle. We then measured from the tight string to the floor timbers at various points in order to make patterns for the engine beds. After cutting and fitting the 2" thick engine beds from the oak salvaged from Phil Shaw, we checked again. Were they the right height? Were they lined up? This was fussy work that made me nervous. If we did not get it right, we would not be able to install the engine and corrections would be difficult. We finally figured that we had done as well as we could, and we bolted the engine beds down to the floor timbers with a combination of carriage and drift bolts depending on the accessibility of the other bolt end for a nut.

We also had to install the propeller shaft, stuffing box and shaft log. The engine was supposed to turn a 16" x 8" left-

190

handed propeller. We checked to make sure that the aperture in the rudder would be big enough – no problem. Soon after we had gotten the engine, we had pasted a scale representation of the engine on the plans in order to help us figure out the length of the 1" Tobin bronze propeller shaft. After both scaling the plans and checking in the field (which was hard without the engine being in the boat), I had figured that the shaft should be 29 ½" long. We ordered it through Sargent Lord and held our breaths. When it arrived we slid the gleaming bronze shaft through long hole bored in the shaft log by the boat builders at Story Marine Railways so long ago, and bolted on stuffing boxes at both ends. "Stuffing boxes" are bronze fittings with greased flax packing through which the propeller shaft exits the hull. The packing is designed to let the shaft turn smoothly while keeping the water out. The length of the shaft looked like it would work, although we would not know for sure until we hooked it up to both the engine and propeller.

"To install the engine . . ." The Volvo diesel weighed about 415 pounds, "stripped". The edge of *Serendipity's* hull was about eight and one half feet off the ground as she sat in her cradle. The challenge was somehow to lift this 415 pound block of cast iron and set it in place in the center of the hull without letting it fall or smash against the sides or bottom which were scarcely built to take that kind of punishment.

The chorus of naysayers rose to a crescendo. "How are you going to get the engine into the boat?" Or, more accurately, "You'll never get the engine into the boat". "You'll have to use a crane." "How are you going to get a big crane out to your back yard?" "Did you ever hear of the guy who built this boat in his cellar and then couldn't get it out?"

Indeed, I thought long and hard of that particular problem. The conventional wisdom, offered by many self-appointed consultants, was to hire a back-hoe to come, pick up the engine with a chain from the bucket, and neatly drop it into the boat. . It would have taken a pretty large machine to pick

191

up that engine, then swing it over an eight-plus foot high barrier, and get it further out over the center of the hull. The ordinary tractor-type backhoe would never do. Hours of rumination, calculation and drawing diagrams on my law school notebooks had convinced me that we could "do it ourselves".

I don't know where I got the idea. Maybe it came from the days when I was working at Prout's Neck, wrestling sailboats and lobster boats around on the "Back Shore" tide flats with block and tackle and car jacks. Maybe it was from my days as "boy engineer" when we rigged up all kinds of mechanical contraptions to build tree forts, rafts, shacks, etc. It probably came from the sight of those two sturdy mast timbers, lying there out under the apple tree, encased in their cocoon of plastic.

Sheer legs! We could use the two mast timbers as a giant pair of sheer legs. They would straddle our ship, providing a purchase point for a block and tackle. We would sway the cast iron Volvo diesel up overhead and then into the bowels of the ship the same way our predecessors had lifted heavy weights in days of old when much bigger ships than *Serendipity* were built on the banks of creeks up and down the coast of New England.

"Bah, humbug", scoffed the naysayers. However, fortunately there were a handful who had faith. My father had an ancient cast iron block and tackle rig which we reeved with new manila rope. A trio of stray wooden blocks, reinforced with epoxy glue here and there to overcome the infirmities of age, made up another tackle and a half. There was a long piece of 3/4" manila and a coil of 1/2" nylon which we had purchased from Al Pendleton for our future anchor rope. With these rude appliances we would build our own crane.

It was a slushy morning in February. The ground was covered with a couple of inches of snow, through which the rotting weeds poked damply. The sky was overcast and gray.

But adrenalin was running high in the Murray household that morning. Today, we would show that it could be done. And risk all in the trying.

We first moved the 32-foot Douglas fir 6 x 6's out so that they flanked the cradle, converging some distance beyond the stern. The overlapping ends we bored and bolted together with a great galvanized eye-bolt that had originally come from a telephone pole. The spread ends on either side of the cradle were also bored and chained to the skids with car chains. This was so that our sheer legs would not splay out suddenly under load.

To the eye-bolt at the apex of the joined timbers, we fastened an old epoxy smeared block. Through this, we rove 150 feet or so of new manila. One end was secured to a pine tree, about 50 feet off the starboard bow of the boat. The other end went to a small sapling at the foundation of the garage, about an equal distance off the port bow.

The idea was that these "stays" would raise the "head" of the sheer legs to a point nearly vertical. The mast timbers, converging high over the stern of the boat, would thus provide a purchase for the old cast iron block and tackle. With the latter, we would hoist aboard the engine.

It was a simple matter to hook the blocks and tackle to the sheer legs. It was much more difficult to actually get the sheer legs erected. As long as the timbers were lying on the ground, we had no angle from which to pull them erect with the forward guys. Somehow we had to get the head of the sheer legs at least partly aloft until we could take the weight of the heavy timbers with the tackles running past the bow. It was heavy. Probably each beam was about 200 pounds, not including the weight of the chains and gear.

We again reached back to the 16th or 17th century. A "gin pole" was the answer. The gin pole was none other than the stout pine mast of *Te Amo*, the flat-bottomed skiff sailboat which I had rebuilt at age 13. *Te Amo's* mast had been cut as a

We are starting the first lift of the sheer-legs with the gin pole. Visible are the chains tying together the ends of the mast timbers, the gin pole made from *Te Amo's* mast, and the dangling tackle with which we would hoist the engine.

dead pine in Wilbraham's forest some 10 years before. For the last five years, it had lain neglected in the rafters of the garage while I busied myself with college, law school, and the glorious new project in the backyard. *Te Amo* now came forth to render one last service to her owner. A simple tackle, rove through the peak halyard blocks on the stout pine mast made a crude gin pole. Now what we needed was manpower.

We mobilized all available human resources for the event. Mr. Randolph, my high school physics teacher from across the street was there. (He was fascinated by the practical application of the principles of physics that he taught). Mr.

Boland, our Sunday visitor, lent a hand. My parents were there, of course. Mark Rollins, a school friend who was in town came down. He was young and strong and a real help, as was my brother, Paul, in this and many other challenges. A key helper was our next door neighbor, Art Taylor. He had a small garden tractor and a trailer. We would use that to move the engine from the garage to where it would be plucked up by the tackle and swung into the boat.

Second lift - the gin pole has been moved along the sheer-legs which have been propped up with old moulds.

So there we were, slip-sliding about in the snow, using 18th century technology and a miscellany of man-power to accomplish a task that 20th century technology could have done in a jiffy. But it all worked.

First, we erected the sheer-legs. Several of us were at the gin pole, holding it erect and in position and then hauling on the tackle to raise the ends of the heavy timbers. At one point, we had got the apex as high as we could, but the angle was still too acute to give the people on the guy tackle enough

195

The sheer legs are nearly erect. The gin pole got them up high enough to give the forward tackle enough purchase to haul them up the rest of the way.

purchase to erect the assembly. We held the ground we had gained by propping the sheer legs up with a couple of the old moulds that we had taken from the hull after it was planked. We then moved the sheer-legs down one of the timbers far enough to gain additional purchase and hauled it up again.

This time we were able to get it high enough so that those pulling on the guy tackle were able to get it to move. The timber ends strained against the restraining chains as we all heaved on the forward tackle. It was moving, it was coming up! The heavy manila falls to the engine dragged like a tail along the ground as the sheer-legs began to make an arrow to the sky. We stopped hauling on the guy tackle when the top of the sheer-legs was still far from vertical. We did not want the sheer-legs to topple over in the opposite direction.

Mighty structure! Towering above us were the thirty-two-foot Douglas fir 6 x 6 timbers, forming a graceful inverted V straddling our beloved ship. The rope falls hung just where we wanted, a foot or two beyond the stern. All that remained was to untangle the dangling block and tackle to have it ready to hook onto the engine. The problem was that the falls' lower pulley block was dangling far above our heads, and the weight of the pulley was not enough to overcome the friction of the twisted new manila tackle. I had to climb up on a ladder held by two stalwart helpers to reach the pulley and untwist the fall before we could drag it down.

Art Taylor is backing his garden tractor trailer with engine aboard under the falls preparatory for the lift.

The engine swings high in the air as we hoist it with pure manpower - aided by the block and tackle.

With some difficulty, we horsed the engine into Art Taylor's garden trailer, and he towed it off to the building site along a path that he had plowed in the snow earlier in the day. The rest of the job was a piece of cake. We hooked the block and tackle to the lifting ring on the engine. With my father and me hauling mightily on the falls, we raised the engine high in the air above the stern of the boat. At this point, the others hauled on the guy tackles to bring the head of the sheer-legs forward far enough so that the engine was swinging over the exact location where it was to be installed. "Lower away!" - and the engine slowly descended down into the hull and onto the beds that we had painstakingly fashioned for it. Everything seemed to fit!

Of course, the engine would have to be shimmed, bolted down, and lined up with the propeller shaft. But the worst was over. It was in. The naysayers had been vanquished. Thankfully and tiredly, we lowered the sheer-legs

Here is the crew that defied the naysayers and hoisted the engine into
Serendipity. From left Mark Rollins, Anita, my mother, Bim Randolph
(behind mother), Mr. Boland, my father, Art Taylor, Art's friend, and my
brother Paul.

which had served us so well, and all stood around for pictures.
By the end of the day, the mast timbers rested once more on the
sawhorses, covered with plastic. From the scene, one would
never know of the great doings that had taken place just a few
hours before.

With the engine in place, we could press forward to
complete the remainder of the deck framing. The sturdy bridge
deck between deck and cockpit was reinforced by an extra
deck beam. Who knows but that we would need all the
strength we could get if a big green comber came aboard
someday. A special stringer was put in along the inside of the
hull upon which to land the cockpit floor beams. The loft plan
and the construction plan provided the dimensions. We
faithfully followed them.

By the time we framed in the cockpit itself and took on the afterdeck, working the white oak had become familiar and relatively easy. By now, I was pretty adept at cutting and fitting the white oak deck structure. Joints which had earlier been simple butts were now carefully morticed and fitted with some nicety. Anita followed, drilling, boring, bolting and always splashing with Cuprinol. We were very concerned about rot, and did whatever we could to make sure that our oak timbers would not fall prey to dry rot.

We had been required to dismantle a part of our roof frame in order to hoist in the engine. We did not bother to replace it, but merely covered the after portion of the hull with plastic when we were not working.

Once the after deck was more or less framed in, we could install the rudder. The rudder post came up through a brass pipe to the deck, where it would be fitted with the tiller.

Anita carefully coats the interior of the hull and the newly-installed deck beams with Cuprinol. The engine is under the plywood cockpit floor.

200

We lined up the pipe with the trailing edge of the horn timber, which would define the leading edge of the rudder. Everything seemed to line up. It was a hassle to try to sculpt the horn timber and deadwood to fit the gudgeon castings for the rudder – a lot of chipping with the big chisel, then sanding with the trusty, but dying, 6" Craftsman disc sander, then chipping some more. We had to be careful that we did not chip away too much or that we did not reveal any of the galvanized drift bolts that held the deadwood together. It was crude, but it would have to suffice. We secured on the rudder gudgeons into the deadwood with some bronze lag bolts (very expensive) – now our ship had a propeller (sort of) and a rudder. We were making progress!

The rudder has been fitted and hangs in place. Our shiny new propeller is on the shaft. Although the seams have been caulked and puttied, the putty has not been sanded. There is still snow on the ground.

A late spring snow blankets *Serendipity*. Fortunately it did not last.

Time was getting short. The deck framing and related tasks had taken most of the winter. As early spring began to come to western Massachusetts, we had a ship which boasted deck framing of oak, but was naked of any further finish. The engine sat forlornly below, unconnected, seemingly superfluous in such a traditional wooden ship. We had to hurry. There were only a few months left before we were due in Maine.

Law school remained secondary, although an enjoyable secondary. To this day I firmly believe that our obsession with *Serendipity* intensified my enjoyment of law school. We certainly had no time to be intimidated by the challenges of academia. We had challenges of our own in the back yard at Wilbraham.

202

But the pressure was on. By March, we could work under the plastic cover no longer. It had already been half breached for the installation of the engine. Although there were still bits and pieces of snow on the ground and dampness in the air, we were glad to tear it off, to saw off the last of the frame heads, to leave *Serendipity* shorn of temporary structure standing proudly in the yard.

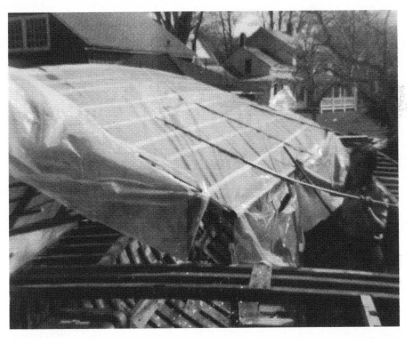

We sawed off the frame heads that had supported the rest of the roof and removed it more or less in one piece.

At this stage, as we put things together, we had to be very mindful to make sure that things were installed in the proper order, lest a premature move made installation of something else more difficult later on. So it was, for instance, with the tanks for water and diesel fuel. At the time *Serendipity* was built, options for boat tankage were limited. Traditionally, boat tanks were made of copper (very expensive and questionable for diesel) or galvanized steel (rust!). So-called "terne plated" (lead over steel) tanks were sold for outboards. It was possible to get stainless steel tanks custom made, but they were very expensive. In addition, finding someone to do this work in Wilbraham, Massachusetts, seemed a bit unlikely.

Ultimately, the best choice for us seemed to be tanks of Monel metal, a combination of nickel, copper, steel and whatever, that was being promoted in the mid-1960's as the answer to marine corrosion products in a variety of contexts. Marine catalogs advertised a line of Monel tanks made by Allcraft Manufacturing Company, right in Cambridge, Massachusetts in a few stock sizes. They were expensive. The plans specified 30 gallon tanks for fuel and water installed under the decks behind the walls of the cockpit on both sides of the boat. The biggest of the stock Allcraft Monel tanks that we could fit in the specified location were 22 gallons. So we had to forfeit a good deal of gallonage. I ultimately decided that the unchallenged resistance to corrosion and the ready availability justified the high price and inflexibility of the Monel tanks. We somehow finagled a 20% discount from Allcraft, who shipped a pair directly to Wilbraham. At $72 apiece, the tanks represented a big item for our diminishing resources to cover.

This was, of course, a time before bank credit cards were in use. In those days, one did not have the option of simply giving a number or swiping a card to make purchases. One had to either establish credit with a merchant and pay invoices for goods shipped by paper check, or send a check for the goods and estimated shipping costs in advance. A surprising number of the people with whom we did business were willing to ship to an impecunious law student couple on "open account" and we made sure to justify their trust by paying promptly. In other cases, however, the need to arrange payment in advance sometimes led to delay and required us to think ahead in ordering, paying for and ultimately receiving needed parts and materials.

As we worked along framing-in the cockpit floor and deck in the after part of the vessel, we had to address a problem that had bedeviled me for some time. How could we handle the exhaust from our diesel auxiliary? The plans had called for a water jacketed exhaust line up to a Maxim style cast iron standpipe muffler. In 1966, the Maxim Silencer Corp., long the producer of the "Cadillac" of marine mufflers, was just tapering out of production. They still made a Monel model. That was, however, beyond our means. The alternatives were crude power-boat style cast iron mufflers from Wilcox - Crittendon, or rubber mufflers which were just then coming on the market.

Serendipity as viewed from the upstairs back window in the barn. Deck framing is almost complete, with holes left for cabin trunk and cockpit.

According to Chapelle and other sources (information was generally scanty), the state of the art was a water-jacketed standpipe muffler that would lead the exhaust from the engine to a high point in the boat at which point it would be mixed

205

with the cooling water and discharged by gravity out the stern. *Serendipity* was built before the invention and wide use of the currently popular "pot type" mufflers which mix the exhaust and cooling water at a point below the water line and use the pressure of the exhaust to lift the water out through a flexible rubber exhaust hose to a port in the stern.

But where should we put this standpipe and how could I get it fabricated? The engine was sited below the cockpit, and the exhaust discharge was located under the after part of the cockpit floor more or less amidships – no room for a standpipe there. In some diagrams, I had seen a standpipes coming up under the bridge deck, with a discharge out the side of the vessel instead of the stern. This would have required a hairpin turn from the exhaust manifold, which was problematical, and I also was concerned about smelling diesel exhaust when sitting in the cockpit with the motor on.

It looked to me as if we would have to lead the exhaust to a high point as near the center line as possible in one of the lockers to the side of the after end of the cockpit. The engine exhaust manifold was on the starboard side. Therefore, it was on the starboard side that we would locate our water-jacketed exhaust.

The question now was how can we fabricate such an item? And what should it be made of? The books spoke of galvanized iron, welded stainless steel and even marvelous Monel metal. These had drawbacks of corrosion, unavailability and cost. Copper had also been used for water jacketed exhausts, but it was unclear how it could be fabricated.

After puzzling over the situation, I ultimately decided that we would make our water jacketed exhaust system ourselves. It seemed to be a simple matter to use standard copper plumbing tubing to contrive a two layered affair with 1-1/2" tubing in the middle and 2-1/2" on the outside. How to do this? Enter George Merwin, plumber of Wilbraham.

George had been our family plumber ever since he came back to Wilbraham after being in the See Bees in World War II. Over the years, he had served the town as one of only two local plumbers. I called him up. Of course, he knew about our sailboat project. And, of course, he would be glad to help.

The trouble was, George was also very hard to get. Many a weekend that spring I called to see if we could get him down. We were completing the deck framing in the stern. It was important that the exhaust system be constructed before we closed in the deck and cockpit in plywood. But it wasn't until spring vacation that he finally showed up.

George soldered together a "Rube Goldberg" angled water-jacketed exhaust riser from copper pipe and brass fittings. It was the best we could do at the time, but did not last.

Although I had thought perhaps that the copper and brass fittings should be brazed together for strength and durability, he insisted that a high temperature silver solder would do the job.

Somewhere, I learned that we would have to provide some flexibility between the engine and the water jacketed exhaust to absorb engine vibration that otherwise would shake the fabrication to pieces. Fortunately, Westerbeke had given us a stainless steel flexible exhaust section when we bought the engine. The latter was designed for rubber flex-mounting. They had suggested it. I did not know enough at the time to appreciate that such a joint would be necessary.

We devised a weird elbow kind of copper water jacket rising to a high spot just underneath the deck on the starboard side of the cockpit. The stainless steel flex section screwed into a brass fitting that was soldered onto a 1 ½" copper pipe. We reamed out a 2 1/2" to 1½" reducing connector and ran the 1½ " pipe right through the center. The outside of the water jacket was a 2½" copper tube that fitted into reamed out reducers at each end. Half inch stubs for the inlet and the outlet of the cooling water were tapped into the reducers. The whole thing had a 45 degree bend in the middle so that it could rise alongside the cockpit to a high point right under the deck at the after end of the starboard cockpit locker. At the high point, the exhaust tube took another bend outside the water jacket (more asbestos tape here) and then cooling water from the jacket was introduced into a heavy rubber exhaust hose running downward to a bronze fitting low on the transom.

George cut tubing, reamed out and tapped fittings, and soldered the whole thing together in a day. It was definitely Rube Goldberg, but we hoped that it would work.

This turned out to be one of the first of our creations that we had to replace. The "silver solder" ultimately did not hold. Exhaust smoke seeping from the water jacket and water seeping into the exhaust required early replacement within the first year or two of operation. But in the spring of 1967, we did not know any better, and sighed a sigh of relief as our makeshift water-jacketed exhaust was screwed and clamped together and then secured to a couple of brackets under the cockpit floor, starboard deck and after deck.

Our next big step was to install the decking. The deck itself was ½" exterior fir plywood, made with waterproof glue.

208

A plywood deck panel on the port side is clamped to the deck beams and ready for nailing. Law school friends Don and Sybil Hebb stopped by and were, of course, put to work.

Serendipity was built before exotic mahogany marine plywoods were generally available to amateur builders. Fir marine plywood was glued up with the same glue as used for exterior construction plywood, but had more layers and fewer "voids". It was also much more expensive. Although Chapelle did not have much to say about plywood, another source frequently consulted, Sam Rabl's *Boatbuilding in Your Own Backyard*, maintained that exterior plywood was plenty good enough for use in building plywood boats, and *a fortiori*, for decks that would be sheathed in fiberglass. So we went with ordinary exterior construction plywood, "A-B" finished sides. A 4' x 8' sheet cost about $8.00.

Cutting out the plywood deck was comparatively easy. We simply laid sheets of plywood on the deck, traced the outline of the hull and cabin sides from the bottom up, and then cut out the plywood pieces with the trusty saber saw. Where two plywood sheets joined along the center-line of the boat forward, aft and on the bridge deck, we let a ½" x 6" oak board into the deck beams to batten the seam. The pieces were joined end to end by plywood scabs screwed underneath the joints.

Once the deck pieces were cut out and lined up, they were screwed down along the edges and fastened to the deck beam with a multitude of 1½" bronze annular ring nails. Each one had to be drilled for. Once driven home, these nails would not come out, so we had to be sure not to make any mistakes in lining things up. The deck-sheer joint was bedded in Caulk-Tex. We had become great believers in the products of Mr. Travers. Caulk-Tex did indeed seem to stick as tenaciously as one could imagine.

The 22-gallon Monel water and fuel tanks are secured in place on the cockpit sole beams by wood strips connected to the beams by 3/8" galvanized rod, threaded by hand on both ends.

We framed in the cockpit at the same time as we did the main deck. We had placed a temporary plywood slab on the 2" x 2" cockpit floor beams that spanned the hull to support our 3' x 5' self-bailing cockpit and the tanks to either side. That was now replaced by a ½" plywood underfloor. The 22-gallon Monel fuel and water tanks were positioned on the beams on either side outboard of the forward part of the cockpit, and secured by home-made galvanized threaded rods to wood battens above each tank. Everything now had to be done in the correct order. If we prematurely closed a part of the boat in before fitting some interior fitting (such as the exhaust system),

Here Anita screws down the cockpit floor to the 2 x 2 oak cockpit floor beams. The hose to the left leads to the Henderson bilge pump that hangs from the beams behind the engine. There is a socket for the pump handle which can be reached through a small hatch in the cockpit floor.

we might have great difficulty making the installation afterwards. There was a lot of thinking involved in ordering the steps that we followed.

The sides of the cockpit were interrupted by small lockers aft of the tanks and by a lazarette in the aft end. These I made of 3/8" plywood, with little square openings for the locker doors. *Serendipity* was built before Morse cables came into general use for marine engine controls. The Volvo diesel had come with a rudimentary brass throttle control with a "Bowden wire" to regulate engine speed. This appeared to be sufficient for our purposes. We figured we could fit the throttle control to the side of the cockpit.

Here I am fitting the sides of the cockpit with the small openings for lockers behind each tank.

The controls for the transmission posed a greater challenge. This was before Morse cable controls came into general use for sailboat engines. The engine had come with a

30" long shift lever with a plastic knob to engage the transmission - great for a small launch, but no good for a sailboat auxiliary. After some serious rumination, the original engine shift lever was replaced by a shorter shift lever made of bar stock. Wilcox-Crittenden had a brass sailboat shift lever assembly that could be installed in the cockpit floor. It was expensive, but appeared to be the only real option for a sailboat at the time. The cockpit shift lever could be removed from a socket in the control lever under the floor. When the shift lever was removed, a small brass fitting covered the hole. The control lever could be linked with the shift lever on the engine by a simple bar linkage.

Before each plywood panel was nailed to the edge of the sheer plank and the deck beams, a layer of Caulk-Tex was applied to seal any joints permanently. This will be the last deck panel.

This arrangement was simple and straightforward, but one had to remember to shift backwards. Pushing the cockpit shift lever forward threw the engine shift lever into reverse, and vice versa. Figuring out and fabricating these controls required quite a bit of ruminating, then various trips to procure parts and get things welded and bored, and finally carefully fitting everything in place before it became difficult to get access to the rear end of the engine under the cockpit.

Once in place and screwed down, the deck got a good sanding, and any holes, screw countersinks, and divots were filled with plastic wood. In those days, boat builders did not have available the myriad of fillers, putties and gunks that are now in use to fill all manner of holes. There was seam compound, and then, of course, Caulk-Tex, to fill seams and bed fittings where movement was expected. But for filling holes that would be later sanded flush, and hopefully disappear, the best product was good old plastic wood.

Fortunately the weather at this time was warm, and the decking process went ahead rapidly. Soon *Serendipity* had a deck, forward, amidships, and aft. But there was still a big hole where *Serendipity's* long trunk cabin would be.

Chapter 10

April 1967. My law school career was drawing to a close. The bar exam would not be far off. I was committed to start my clerkship with Judge Gignoux in Portland, Maine, the day after Labor Day. There were less than five months left to make *Serendipity* ready for the sea. Where were we? There she stood in the back yard in Wilbraham. Around her graceful hull the trees were in bud and blossom. The plywood deck had been nailed in place. The cockpit also had been roughed in, with plywood sole and sides. I'd even cut little square doors for lockers on both sides and aft. The Monel tanks nestled concealed under the deck on either side of the cockpit. Nothing was painted. The hull was rough sanded. Any raw wood was sealed with Cuprinol or red lead or both. There was a lot left to be done.

......a lot left to be done.

I don't know how we really scheduled all that we had to do to finish *Serendipity* that spring and summer. As school pressed on toward exams, my level of activity reached a fever pitch. I must have been running on pure adrenalin. Every minute was precious. During the week, I struggled to complete my studies and prepare for legal challenges to come. On the weekends, we labored to bring to fruition the great Task of the last three years. Anita gamely hung in there, and put her shoulder to the wheel as well. My parents rolled with the punches and helped as they could.

We had several projects going at once, depending upon drying times for glue or fiberglass, the weather, and the order in which things would have to be done to keep the thing moving at best efficiency.

With the exception of that red-letter day in February when our 6 x 6 Douglas fir timbers had served as sheer legs to hoist the Volvo engine in place, during the time we worked to complete the hull and deck, the timbers that were destined to become *Serendipity's* masts lay covered on sawhorses awaiting our attention.

But the time was coming when we had to make good on our brave intentions and actually shape these square timbers into round, and to some extent tapered, masts. A weekend visit by Peter and Pam Plumb provided the catalyst to get the job done. Of course, I had read about mast-making in Chapelle over and over. The idea was first to make a 45-degree cut along each edge of the square timber at just the right place so that the resulting cross-section would be an octagon, with eight equal sides. Chapelle gave a formula for this. We would have to compute the sides of right triangles so that the hypotenuses would form the equal sides of the octagon.

We approached the mast making with some trepidation. Suppose we did not get it right? Maybe we would ruin these great mast timbers? They were so massive. The idea of sawing them into octagons and then planing them perfectly round seemed like a lot of work. But we could not put it off forever. So on a weekend in early June, and a perfect weekend at that, we went to work. Despite our fears and trepidation, mast-making turned out to be a piece of cake.

We did just what Chapelle described. First of all, we had to reduce the size of the foremast from 6 x 6 to 5 x 5, as specified by the plans. This was accomplished by a couple of passes with a borrowed Skil saw and then cleanup with the big fore plane. By now I was pretty good at hand planing and Douglas fir was a lot easier to plane than either mahogany or oak.

First cut on the mast - 45 degrees along chalk lines snapped according to Chapelle's formula.

We then applied Chapelle's formula to determine where to make the 45-degree cuts. From the points laid out on the ends of each timber, tightly stretched chalk lines extended the lines the length of the timbers. Here we go! The Skil saw blade was set to cut at a 45-degree angle. The saw whined as I carefully guided it along the blue line left by the chalk. One of

217

the others held onto the triangularly shaped waste strip as the saw crept forward. But as I reached the end of each cut and as the waste strip fell away, we could all see that it was working. The square timbers were becoming octagons!

It ultimately took only a couple of hours to make the saw-cuts on both masts. It was a little tricky at the top of the foremast, where the last 6 feet or so tapered from a 5 x 5 down almost to a 3 x 3. But the formula worked there too, and that part of the mast became a tapered octagon right before our eyes.

Two cuts - the square timber is becoming an octagon.

The next step was to use a tool called a "draw-knife" to plane the corners of the octagons to make the timbers 16-sided, almost round. A draw-knife is essentially a blade between two handles that the craftsman uses to remove stock by pulling the handles toward him. I had acquired one of these back when I was building *Te Amo* and used a dead spruce tree for her mast. I then used the draw knife to remove the stubs of the many

218

branches to make the trunk smooth and round. Out it came again for the building of *Serendipity*. This was one of a very few times that we used the draw-knife on this project. It was one of those tools that one uses seldom, but is very handy when it is needed.

Working with the drawknife to make 8 sides into sixteen.

It took a relatively short time to plane off the edges of the octagons with the draw knife. The knife was sharp and the Douglas fir planed easily. The only problem was occasional splinters. Unlike Sitka spruce (or even oak or mahogany), Douglas fir is a very splintery wood, and before we got the masts done, all of us had splinters in our hands. But no matter, the mast work was going rapidly, and that is what counted. By the end of the first day, we had both masts "roughed out" and planed with the drawknife in this fashion.

The penultimate step was to plane the many-sided mast timbers smooth and around with the long fore plane, the same plane I had used to plane the edges of the planks the previous summer. This Craftsman plane was the one hand tool on which we had spent a little money. But it turned out to be well worth it. It did a lot of work.

We had only one fore plane, so I did almost all the planing. But it went pretty fast. As I went up each timber planing off the ridges from the saw and draw knife, the others rotated the mast stock to expose new surfaces. Planing each mast was a matter of a couple of hours, not days as I had thought beforehand. And the planed masts looked so good! Even without sanding, they look almost like finished masts. We marveled at how well they were coming out and how easy it was to make sturdy square timbers into graceful round masts.

Planing the foremast at the tapered end. The Craftsman fore plane made short work of the Douglas fir - at the expense of sore shoulders.

The last step was the sanding. This was all done by hand. But there were many hands. Here all of us took sheets of sandpaper, wrapped them around the mast timbers, and sanded away. Our hands formed the sandpaper to the round timber. Yes, we did get splinters, but no matter, we were getting the job done.

The whole crew turned to for the sanding - all by hand. Our sanding machines would not work on the soft round surface of the Douglas fir. Peter Plumb is sanding the top of the foremast, followed in order by Pam and Anita.

I had anticipated that the process would take days; it actually took hours. Almost before we knew it, the masts felt round to the touch. Sanding, sanding, and more sanding by everyone rounded the last little ridges from the many passes of the plane. We started on Saturday morning. By mid-day Sunday, the masts were rounded, planed, and sanded - even tapered at the tops. We hastened to put on a coat of sealer, and then a couple of varnish.

221

Back to the hull.   Now we were faced with the challenge of building the cabin. *Serendipity* was designed with a long, relatively substantial trunk cabin which promised generous headroom and comfortable quarters below. I was a little concerned that the cabin top would not be strong enough to provide bracing for the mainmast which pierced the cabin roof just forward of the companionway. All the books had said that a schooner should have a divided cabin, with a sturdy bridge deck to reinforce the main mast partners. *Serendipity's* designer had sacrificed this structural feature in favor of larger, more commodious quarters. Had it been the right decision?

But I didn't second-guess Crockett. We stuck with his design and next addressed the building of the cabin trunk. The plans called for 1-1/2" mahogany for the sides.   Winde-McCormick again was the source. We ordered, and received by common carrier, two long wide Philippine mahogany planks from Winde-McCormick. They were 1½" thick, rough and almost 15" wide. The yard advised us that if we wanted to be sure that we would end up with a full 1½" thickness after planing, we would have to get 2" rough stock and plane it down. Winde-McCormick did not have much 2" rough stock in the sizes we needed. What they had was very expensive. They assured us that the "6-quarter" (1½") stock was on the generous side. It should plane out to almost 1½" if we were careful. So we took it.   Sure enough, when we passed it through Mr. Merrick's planer, we got smooth planks at just about 1 7/16", near enough to 1½" that we did not worry.

The plans called for the cabin sides to be set on edge along the deck, and secured by long threaded rods going down through the wood sides, the deck and the deck carlin below. The cabin sides were not straight, but curved to match the curve of the hull. They were not quite vertical, but canted in just a little bit toward the center.

Now we had to take these massive planks and form them to meet the curve of the sheer and then somehow bend

222

them to follow the curve of the outline of the cabin. How were we going to bend these thick and heavy mahogany planks to follow the curve of the carlin? Suppose a plank cracked? How were we going to bore holes down through the planks edgewise to secure them to the deck and the carlin below. What would happen if our drill wandered out through the surface on either side? Suppose the heavy 1 ½"" thick lumber would not bend to follow the curve of the cabin sides? Tension rose as we contemplated the construction of the cabin.

Of course, as these big steps were being taken, we were also working many smaller projects. One of these was fashioning galvanized steel hardware for *Serendipity's* masts and rigging. Mr. Crockett's plans specified galvanized mast bands, chain plates, travelers, cleats, belaying pins and deck hardware. Perhaps such items had been available in 1955, when he first drew and published the "*Nimble*" plans. But by the mid-1960s, many items of galvanized marine hardware, such as eye-bands and chainplates, were impossible to find. Indeed, even bronze chainplates were limited to sizes suitable only for small sailboats such as Blue-J's or Lightnings. Larger chainplates and eye-bands for round masts were unobtainable in any metal. We had no choice but to make what we needed.

My pencil and notebook had been busy that spring. We needed several 3" eye-bands with from 1 to 4 eyes, a 5" eye-band for the foremast, an elaborate iron fabrication to secure the head of the mainmast to the fidded topmast, a bunch of eye-bands for the gaffs, boom-bails to secure the sheets to the booms, travelers for the deck, and chainplates for shrouds and bobstays.

I went to a steel supplier in Cambridge. Yes, he could give me 1 1/2" lengths of 3" and 5" steel pipe, which would make the basic bands for the eye-bands. He was even willing to cut 2" x 1/4" stock into 24" lengths for the chainplates. With a little wheedling, his automatic hacksaw nipped off a couple of dozen little 1-1/2" square x 1/4" "ears" which we could weld on to the round bands for the eyes. Another burlap bag full of oily, gritty bits of iron cost me little in money and a lot in time. It was undoubtedly a nuisance to provide. Thank you, Mr. Steel Company.

The chain plates were relatively simple. We had 10 - ¼" x 2" x 24" steel straps, cut to length. These, slightly bent to conform to the sides of *Serendipity's* hull, would become the chainplates to which the 6 main shrouds and 4 fore shrouds would be secured.

The eye-bands were more difficult. "Eye-bands" are round metal straps that encircle the masts or bowsprit at key points in order to provide strong points to secure standing or running rigging. I carefully estimated the diameters of the fore and main-masts where we would need eye-bands to anchor stays or running rigging. We would need 3 eye-bands each of 3" in diameter, and each with four ears. "Ears" are the little tabs with holes on the eye-bands to which the rigging is shackled. We would also need a larger 5" eye-band for the foremast to provide the purchase for the fore throat halyard.

The situation was a little more complicated on the main mast. The plans called for a picturesque traditional "fidded" topmast overlapping and surmounting the main mast. The overlapping joint was secured by wooden structures including the cross trees and the spreader at the bottom, and with a metal fitting at the top. This metal fitting was supposed to be square on one side to take the squared end of the main mast and round in the diameter of the topmast at the other. We would somehow have to fashion it out of steel strapping.

In the absence of any metal-working capacity (or ability!) whatsoever, we had to rely on the good-heartedness of those who had such capacity. With our bagful of oily steel strips, rings and bits, we went in search of someone who could help us bore the necessary holes for bolts and fittings in the stock and for someone who could then fabricate the mast bands and the all-important topmast fitting.

Jeffrey Wood, one of my childhood friends who still lived in Wilbraham, had a small bench-mounted drill press. Although it was a bit on the light side for boring scores of 3/8" holes in quarter-inch steel stock, it was a lot better than our ¼" and 3/8" portable electric drills. We bought a new 3/8" drill bit, set up the drill press on the floor of Jeff's garage, and went to work, taking turns with the somewhat overloaded tool to bore the holes, squirting oil as we did so. By the end of a long evening, the drill bit was pretty well worn out and the drill press was smoking, but we had bored all the holes we would need in the chain plates and the little tabs that would become the ears on the eye-bands.

The next stop was at Eddie Dearborn's garage in Ludlow. Eddie was a gifted auto mechanic who had repaired my father's cars and had coached me in the rebuilding of the engine on my 1931 Studebaker back in 1960. He was also a capable welder and had gas welding equipment right at his shop. He agreed to meet us there off-hours on the weekend to see what he could do. He was ultimately able to weld the little ears with pre-drilled holes onto the pipe rings to form instant eye-bands and even to fashion a crude D-shaped fitting for the topmast. We were making progress. I don't remember whether we had to pay Eddie anything for his couple of hours of work. If so, it was nominal. Like many others along the way, he was intrigued with our project and wanted to help us as he could.

So now we had a bunch of bored straps for chain plates and some crude welded-up eye-bands – in raw steel. In a salt-water environment these would rust away before we knew it. We would have to get them galvanized.

Back in the "old days" before World War II, there were zinc kettles for galvanizing marine hardware in every port. By 1967, various forms of stainless steel and plastics were in the process of replacing galvanized iron and steel in many applications. Many galvanizing shops had shut down in the face of diminishing business and increasing safety regulations.

225

However, the Yellow Pages came through. I found the New England Galvanizing Company in Everett, Massachusetts. The vast zinc kettles of that concern, served by chain-falls, could galvanized mighty tanks, great weldments and massive fabrications. My pitiful burlap bag was practically a joke. But my condensed tale of the building of *Serendipity* had the usual effect. They were glad to help. While I watched, they dumped my bits and pieces into a wire basket, which in turn was dipped in an acid bath. This was to remove the oil, filings, and surface accretions that would interfere with the adhesion of the zinc to the steel. When I came back a few hours later, my ironwork glistened with the bright zinc shimmer of a new pail. Crude and inartistic, but rugged and cheap, these were the fittings with which *Serendipity* would put to sea.

Although the dollar cost of our metal fittings was not great, the number of steps we had to go through from sourcing the steel in the first place, to cutting, boring, welding and then galvanizing, each involving a separate purveyor, would have been exhausting and dispiriting to anyone except for a young man with a dream. What counted was that at the end, we had the special galvanized fittings that we would need to rig *Serendipity's* new masts.

Serendipity's booms and gaffs were another matter. We needed eye bands on the booms for sheet connections ("boom bails") and on the gaffs to secure the halyards. Boom bails are not simple eye-bands, but generally include a curved rod so that on each tack the sheet tackle can lead from the correct side of the boom. The steel pipe segments would have been too heavy and clumsy for these purposes. By rumor, I had heard that the Atlantic Marine Exchange, on Atlantic Avenue in Boston, still had a few galvanized eye bands left from the olden days when they were a staple in any ship chandlery.

On one of my last days in Boston that spring, I hurried down to Atlantic Avenue. James Bliss & Company, not far away, had already become "yuppie". Everything there was packaged in plastic and sold at high prices. But its neighbor down the block still had a little flavor left of the old days. Hanging from nails in the naked beams of the ancient and dusty Boston warehouse were indeed a number of galvanized eye-bands. Apparently never used, they had probably been forged and dipped 30, 40, or maybe 50 years before. They were willing to part with them for $1 apiece. We could get them down with a small stick with a hook on the end.

I measured carefully, comparing the dimensions with our list. Yes, they had galvanized eye-bands in the sizes needed. I picked out enough to secure the halyards to the gaffs. I even found a 3-1/2" boom-bail for the main boom. The latter, though cracked, crude and light, was better than anything else I had seen. I was happy to pay $1.50 for it.

Harold Koncitek brings our last order of white oak boards. We were grateful for his willingness to go out of his way to find and saw good white oak for your project and at a very economical price.

Despite diligent searching in Atlantic's musty warehouse, we did not locate any boom bails for the fore or jib boom. Those we had to fabricate by taking some steel pipe clamps and bending bits of 3/8" galvanized rod, threaded at the

227

ends, to take the place of the bolts on both sides. They went into the galvanizing kettle along with the other fittings.

Sourcing the standing rigging and the cordage was also in progress at this time. The plans called for 5/16" wire rope, with spliced eyes and speltered terminals for the shrouds and stays. Learning how to splice wire rope and pour molten lead to make speltered terminals seemed at the time to be beyond our available time and skill level. While it was possible to make cold-pressed eyes with 'Nicopress" sleeves in 5/16" wire rope, the necessary equipment was not generally accessible to us and the wire itself was very expensive. On the other hand, 1/4" wire rope and the necessary tools and fittings to make Nicopress loops were readily available – and at reasonable cost. Would ¼" wire be strong enough to stay *Serendipity's* masts? I called Mr. Crockett. "Oh yes," he said, "Quarter-inch wire rope would be plenty strong." He had specified the 5/16" for the sake of obtaining a more traditional appearance.

Now we had to obtain the wire rope and the fittings. Our friends at Sargent Lord were not particularly competitive on either wire rope or on manila for the running rigging. They would be able to give us a discount, but not much. We must be able to do better than that. Maybe someone in Boston could give us a good deal.

At that time the "Yellow Pages" of the telephone book served as the best place to look for almost any kind of goods or services available in the locality. Among the listings for wire rope distributors was "Al Pendleton Supply", downtown in Boston near the waterfront. I took a trip down there on the subway. Al Pendleton was an elderly man in a little musty office in a street or two away from the water. His business had seen better days. There were a few coils of wire rope around and some miscellaneous fittings. He sat at an old oak desk with a telephone and a pile of catalogs. But he had the key contacts and distributorships that enabled him to offer us good discounts on both wire rope and manila cordage. I ordered the

¼" 1 x 19 stainless steel wire rope we would need for the shrouds and stays, plus 5/16" and 7/16" manila for the running rigging. At that time polyester (Dacron), strong and rot-proof, was in general use for running rigging on sailboats. But for traditional *Serendipity*, only natural manila would do. Besides, manila was quite a bit cheaper than Dacron. It was not until later that we experienced manila's tendencies to shrink in wet weather and stretch in dry, and its relatively short life due to rot.

Al Pendleton was also a distributor for Merriman yacht fittings. Merriman, the manufacturer of the best yacht blocks and bronze hardware from the time of N. G. Herreshoff, was on its last legs. Like many traditional family businesses, the company had been sold by the heirs of the original Merriman Brothers to a "mini-conglomerate", which proved to be completely incapable of operating a traditional sailing yacht hardware business in the changing post-war world, when wood gave way to fiberglass for hulls and to aluminum for spars, and when bronze gave way to stainless steel for most fittings. We looked through the Merriman catalog together. Most of the fittings that were still available were way outside of our budget. However, aided by Al's generous discounts, we resorted to Merriman to solve one technical problem that had bothered me for some time.

Serendipity's plans called for a single loose-footed but boomed jib on a traveler. This arrangement was perhaps slightly less weatherly than the more customary overlapping jib or jibs, but incomparably easier on the crew when tacking. There is no need to release the jib and haul it in on the new tack when going about. It simply slides over on the traveler by itself just like the fore and the main.

The problem was that in order to keep the jib tight when raised, yet allow it to be raised and lowered easily, it was necessary to be able either to slack the ties that secured the sail to the forestay, or to slide the boom fore and aft. *Serendipity's* designer had opted for the latter, and had specified an elaborate galvanized fitting with a carrier sliding on two rods for the tack end of the jib boom. When we had sailed with Mr. Randolph on the *Elise*, I had seen one of these and observed how it worked - which was not very well. It was bulky and ugly and tended to stick when one wanted to either slide the boom forward to raise or lower the jib or slide the boom aft to flatten it out once raised.

Our solution would be simpler and more elegant than the galvanized rod fitting. We would use a short section of bronze genoa jib track and a genoa "car" to which we would secure a swivel eye that could engage with a set of turnbuckle jaws in the end of the jib boom. Al Pendleton undertook to get us the 2' section of genoa track, the end stops and a Merriman bronze Genoa car for this apparatus.

It was the same with the sourcing of everything that went into *Serendipity*. Marine equipment then, as now, was expensive, partly because of generous markups at every level of the distribution chain. The only way we could afford much of what we needed was by finding a supplier who was prepared to extend to us discounts from "list" or "retail" prices that were usually available only to dealers or boatyards. We always made it clear that we were building our own boat as amateurs. Some suppliers refused to extend us any discounts. But many others, starting with Sargent Lord in Portland, were understanding of our situation and were willing to give us substantial discounts that saved us in the aggregate many thousands of dollars in the cost for *Serendipity's* materials.

Back to the hull once more. We had planed the generously rough-sawn "6-quarter" Philippine mahogany planks to about 1 7/16" on Mr. Merrick's planer. How would we be able to bend them to follow the curve of the cabin carlins, which, in turn, followed the curve of the sides of the hull? How would we bore the holes for the long bolts that would run down through the width of these planks to secure them to the deck and the cabin carlins without the bit wandering out through the sides?

We started with the forward and aft ends of the cabin trunk. Those were straight across. The forward cabin trunk end was glued up out of two narrower planks, and then sawn on one edge to follow the camber of the deck, and on the other edge to follow the more pronounced camber of the cabin top. We fit it several times to minimize the seam between deck and cabin side and then clamped it in place using our trusty pipe clamps.

Now for the boring. Somewhere, probably in Chapelle, I had read of how one can make a jig for boring long holes in plank edges to minimize "bit-wander". It was basically a block of wood the same thickness as the plank and with a hole in the center of the same diameter as the bit fastened to two "legs" of strapping material. The legs would be clamped to the sides of the plank so that the block and the hole would be some distance from the plank. The idea was that the bit would be inserted through the hole, which would keep it straight as it went into the plank. As the bit went deeper, the clamps could be adjusted to bring the hole closer.

We also used special barefoot "ships augur" bits that were designed to bore deeply without wandering. Conventional bits had screws in the ends that would pull the bit into the hole. The problem was that the screws could lead the bits astray. For the longest holes, the bits were "barefoot" – without screws in the end. This meant that they were not self-starting. One had to drill a starter or "pilot" hole with another drill before inserting the ships augur via the aforementioned jig.

This may sound complicated and many-stepped, and it was. But we could not afford to have a drill hole break the surface of our cabin sides – it would not only ruin the appearance of the cabin, it would also fatally compromise the strength of this structural member.

231

Before we drilled and installed the forward end of the cabin trunk, we cut out holes for two forward-facing port-lights. The plans called for 4" round bronze opening port-lights in the forward end of the cabin trunk. Always concerned about ventilation, we opted to enlarge them to 5". The plans also called for 5 fixed windows or "lights" along each side of the cabin trunk. This would provide plenty of light, as we could see when we went sailing with Mr. Randolph, but no ventilation. Wouldn't it be nice if we could get some opening port-lights or rectangular marine windows for the main cabin? The problem was that bronze marine windows of a size comparable to the fixed rectangular lights specified in the plans were fantastically expensive – $150 or so apiece at the time.

We turned to Rostand. Unlike other manufacturers such as Wilcox-Crittenden (then on its last legs in Middletown, CT) or Perkins Lamp and Marine (Perko), which had moved from its traditional factory in Brooklyn, NY to Miami, Florida, Rostand did not sell its marine hardware through dealers or distributors. It dealt directly with boat builders and manufacturers. Among many kinds of cleats, stanchions, hawse pipes, block, and whatever, Rostand offered several different models of marine windows – and at net prices that we could conceivably afford. I called them up and spoke to Mr. Cameron, Rostand's sales manager. After hearing my spiel about our project, he agreed to supply us with their products at the same net prices paid by boatyards. I went ahead right away and ordered the pair of 5" round port lights and two 8" x 16" rectangular windows for the cabin sides.

Why did we order just two rectangular windows when the plans called for 5 windows on each side of the cabin? We were running low not only on time, but also on money. Even at Rostand's net prices, the windows would cost us something like $80 each. Why don't we start out with a single window in either side of the cabin trunk and add more later on as we could afford them? We also ordered a pair of bronze chock fittings

The forward end of the cabin trunk was made up of two pieces of mahogany glued together. Here, I am rasping out the hole for one of the port lights. The other is already installed. The port lights and windows were installed without "finishing rings" on the outside, so that the fits had to be exact.

that could be recessed into our cap-rail forward. Although the Rostand prices for such other necessities as bronze cleats, blocks and turnbuckles, were most attractive, we stuck almost entirely with galvanized fittings from Sargent Lord, which were cheaper yet and just as strong, if not just as pretty.

At this point, we discovered something else about Rostand. They were terribly over-committed and could not meet their promised delivery schedules. Calls to Mr. Cameron were usually not returned. When we reached him, his promises and assurances turned out to be over-optimistic and hollow.

233

Apparently we were not the only customers whose orders were unfilled. In one conversation, Cameron disclosed that outside his office in Milford sat several "expeditors" from government contracting customers whose job it was to sit there and make themselves obnoxious until the promised order was completed and delivered. This was what my telephone calls were competing with!

Somehow, however, Mr. Cameron was able to get our order processed, and in due course a large carton appeared on the porch of 477 Main Street. When we opened it, it was like Christmas. The port lights and windows were gorgeous gleaming works of art. We were thrilled. Of course, we wanted to order more right away. But sober consideration of the priorities convinced me that we should install what we had and wait to order additional ones until we could afford them and had the time to put them in.

As it turned out, we almost waited too long. At the time we were dealing with Rostand, that ancient Connecticut manufacturing company was on its last legs. Within 5 years it was no more. Fortunately, we had been able to purchase four additional marine windows and some splendid bronze stanchions in the interim, so *Serendipity* ultimately did not suffer by reason of its closing.

Although we installed the port lights in the forward side of the cabin trunk before we bolted it in place, we held off on the marine windows. They were large and could affect the flexibility of the cabin sides which still lay before us. It would be a terrible shame, and likely a fatal delay in the construction period, if one of the sides broke at the window opening as we were trying to bend it in place.

Before we tried to bend in the two cabin sides, we also built up and bolted on the aft end of the cabin trunk. This was in two pieces, separated by the companionway. Each piece was cut to the camber of the deck on the bottom and to the camber of the cabin top at the top. Installation should have been simple and straightforward.

Perhaps it was too simple. As we clamped the cabin end pieces in place, with the deck joint well bedded in Caulk-tex, I failed to notice that the two halves of the rear wall of the cabin house were not at the same angle to the deck. One was almost straight up, the other was tipped forward just a bit. Either way was correct – but they both should have been the same. The difference was about ½", but it turned out to be a half-inch that has plagued me for the 50 years since.

Here Anita drives the threaded rod through the hole in the starboard rear end of the cabin. If only I had thought to make sure that both of the sides were at the same angle to the deck!

235

Our boring jig and ships augur drills worked well to bore the long holes for the galvanized rod that secured the cabin ends in place. We made our own threaded rod. The stuff that you could buy then in the hardware stores was cheap electroplated stuff that would rust in a minute. Not for *Serendipity*! What we used instead was 3/8" hot galvanized rod that we bought from Sargent Lord in 4' lengths (20' lengths cut in five pieces for transportation) like the half-inch rod from which we had fashioned the drift bolts that tied the various pieces of deadwood and the horn timber to the keel. Cutting the 3/8" rod to the proper lengths with our Craftsman sabre saw was easy. The hard part was putting threads on both ends of each bolt. All we had to work with was a small Sears Roebuck die set and a lot of energy. We would clamp the piece of rod in the old wood vice in the tiny workshop by the barn, file the end just a bit so that we could start the die, douse on a little cutting

My brother Paul and I are carefully bending the port cabin side around our impromptu moulds with various clamps. Once we had the wide mahogany plank bent into place, we bored holes edge-wise down into the oak cabin carlin underneath and bolted it down with threaded rod.

oil, and then laboriously cut the threads by hand – a quarter-turn of the die, then back to clear the cuttings, then forward again, with perhaps another squirt of oil. It would have been nice to have the proper tools, including a power thread cutter, but those were simply out of the question. If we could somehow do it with what we had, or could buy for little money, then we made do.

Taking out the cabin side moulds. We left a couple of temporary cross spalls until we could install the cabin top beams.

Once we had the cabin ends bolted on, it was time to fit the cabin sides. We had spiled the sheer curvature of the deck carlin and made a pattern for the lower edge of the cabin sides. The upper edge was supposed to be straight and level, fore and aft. Somehow I figured out how it had to be and cut and planed a smooth curve along the lower edge to fit the deck. From available scrap, we made a set of three of moulds to hold he sides of the cabin apart at the middle while we bent the ends in fore and aft.

237

Bending the nearly 1½" thick mahogany planks to form the curved cabin sides turned out to be easier and more straightforward than I had feared. We did it with pipe clamps hooked around the cabin ends drawing very slowly on each end of the cabin side plank. My heart was in my mouth . . . . suppose one side had cracked! But the sides came gradually, inexorably ever closer to the corner posts that I had screwed to the cabin ends. At the bow, we could finally fit a deep-throated clamp from the top to hold the side to the corner post. At the stern, we had to continue to rely on the pipe clamps.

Once we had bent the cabin sides in place, we needed to bore the long holes down edge-to-edge for the rod bolts that would tie them securely to the deck and the oak carlin below. This was also a tense exercise. If our bit were to stray and emerge from the mahogany plank en route, the whole cabin side might be spoiled. We could scarcely contemplate what that would mean in terms of getting our boat done on time.

But we were careful – and lucky. Guided by our impromptu jig, the 3/8" ships augur bit emerged more or less centered in the oak carlin. We counter-bored on each end for the nuts and took up on the bolts to draw the cabin side firmly down before fastening it with screws to the corner posts.

Here, of course, we should have noticed that one side of the after wall of the cabin was at a slightly different angle from the other. But we didn't, and bedded everything together with Caulk-tex, screwed the side planks to the corner posts, and sawed off the ends of the planks flush with the fore and aft cabin ends. The new cabin sides greatly increased the sturdiness of our side decks, acting as fore and aft girders to give them stiffness. When we took out the molds, the graceful curve remained.

With cabin sides in place, *Serendipity* began to look like a real yacht! We stepped back from the building site a bit to admire it. Once again we followed the advice of our boatbuilding books that recommended that the amateur builder take the time frequently to admire the work as his creation is taking form. It was good advice. The exhaustion and frustration that inevitably accompanies a project of this sort would become a little less onerous when we stepped back at the end of the day – or the beginning, or the middle, or at any time – and admired the beauty of our growing boat.

Chapter 11

By now it was June in Wilbraham, and we were acutely aware that in just three months, I was due in Portland, Maine. The key date was September 3, 1967. Between now and then, we had to get *Serendipity* finished, or finished enough to sail, and up to Maine. Law school graduation in the first week of June was a distraction. So was the Robinson Bar Review course, a genteel 3-week affair at the Parker House in downtown Boston, where Clements Robinson, a lawyer from Lowell, Massachusetts, attempted to instruct some 30 potential Bar Exam candidates in the fine points of Massachusetts law, at least those that were likely to appear on the Bar Exam in late July. These were the realities of life around which the main effort of getting *Serendipity* finished had to be configured.

We moved back to Wilbraham for the summer. To be sure, there would be the minor interruptions of bar exams in Massachusetts and in Maine. But the real business at hand was finishing the myriad of details, big and small that would make our still half-finished hull into a sailing ship - by Labor Day.

In the Connecticut Valley, the month of June is a time of lushness. Everything is a rich heavy green. The grass is green. The garden is green. So are the leaves on the trees. The damp, moistness of spring has not yet left the air. The days are warm, yet not with the baking heat of July. This was the way it was back in 1967. I rapidly threw aside my cap and gown and my law books for my ancient chambray work shirt and my "Can't Bust 'Ems" longshoremen's pants from San Francisco. By now my clothes were stiff with Cuprinol, glues and "gorps". My tools fit the callouses on my hands.

You can always tell a boatbuilder by his hands. For more than two years, my hands had never been without blisters, nicks, cuts, bruises, or marks of indelible paint. At 24, my hands looked practically gnarled from the aftermath of tiny accidents, poundings, scrapings, and nickings, which are inevitably a part of boat building, especially boat building in haste. I don't mean to say I was consciously careless. Nor was the project a frenzy. But the pressure was on. *Serendipity* would not become a relic in my parents' back yard. We would not leave *Serendipity* behind when we went to Maine. We were determined. When we went to Maine at the end of that summer, we were going in *Serendipity.*

There were so many things yet to be done! The cabin trunk yawned without its roof beams and roof. The cockpit was just roughed out – we needed to complete the framing and cabinet work for the three lockers on the two sides and aft side of the cockpit. Then there was hull fairing, priming and painting, topsides and bottom. Fittings had to be bedded and installed. If I tried to think of everything, my head would swim. Our only choice was to plug away, "one day at a time," and get as much done as we could. Somehow we would get the boat finished enough so that we could take her with us to Maine.

The first task was to cover our plywood deck with fiberglass cloth and epoxy resin. When Vere B. Crockett originally designed the 30' "*Nimble*" schooner in the 1950s, the standard for decks was plywood covered with canvas soaked in paint. Technology had evolved since then, and by the mid-sixties the process of covering wood decks and hulls with fiberglass cloth was in general use and had found wide acceptance. When I rebuilt *Te Amo* in the later '50's, I covered the hull with fiberglass cloth and polyester resin to provide strength and abrasion resistance as well as to make the leaky old skiff watertight.

The problem with fiberglass covering was getting a good bond between the glass cloth, which contained the strength-giving fibers, and the wood of the deck or hull, as the case may be. Polyester resin, which was generally used for this purpose, formed a strong fiberglass shell, but adhered poorly to wood. There was the risk that over time, water could creep in between the glass and the wood subsurface and develop hidden pockets of rot.

My experience with *Te Amo* and my readings in contemporary literature had convinced me that polyester resin just did not stick well enough to wood and that we should incur the extra expense for epoxy resin, which bonds powerfully and permanently to any wood surface. Developed during World War II, epoxy resin was just coming into use for marine applications. It was still very expensive. Once again, we turned to Ralph Travers, who manufactured at the time a high quality epoxy resin under the name, "Liquid Marine Tex". He was kind enough to sell us enough to do our decks and cabin tops at a substantial discount. We picked up several gallons at the plant in Chelsea.

There was only one problem with the epoxy resin. It turned out that Anita was terribly allergic to it. Any contact, even smelling it, would cause a terrific reaction. She would puff up all over and have difficulty breathing. Therefore, since I did not seem to have any particular sensitivity to the resin, it was I who had to apply the fiberglass cloth and resin to the deck.

The deck got a good sanding, then Anita retired and I went to work with the fiberglass cloth and the resin. Of course, Ralph Travers specified a special kind of Xynol-treated fiberglass cloth to use with his marvelous Liquid Marine Tex. Fortunately, it was generally available, and we were able to get a good deal on enough 10-ounce fiberglass cloth to cover the deck. The first step was to give the whole deck a coat of Liquid Marine Tex that would soak into the deck and form a strong bond with the cloth to be applied. After this first coat had hardened (usually overnight), I spread the cloth on the deck and cut it more or less to size, with overhangs all around.

We cut pieces of the heavy 10-ounce fiberglass cloth to lap over the edges of the deck and up against the cabin sides.

The cloth was lapped slightly up on the cabin sides to make the joint between cabin side and deck more watertight and secure.

Once the cloth had been spread on the deck, I then wet it out with another coat of resin. For some reason, we did not staple the cloth down. The wet resin held it to the deck and it dried in place. Finally, a third coat of resin was brushed on the cloth to even things out and give it a smooth finish. When I had sanded the rough spots smooth, I was sure we had a deck that would be as tight as a nut against the onslaught of the sea.

With cabin sides in place, we went to work on the roof of the cabin with its forward hatch and aft companionway. The boatbuilding books told us that traditionally cabin top beams are sawn out of spruce to save weight above-decks. I had not ordered any stock for the cabin roof beams. It was probably because I didn't know where I could conveniently get the clear

243

The cabin top beam laminating jig was cut to the camber of the cabin top beams. It could hold up to four beams at a time.

spruce prescribed by the specs. Therefore, when it came time to put a roof on our lovely curving cabin, we had to cast around a bit. The mahogany scrap pile from our planking lay in plain view. There was a plethora of long, narrow, pointy scraps left over from the sawing of curved strakes from straight mahogany planks. If I sawed them in pieces about 1-1/2" or 2" wide and about 3/8" thick, I could get enough mahogany strips to make laminated deck beams. The old table saw whirred, spitting out long daggers of scraps as we made long triangles into narrow rectangles. We then turned them on their edges and sawed them again, producing from each plank scrap two rough battens each about 1/2" thick. Mr. Merrick's planer did the rest. In a weekend's time, we had a great stack of 7/16" mahogany battens each about 8' long. From these we would laminate our cabin top beams.

Back at the ranch, we next made a jig for laminating the strips. A couple of wide scraps cut to the camber of the cabin roof made up the sides. They were joined by a number of 2 x 2

244

cross-pieces to which we could clamp the layers of strips while the glue dried. Each cabin top beam was composed of three 7/16" thick strips.

We glued them up in bunches of three or four at a time using Liquid Marine-Tex for the laminations. In a couple of days, we had enough raw blanks to make up the 16 cabin top beams, plus some scraps for the half-beams in way of hatch and companion way. Both sides of each laminated beam then

The laminated cabin top beams rest in notches in a deck beam carlin that is clamped to the cabin sides. The batten on top will be let into the beams along the centerline of the cabin top.

had to be planed (by hand) to remove the excess glue and even up the edges of the laminating strips. We finally were able to fit the deck beams into a crude notched carlin screwed to the tops of the cabin sides. Another pause to admire. How handsome our (Philippine) mahogany cabin top beams looked in the summer sun!

There was no time to give much consideration to the interior of *Serendipity's* cabin before launching. We knew that we would be doing well to get a bare hull completed by the time we had to be in Portland, Maine. However, we did decide to try to fit the main bulkhead separating the main cabin from the forecastle. We cut this from two pieces of ¾" exterior plywood and secured it to the frames and cabin sides. It was a bit of a trick to get the right curvature of the edge along the hull. We had to work from the existing mould patterns with

The plywood cabin bulkhead is now in place, secured to the cabin sides and the hull. The frame for the fore hatch opening is visible as well.

some in-place spiling to make each half more or less fit.

The plywood cabin top came next. This time we used 3/8" exterior plywood to be covered with a lighter weight "Vectra" fiberglass cloth. The idea was to save weight topsides. We did not want *Serendipity's* superstructure to be unnecessarily top-heavy.

Cutting and fitting the plywood, was like fitting the main deck – with one difference. We let a 7/16" strip into each deck beam along the centerline to take the seam of the plywood sheets. It was easy to clamp the first sheet on each side along the center line until we could secure it to the center-board with screws and ring-nails. However, when we came to fit the second sheet, there was no place to clamp except at one end. Ultimately Anita stood on the edge of the plywood panel until I was able to get enough fastenings in to hold it firmly on the beams. We drove in a multitude of 1¼" ring nails to nail the cabin top firmly to all beams and carlins and to the cabin sides themselves.

Here I am nailing down the plywood cabin top to the laminated cabin top beams. It took a vast number of 1 1/4" bronze ring nails.

At this point, we first noticed that the rear edges of the cabin roof did not exactly line up. My error in aligning the rear sides of the cabin had come to light. But by now we had the cabin sides fitted and the cabin roof fitted and nailed down. To take everything apart to redo things "right" would have been a lot of work and a lot of very scarce time. It was not a big error – scarcely noticeable to most people. We decided to let it be. We could live with it.

Live with it we have. But we should have taken the time to fix it. The result of this asymmetry in the after end of the cabin, is that the companionway does not really close right, and the screen doors in the companionway opening do not fit right – defects which remind me of my error every time I am on board.

We had no time to ruminate on these matters at that time. We had to go forward. Bowsprit and cockpit floor came next. The plans called for a bowsprit of oak bolted through the deck and butted into a four-by-four oak Sampson post rising from the stem and through the deck. We had installed the 4 x 4 for the Sampson post when we framed the deck beams. A 4" x 9" blank for the bowsprit had been included in the original white oak order with Mr. Koncitek and had been sitting seasoning in the garage ever since. When we went to retrieve it, however, we found that it had hopelessly checked and cracked despite being coated with linseed oil at the time we had put it in there. We couldn't use it. Now, we were in a pickle. There was little time to look around or even to get Mr. Koncitek to come up with a new blank. We had to make do with what we had.

What we did have was one more oak timber. This was checked along one side, but it appeared that there might be enough good wood from which we could re-saw some kind of a bowsprit. To be sure, the piece contained a large knot that could undermine its strength under extreme conditions. However, there appeared to be enough good wood that we figured the knot would not make much difference. And we did not have much of a choice.

A somewhat awkward photo of installation of the bowsprit. One of our home-made galvanized eye-bands is on the end. This made *Serendipity* look like a real ship!

Laborious re-sawing with complementary Skil-saw cuts from both sides produced a rough 3 1/2" x 7" timber more or less free of checks and cracks. We couldn't avoid the knot though. We would have to live with it. We took comfort in the fact that the bowsprit would be stoutly stayed with chains so that the actual strain on the timber itself would not be too great. Rounding the hard oak bowsprit with draw knife and plane was not the picnic that we had with the masts. The wood was fairly dry and getting tough and hard. It was not easy to plane the big knot, either. And it was getting hot!

Eventually we got it planed more or less 3" round at the outer end, while maintaining 3½" x 6" rectangular at the inboard end. We butted it to the Sampson post, bedded it in

249

The cockpit deck was made of thin strips of teak, caulked with "Black Caulk-Tex". Visible in this picture is the hole in the cockpit floor for our Danforth compass, the small slot for the shift lever, and the holes in the cockpit walls for instrument panel and starboard locker.

Caulk-tex and bolted it to the deck beams with ½" galvanized bolts, heads plugged with oak plugs. The plans had called for an 8" wide bowsprit terminating aft of the Sampson post with a 3½" square hole so that the bowsprit would fit over the Sampson post and be bolted to it. However, the usable wood in the replacement blank was not wide enough, so we had to make do butting the bowsprit instead. We gave the new bowsprit a coat of sealer for the time being.

Although I probably would have liked to, I couldn't really forget that I was supposed to be a lawyer, or at least was in the process of becoming one. Fortunately, my Massachusetts bar exam preparation overlapped my last days in Cambridge waiting for Anita for finish her career as an elementary school librarian. But at the end of June, I had to go back to Boston and take the bar exam. How I begrudged those two days I spent trying in writing to convince the Massachusetts bar examiners that I was fit to be licensed to practice law in the Commonwealth. I had to do all I could to concentrate on the hypothetical legal conundrums that are devised for the annual process of sorting sheep from goats in the licensure of lawyers. But before I knew it, we were back in Wilbraham again, and it was July. It was a hot July. Every day counted now, seven days a week.

The premier material for yacht decks then and now was and is teak planking. Not only does the sanded teak set off by wide black seams look great, but it is also naturally "non-skid" when wet, a very important attribute for a boat deck. But teak decking was then (and still is) very expensive. Fitting teak deck planks to follow the curves of a vessel's sides is also very time consuming and tricky as a matter of workmanship. So we didn't really consider teak for *Serendipity's* decks.

However, the sole of *Serendipity's* 3' x 5' cockpit was another matter. The plans called for plywood covered in canvas or fiberglass. Mr. Randolph's schooner had a teak grating in the cockpit, which improved footing, but accumulated dirt and debris. Why not install a teak deck over the plywood in the cockpit only? That would involve only a small quantity of the precious teak lumber, and all the planks would be straight. It should be a piece of cake. And, comparatively speaking it was.

We purchased the requisite number of 7/16" x 2 ½" teak deck planks to cover the 15 square feet of cockpit floor from some maritime lumber source along with a bunch of teak plugs for the heads of the screws to hold it down. We laid the planks in a special kind of black Caulk-tex that is specially formulated for bedding and caulking laid decks, screwed them down, and plugged the heads with the teak plugs. The caulking took overnight to cure. We then sanded the teak with our trusty old 6" Craftsman rotary sander – now clearly on its last-legs. It

251

looked great with the bright glow of the sanded teak set off by the black bands of the caulked seams. When we laid the deck, we left a small rectangle above the hole for the bilge pump handle. This we filled with a removable rectangle of teak decking in which I let a small bronze ring pull, so that it was flush with the rest of the deck when in place.

We tried not to call on my parents for help on the boat too often. But when we did, they were there. Father is patient as he holds the aft end of the toe-rail aloft with one of the gaffs and puffs on his pipe as we try to secure the forward end with 5/16" drift bolts into the sheer strake.

We also cut a six-inch round hole in the floor of the cockpit for our Danforth flush-deck mount compass. After some mulling, it seemed as if the best place to mount the main steering compass would be below the floor of the cockpit. There was no room for a proper binnacle. Having the compass project from the aft side of the cabin or the forward wall of the cockpit were the alternatives. These seemed too intrusive. Danforth made a nifty bracket with which one could mount the compass below a glass bullseye in the deck or cockpit floor. It was not an ideal location, since one had to look way down to see it from the usual steering position at the helm. The compass was also very close to the iron mass of the engine, which would make it hard to correct. But it was the best we could do at the time. It was exciting to be seeing things actually look finished!

A particular, long-dreaded challenge was making and installing the 1 1/8" x 2 ½" oak toe rail along the edges of the deck on each side. First, we had to join two 16" lengths of 1 1/8" x 3" white oak (our pile from Mr. Koncitek was almost exhausted) with an edge scarf bolted with 5/16" galvanized bolts. Then I had to take the trusty fore plane and bevel the lower edge of the forward end of each toe rail so that the rail would toe outward and follow the surface of the flaring bow. We almost forgot to notch the underside of the toe rail for the deck scuppers, so that water on the deck could run overboard freely. Out came the saber saw to make small 3/8" x 2/1/2" notches at regular intervals along the bottom edge of the battens. Another mistake! We did not need scuppers forward,

We pause to catch our breaths and to admire the newly-installed toe rail.

253

where the sheer was elevated, but we needed more scuppers amidships where the water would tend to collect. I eventually laboriously chiseled out an additional scupper on each side at the low point of the sheer amidships after the toe rail had been installed.

The hard part was fastening the toe rail along the edge of the deck. How could we secure the long floppy oak battens exactly along the edge on each side? The toe rails had to be secured in some fashion while we bored them and fastened them down through the deck and into the sheer strake with 6" x 5/16" galvanized drift bolts. We had these made from carriage bolts with some of the threads ground off. The problem was, there was nothing to clamp to. The tough oak toe rails took both a curve and quite a twist forward and aft.

We ultimately screwed a row of blocks to the deck 1 1/8" back from the edge on both sides to which we could clamp. It was trickier up near the bow where the toe rail was slanted. There we screwed pieces of old rib ends to the outside of the hull so that the toe rail would be precisely lined up with the angle of the planking. We started securing the toe rail in the bow by cutting the angle of the end where it screwed to the bowsprit.

As we worked our way aft, bedding the toe rail in Caulk-Tex and clamping it to the blocks, it was necessary to hold the free end aloft at the level of the deck. Ultimately, Father had to be recruited from his study and Mother from her garden. Using one of our future gaffs like a trident, Father held the aft end of the toe rail batten up in the air at deck level but some distance out from the side of the boat. Anita and I tried to secure the bow end in place with whatever clamps and cleats we could jury rig until we could bore holes and drive the drift bolts properly home. Then gradually, oh, so gradually, Father moved in closer, holding the toe rail aloft in the gaff jaw as we worked our way aft with drill and bolts. We got the rail to twist by clamping sticks cross-wise at strategic points and then

Wetting out the Vectra cloth on the cabin top. We chose Vectra rather than fiberglass because it was lighter and we did not want *Serendipity* to be top-heavy.

using the leverage to twist the oak batten. Once the toe rail was clamped in place, we carefully checked to make sure it all was in line, then bored the 9/32" holes into which we drove the drift bolts.

Whew! It was finally done. A task that I had worried and mulled about for some time was accomplished! Although the fit of the oak toe rail to the deck was not perfect, Caulk-Tex covered a lot of sins. We paused briefly to relish the feeling of accomplishment and then pressed on.

After giving the cabin top a good sanding with the old Craftsman 6" sander and a sanding disk attachment to our ¼" drill, we cut the Vectra fiberglass cloth to fit and went ahead to wet it out with Liquid Marin-Tex epoxy resin. This time, Anita covered up with long sleeves to help as best she could, and paid the price in terms of an itchy rash. Although the epoxy resin was expensive, and apparently highly toxic, we could see

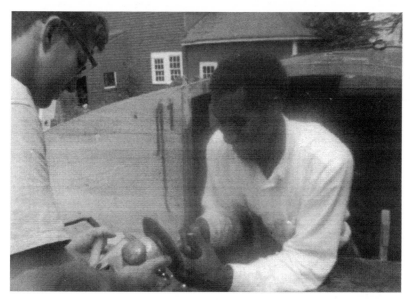

Here is Arthur Thomas as we use the ancient Sears disc sander to round the corners of a chain plate before bolting it in place. It was a hot day!

that it was doing the job and strongly bonding to the wood surfaces of the cabin top and deck.

It was great fun to put in our two marine windows. Lifting them reverently from the excelsior, we traced out their outlines on the unbroken surface of our heavy mahogany cabin sides. With the drill and saber saw, we carefully cut out the apertures. We had decided to fit them without "finishing ring" so that the smoothness of the mahogany exterior would not be interrupted by a bronze ring with bolt heads. This particular vanity required a nice fit of the spigot of the port in the hole. Caulk-Tex insured a watertight bedding. How beautiful they looked screwed in place! Anyone but ourselves would have viewed our cabin with only one port per side as incongruous to say the least. But we were looking at the positive, and they were positively beautiful.

Of course, we had no illusions about being able to finish the interior of *Serendipity* before we headed north. That would be a project for a future season, once we were settled in Maine. For now, it would have to remain a great open cavern, smelling faintly of Cuprinol, in which the engine stood proud and alone. We rigged a temporary sole on the floor timbers. We clambered in and out on a makeshift ladder from an old bunk bed set.

Former college roommate Arthur Thomas came to Wilbraham for the third time (the first time was our ill-fated trip to bring the planking lumber) to help fit our shiny newly-galvanized chain plates. The chain plates were 18" straps of 1/4" x 2" galvanized steel that we had bored for bolt holes and turnbuckle jaw-pins. They had to be bolted in place along the sides of the hull before we put the rub-rail in place. In order to spread the forces from the shrouds, we had fashioned oak backup boards, two layers each 7/16" thick so that the backup boards would bend to the contour of the hull.

The problem was that we had bored the bolt holes in the chain plate blanks before we knew where they would be on the sides of the boat. It turned out that the uppermost bolt hole on each chain plate was behind the sheer clamp near the top of the sheer strake. Fitting in the backup boards and then a washer and a nut in this cramped space called for particular talent. Arthur took on the challenge. While I bored the holes and drove in the 3/8" cap screws from outside the boat, Arthur held up the backup boards and then held the nuts and washers on the inside. We had to coordinate perfectly in order to get the nuts on the top bolts. The bolt had to be driven in just enough so that the tip just cleared the backup board. Arthur then had to feel with his fingertip the emerging bolt in the ¾" deep space between the backup board and the sheer clamp and somehow get a washer and nut in position. It required a couple of light taps on the bolt from outside to get enough threads through so that Arthur's fingers could get the nut caught. The rest was comparatively easy – with a carefully-inserted open end wrench Arthur could hold the nut while I tightened down from the outside.

It was hot! Sweat streamed down both our faces, especially Arthur's, cooped up in *Serendipity's* dark enclosed interior. Sometimes it took several tries to get a nut on one of those top bolts. I regretted bitterly that I had not thought more carefully about the locations of the bolt holes or how I would install them when we had bored the chainplates in Jeff Wood's cellar. But we persevered. We had no choice. And by the end of the weekend, we had the 10 shroud chainplates firmly bolted on. Arthur certainly earned his keep, and many future sails, by his work that weekend.

By now we were well into July. The bar review course and the Massachusetts bar exam were finished and my law school graduation was a distant memory. We were working full time. The only distraction that would remain before launching was the Maine bar examination conveniently scheduled for two consecutive days at the end of the month.

At this stage of the work, we were climbing on and off *Serendipity* almost continually, as we went from task to task in the progressively finishing hull. From the beginning, our means of climbing aboard had been impromptu and crude. We had no scaffolding or work platforms, but had to improvise when we wanted to go aboard. Most of the time, we used an old straight ladder that had hung in the garage since time immemorial. We would prop the ladder up against the hull wherever we could. It was precarious and inefficient, but it was what we had.....

Until, of course, my father came to the rescue. He had noticed our difficulties with getting up on *Serendipity*. One day in July, he drove into the yard with a large wood fruit-picking ladder strapped to the roof of his car. This was like a giant stepladder, with a single forward leg and the two sides of the ladder itself splayed out so that it would be steady in most positions on most kinds of terrain. It was exactly what we

With her new oak rub-rails *Serendipity* is beginning to take on a finished look. Spencer Moore inspects from above. To the left is the marvelous fruit-picking ladder that my father found and gave us to ease embarkation and disembarkation.

needed. Now we could set the new ladder up alongside *Serendipity* and mount it like a set of stairs, stepping confidently off onto the deck when we reached the top. It made the rest of the work on the boat incomparably easier. We were grateful for this thoughtful contribution to the effort. Now nearly 50 years later, the ladder is still in use every spring and fall for work on *Serendipity* and brings my father and his generosity to mind every time.

Although the hull and the cabin of *Serendipity* were more or less roughed out, there were a million things left to do before we would be ready to launch *Serendipity* at the end of August. We had figured backward from September 3, the day after Labor Day and the day I was to start work in Portland, Maine. Realistically speaking, we would have to launch the boat by mid-week of the week before in order to have enough time to iron out inevitable bugs and then sail the boat to Portland by Labor Day weekend. During the course of the project, we had considered various alternatives for launching *Serendipity* - from the Connecticut River to Massachusetts Bay or even having the vessel trucked all the way to Maine. The last would be necessary if we did not get the boat sufficiently completed to launch before we had to be in Maine.

Relatively early on in the project, I had visited Graves Yacht Yard in Marblehead for some reason and had noticed the bronze tiller-head fitting that they were using on their 30' Constellation class sailing yachts. At that time, I bought one for $40, a high price then, but there were few alternatives. Now as we were considering how we would launch *Serendipity* near the end of August, Graves came back to mind. I got back in touch with Selman Graves.

Graves had a large crane on rails with which they launched even large yachts using strap slings dangling from a square frame. Would they be willing to launch *Serendipity* from a truck? I told them the story of the project. Like many others, Graves were willing to help. Late August was not a busy time for them. The fall hauling season would not start for a couple of weeks. Yes, they would be glad to launch *Serendipity* if I got her there during the week before Labor Day. So the plan was made. We were working against a deadline of the last week in August when *Serendipity* hopefully would be trucked to Marblehead and launched at Graves. How she would be trucked there, was yet to be determined. We left that for later determination and plunged ahead with the next stages of the construction.

The plans called for a 2" half-round oak rub rail covering the joint between sheer strake, deck and toe rail along both sides. The problem was that 2" half-round white oak moulding was simply unobtainable – anywhere. After several fruitless efforts to locate a stock product, we turned to our old friends, Roy Lumber in Willimantic. Yes, they could make a moulding cutter and manufacture 80 linear feet of white oak 2" half-round for us – which they did. One morning, the Roy truck rolled up and delivered to us six 14-foot lengths of beautiful clear 2" half-round – exactly what we needed. At various key points in the project, Roy had come through with invaluable help – such as with the band-sawing of our oak backbone pieces, to supplying rough 5/4" pine boards from which we made the moulds, to planing our mahogany planking, to band-sawing our deck beams, and finally to providing the rub rail - in each case at reasonable cost. It is hard to imagine that we could have actually built the boat without the sympathetic cooperation of many suppliers and sources along the way.

The white oak moulding was still somewhat green. It bent smoothly and easily along the sides of *Serendipity*, neatly covering the ugly joint and accentuating the graceful curve of the sheer. We bedded it in Caulk-Tex and screwed it on to the sheer plank with 2" x 12 bronze screws. This heavy finish molding added not only a touch of finish, but a smack of ruggedness. Pilings, docks, and other boats, watch out! We were protected.

There came the day when we accomplished the many tasks to complete the installation of our solid Volvo diesel and test it in operation. Lacking the proper tools and equipment, every step in the installation had been a hassle. Even the simple matter of a fuel line from engine to tank, for example, required a trip to Westerbeke for a special "banjo" fitting which had been omitted when we originally picked up the engine. Then, I had to go to a special hose place in Cambridge. Finally, we stopped at our local gas station for a small piece of copper pipe to connect the Swedish banjo fitting to the special American hose. Battery cables had to be made up in similar fashion. Painstakingly we tried to shim, wedge and level the engine to avoid the anticipated horrors of "misalignment". The books warned ominously of possible shaking, wear on the bearings, excessive leaking of the stuffing box, and perhaps a total failure of our means of propulsion!

I installed the crude Swedish Bowden-wire throttle control that was supplied with the engine. I didn't know, however, that I had hooked it up so that wide open, the motor would only be running at about one-third speed.

The shaft had been carefully lined up and the engine had been adjusted on its flexible rubber mounts. Our "Rube Goldberg" water-jacketed exhaust system had been bolted onto the appropriate flange on the engine. A piece of special wire-reinforced exhaust hose had been installed to lead the fumes, mixed with the water from the water -jacket, downhill to a bronze exhaust through-hull fitting in the transom and then out. The crude control wire provided by Volvo had been let to the cockpit and the control lever bolted on the side. The shift linkage had been hooked up and seemed to work. I ran a fuel hose from the tank to a large external filter. From there a copper line led through a loop (to dampen vibration) to the engine.

Electrics were very simple. The Volvo MD-2 came with a starter-generator double-belted to the massive flywheel on the front of the engine. It functioned as a starter to get the engine going. Once the engine was running, it went into generator mode and provided a trickle of charge to the single battery, secured in a box screwed to the frames beside the engine. The modest instrument panel was let into the forward wall of the cockpit and the charge controller screwed on behind. That, with an "on-off" switch to the battery was about all there was.

By mid-July, we were ready to test the engine. Of course, we could not run it dry. I borrowed every hose I could in the neighborhood to bring water from the house all the way out to the garden and to *Serendipity*. Hooking up the hose to the water intake on the engine, we followed the owner's manual step by step through the engine starting procedure. Our gleaming tank held five gallons of diesel fuel, fetched from a nearby gas station. The sump had the requisite amount of oil. The battery was newly charged. Had we done everything right? Would our brand new engine, sprayed with its coat of gray paint and never yet started, run? We turned on the water. At first, nothing happened. Then I could hear the water gushing out of the exhaust port on the transom. There were no apparent leaks. I turned the key and pushed the starter button on the instrument panel, newly screwed to the forward wall of our tiny cockpit. "Keelumpf-keelumpf-keelumpf". The little starter-dynamo strained to turn over the great cast iron flywheel and overcome the compression.

Over and over the little engine turned, but no results. Was it dead? Was something wrong? Was the fuel getting to the engine? We stopped for a minute, discouraged. And then we tried again. "Keelumpf-keelumpf-keelumpf . . . chunk, chunk, chunk". It started! It was running! "Chunk, chunk, chunk". The water sprayed out the stern mixed with puffs of smoke. Mother looked up from the garden. We ran into the house to get Father. The engine was running! The flywheel spun around, and the lamps and gauges on the panel did what they were supposed to.

Of course, we didn't dare put it in gear. The shiny propeller remained motionless in the aperture. But we knew that the Volvo would run. Hallelujah! A great weight was off our mind. We pressed forward with renewed zeal.

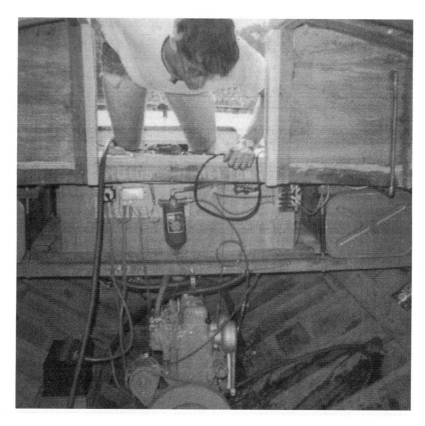

It was very exciting to finally test the Volvo engine. Amazingly enough, it ran on the first try! As can be seen in this photo, the installation was very simple and rudimentary.

Sometimes in a project of this kind, one tends to put off a task thinking it difficult and complex, only to find it easy and rewarding once it has been tackled. So it was with the construction of the cross-trees and spreader which joined the main mast and its fitted topmast. The traditional topmast had been one of the many charming features that had endeared this design to me from the beginning. However, in late July as we hastened toward launching, the structure itself looked complicated. There was this unusual bit of ironwork which we had somewhat crudely approximated with Eddie Dearborn. In addition, the construction of the wooden frame at the base of the topmast and the spreaders looked complicated and difficult.

Mark Rollins helps bolt the oak cheek-pieces that hold the spreader and topmast to the squared head of the lower main mast.

But once we got down to it, we found that the spreader was nothing more than a simple oak 2 x 2. The same was true with the stock out of which the rest of the framework was constructed. Going one task at a time, we bolted the cheek pieces onto the square head of the mainmast where it began to taper. In a jiffy, we had the frame for the foot of the topmast completed, bored and bolted as well. The spreader then naturally crossed in the back. The base of the topmast settled down snugly on the support frame in front. Although our crude ironwork was not quite straight, we managed to align the topmast, more or less, with several blows of the mallet. I installed one of our home-made 3" galvanized eye bands on the top of the topmast. There, before our eyes, was a real mast of a gaff rigged ship. The daunting task had been done in less than an afternoon.

The masts were nervously cut to length and squared at the butts to fit in the slots in the forward and main mast steps. There was no way to correct this if my scaling off the plans was wrong. Friends such as Spencer Moore and Mark Rollins stopped by to check on progress and even help a bit as we went along. With a coat of sealer, the completed masts really looked pretty good.

Cutting off the excess length of the foremast was a little scary. There was no going back. Suppose I had not measured correctly? Suppose it turned out too short?

We needed a tiller. Turning to the wood pile, we didn't find much left. I dragged out a half of an oak deck beam left over from the work which we had been doing that winter and spring. It now seemed years ago. However, the rough oak piece seemed to be about the right curve. Although heavy and clumsy, maybe it could be planed to shape. It took a lot of planing, but it looked mighty good with a coat of varnish, bolted to our bronze rudder-head fitting from Graves. Simple and sturdy, it would do the job.

Hatches we had to have to keep out the rain, the spray, and the sea. The fore hatch, a simple square affair, was not hard. Following Chapelle, I made a simple hatch frame with a rabbeted edge to keep out the water. The hatch cover was a simple box made out of scrap mahogany from our rapidly dwindling pile. Remaining bits and pieces from our planking, no matter how small, were kept and "recycled" into bits of trim, hatch frame or whatever was needed as we pressed ahead. As with all of our work, it was not fine cabinetwork, and the craftsmen at Graves would likely have cringed at our workmanship. But it was the best we could do, and to us it looked great. We stained the Philippine mahogany to a uniform red-brown color before varnishing it.

Here Anita sands the rectangular fore hatch, made of Philippine mahogany scraps from planking. The finish sander was borrowed.

The companionway hatch was more difficult. I cursed the error that I had made in misaligning the aft cabin walls on either side of the companionway. Our companionway opening was thus not quite rectangular, but had an odd angle at the after end. Fortunately, the difference was less than half an inch. It caused the hatch to be not quite square, and to run not quite true, and to close not quite straight. But it was an imperfection with which we would have to live.

This picture shows the stage of completion by late July. The hull is surrounded by lush green summer vegetation.

In building the hatch itself, I became a little daring. Planing the mahogany bits and pieces to half-inch thickness, I made the frame curved so that the hatch would be crowned like the cabin top itself. The mahogany boards were edge-joined by liquid Marine-Tex glue, specially formulated by Mr. Travers for gluing wood rather than laminating fiberglass. The belt sander did a job in smoothing off the planks and bringing out the beautiful grain of the mahogany itself. I again used stain in an effort to deepen and enrich the color. With the final coats of varnish, our hatches looked pretty darn good.

The end of July came. In a few days, I would have my Maine bar exams. We were counting our remaining time in days. The tools were hot in my hands. Our list of things to do was still long. Our hull was still raw, unpainted. We still lacked rigging, fittings and finish. There was sanding and smoothing, that was yet to be done. However, the days and hours were few.

Chapter 12

Time was precious now. Every day counted. I remember that I took the Maine Bar Exam on a Monday and Tuesday at the very end of July or beginning of August. In those days, the number of applicants to the Maine bar were few, 40 in 1967. The bar examiners corrected the papers as soon as they were written and usually notified the applicants within hours of completion of the exam. When I got my call on Tuesday night, I was already back in Wilbraham, and in my work clothes. Yes, I had passed. I sighed with relief, and once more turned to the job at hand. The results of the Massachusetts examination would not be available until

Anita paints a band of red lead primer along the lower side of the waterline. In the background to the left is the trusty fruit ladder with a cross spall clamped on at the precise altitude of the waterline according to the loft plans.

October. All of this was more or less incidental to the task at hand – finishing *Serendipity*.

By now things were happening thick and fast. It was finally time to start painting the beautiful hull which had somehow come into being in our parents' back garden. We gave it all a final sanding with our puny equipment. The old Craftsman disc sander was on its last legs. Looking back, it is amazing to me that we had the temerity to tackle a job like building *Serendipity* with the inadequate tools that we had. But somehow we got it done.

Serendipity has a galvanized chain bobstay and chain whisker stays on either side to support the forestay loads on the bowsprit.

Before we started to paint, we had to determine and strike *Serendipity's* waterline. We went back to the loft plans to get the measurements from the "baseline" represented by a

271

wire stretched fore and aft between two stakes below *Serendipity's* keel. We then measured up to the altitude of the waterline and clamped a two-by-four to our increasingly trusty apple-picking-ladder set up under the bow. We did something similar under the stern, so that we had two-by-fours athwartships at the waterline elevation at both bow and stern. With these reference points, it was relatively simple to stretch a wire between the two-by fours and mark the location where the wire touched *Serendipity's* side. By adjusting the position of the wire on the two by fours, we were able to get a succession

The white undercoated on the topsides gave *Serendipity* a real finished look. Our single cabin window on each side is installed and the mahogany cabin sides are stained for varnish.

of points on each side that we could join with a batten to get a smooth base waterline. We penciled in the waterline, foregoing graving it into the planks for the time being so that we could adjust it if necessary based on the actual event. Then we painted a narrow band of red led primer along the lower side of the waterline so that we would be able to see it clearly as we went ahead with the next steps.

At this point, we also fitted the chain bobstay between the 3" home-made eye-band at the end of the bowsprit and a crude Eddy Dearborn welded and galvanized eye-fitting bolted to the stem beneath. Now *Serendipity* was really beginning to look like a ship!

How exciting it was to apply the first paint to our beautiful hull that had been unpainted wood for so long! We had thought long and hard about the color. The traditional colors for the old coasting schooners after which our design had been modeled were black hull, white cabin and trim and grey deck. Those were the colors of Mr. Randolph's *Elise*. But they were too dark and drab for our dream ship. We ultimately decided on a dark green hull and, after much hesitation, a light green deck. We used conventional Petit marine paints – Pine Green for the hull and Green Mist for the deck. This was

Even my father turned to when we were painting the red lead primer on the bottom. Time was getting short and we appreciated any help we could get.

273

before the days of polyurethanes, epoxies, Awlgrip and the like.

We had to start with primer – red lead primer for the bottom and the iron keel and white under-coater above the waterline. Out came the gallons of white yacht under-coater which had arrived from Sargent & Lord months before. The painting went fast. In a single afternoon, the topsides were coated with white. What a sight!

Everyone helped put on the red lead primer. Everyone stood back, bespattered, and admired. The bottom of *Serendipity* gleamed orange in the late afternoon sun.

How good our boat looked as we carefully struck the waterline, white above, red below! Once the topsides had been painted with under coater, we had to strike the 2" white waterline stripe just above the actual waterline. This we did with a 2" block of wood with a pencil taped to the top. We held the block level with the bottom at the actual waterline, and scribed along, creating a second line that was 2 vertical inches above the first. The actual surface of the stripe was, of course,

The first brush of green on *Serendipity's* topsides. We are on the home stretch!

274

greater than 2" in places where the hull was slanted out, such as at the bow and under the transom. It has to be that way in order to give the visual impression of a stripe of uniform width the length of the boat.

With "boot-top" stripe struck, we could paint the dark green of the topsides. Wow! Suddenly *Serendipity* looked like a yacht! The glossy new paint gleamed in the summer sun in the back garden. After we had finished, we looked at the hull from many perspectives, and took many pictures. We alternated, bottom and topsides in those last few days. We paused for brief, but intense, admiration sessions and hurried forward. How that Pine Green top coat gleamed when we set the first brush of finish coat to *Serendipity's* topsides. While the topsides dried, we painted the deck, a light "Green Mist". It set off the rich varnished mahogany cabin sides beautifully.

The cabin sides were a special case. The design called for them to be painted white. But the more we looked at the lovely Philippine mahogany the less we liked the idea of covering it up with white paint. When we bolted the cabin sides to the deck and carlin below, we had located the edge-bolts so as to avoid the locations of the five ports per side shown on the plans. We now had to install our two precious bronze opening marine windows – all we could afford at this stage of the project. We elected to install the windows without external bronze "trim rings" around the outside of the windows. These trim rings can cover a multitude of sins in fitting the window in its opening. Without them we would have to be very accurate in cutting the holes, especially if we wanted to finish the cabin sides "bright" (with varnish only – no paint).

After carefully tracing the "spigots" of the windows centered on the respective sides of the cabin trunk, I went to work with drills and our trusty saber saw. We were a little conservative with the sawing, so there was a lot of rasp work to enlarge the openings just enough so that the windows would snugly fit. They were secured with bronze screws from the inside. We stained the Philippine mahogany in an effort to get a uniform shade for all our brightwork and then applied a couple of coats of varnish. It was really beginning to look good.

Here Anita is painting "Green Mist" on the cabin top. Visible are our crude grab-rails, the bent galvanized traveler for the fore-sheet, the stained and varnished fore hatch, and the slides for the main companionway hatch. The edges of the cabin roof are finished off with half-round stock.

By now we were rushing – we were down to a matter of days before our anticipated departure. There were many details to accomplish. We fit ¾" half-round molding around the edge of the cabin top to cover the joint between the plywood and mahogany cabin sides.

According to the plans, the many halyards, toping lifts and lazy jacks which serviced *Serendipity's* intricate spars and rigging were secured to galvanized belaying pins in wooden pin rails clamped in the fore and main shrouds at waist level. However, galvanized belaying pins, like galvanized ironwork, were not readily available in 1967. I had been lucky. At the Atlantic Marine Exchange, they had six or seven. I bought them all for something like $1 apiece. However, I needed 14. Scan as I might, the many catalogs which had piled up in my Cambridge apartment failed to yield a clue as to where I would find these essential components of our rig.

The Alan Clark Company, New York, New York, was one of the sailmakers who had bid unsuccessfully on *Serendipity's* sails. With their bid, they had included some kind of a flyer advertising their sail-making and rigging supplies. Almost by chance, I called them in New York. Did they have belaying pins? Yes, they did? Galvanized belaying pins? Well, they thought so . . . The Alan Clark pins cost $1.65 each. By that point, I was really glad to get them. I think they were the last galvanized belaying pins to be available on the East Coast for the next 20 years.

The pintails will be secured to the shrouds on both sides of each mast. The galvanized belaying pins act as cleats for the many halyards needed to raise the various sails. Here they get a quick coat of varnish as we hurry to complete many final tasks.

By this point, we were working as fast as we could. We didn't have the time to finish things as nicely as we wanted to. For instance, the oak grab rail along the top of the long trunk cabin was an important safety feature. Crew members going forward or aft on *Serendipity's* exposed deck would have something to hold on to in case of a sudden lurch or slip. We didn't have the time to make the gleaming kind of finished handrail that one sees on modern fiberglass yachts or even on older wooden ones. I made a crude cutout pattern, scalloped a piece of 1 x 2" oak with the saber saw, and we bolted it down with 1/4" galvanized bolts backed up by little oak squares on the inside of the plywood cabin top. Even two or three coats of varnish could not conceal the crude and unfinished appearance of our grab rail.

The pin-rails were also crude. The four of them, for the 14 belaying pins, couldn't have taken more than two hours. Sanding was skimped. Corners were left square and sharp. Fits were far from perfect. Varnish was slapped on. But they would have to do the job, for we didn't have time for better.

The travelers we made and bent ourselves. They were unexpectedly easy - 1/2" galvanized rod bent in the vice. The ends were threaded by a hand-turned die and plenty of cutting oil. A nut on the outside and a nut underneath, taken up snug, left them rugged and strong. They looked neat, too, belying our haste in making them.

Throughout the project, we had visitors at the building site. By the summer of 1967, the visitors had become a steady stream – on most days we had at least one, and sometimes more than one friend stop by to see how things were coming along, and occasionally to help. Some visitors came to see, and

One of the ways my mother (facing camera) helped us a lot was by acting as tour guide for the many visitors who came to see *Serendipity* as she neared completion. That left us free to continue to work.

ended up being pressed into service. "Can you hold this?" or "How about coming with me to get that?" Mr. Boland had been coming Sundays for some time. Now, as the project was nearing completion, he came more frequently. We were glad to see him and appreciated his interest. However, he did like to talk, and we did not have much time for that.

During my brief visit in Maine to take the bar examination, I had stopped at the U. S. Customs Marine Documentation Office in Portland to register *Serendipity* as a vessel of the United States. Then, as now, pleasure vessels of at least 5 net tons could be either registered under state law, in which case they would have to display 3" numbers on their bows, or registered under the laws of the United States. A U. S. registered vessel was not required to display any numbers externally, but the registration number had to be carved indelibly into the "main beam" inside the hull. Since we were

279

moving to Portland for at least the next year, it made sense to register *Serendipity* there.

I first had to measure the hull – length, times breadth, times the depth inside the hull to the sheer, times a formula – to develop *Serendipity's* "net tonnage". Only vessels of 5 net tons or more were entitled to be registered. Fortunately the measurements and formula worked out to a little more than 6 net tons, so we were eligible.

The Marine Documentation Office was located in the historic U.S. Customs House on the Portland waterfront. By the 1960's, that formerly bustling government agency had become quiet and sleepy as waterborne commerce diminished and died in the Port of Portland. The customs official took me through the various papers needed to register the boat. I signed oaths as builder, owner and captain of the new vessel. All was typed up laboriously on a large form preprinted on heavy document paper. *Serendipity* was duly registered as a yacht of the United States with home port of Portland, Maine – registration number 510,105.

We were required to display the name of the vessel and its home port on *Serendipity's* stern in 3-inch letters contrasting with the background color. Probably we could have found a sign-painter to come and paint the name and home port on the transom. For some reason, that seemed impractical at the time. However, our friends at Rostand sold polished brass letters and numbers that gleamed when we unwrapped them from their protective tissue wrappings.

After some puzzling, I decided to grave the official number in the forward deck beam of the bridge deck right inside the companionway hatch. My work, in some haste, with mallet and chisel, was far from artistic. But it would have to suffice. There was no time left to be artistic in such things.

Serendipity's legally-required navigation lights included a pair of red and green (port and starboard) side-lights that we decided to locate on the sides of the cabin. We carefully bored

One of the myriad of tasks we had to complete before our dream ship could be launched was installation of the cockpit locker doors with their brass hinges, vents and latches.

holes for a pair of teardrop-shaped bronze "Wingtip" navigation lights about half-way up the sides of the cabin about amidships on each side and bolted our new lights in place. As we surveyed the finished installation – another mistake! From their positions half-way up the cabin sides, the lights would be obscured from visibility ahead by the rising sheer of the bow.

Ugh! We did not have time for mistakes at this point. If we moved the lights, it would be very hard to conceal the holes we had bored in our new cabin sides. But we had no choice. We could not go to sea without properly functioning navigation lights. Sadly, reluctantly, I unbolted the new lights and filled the holes with hand-made plugs of Philippine mahogany chosen to match the surrounding wood. It looked crude. I re-bored new holes near the top of each cabin side – high enough so that the lights would be visible from ahead above the sheer of the bow. The lights were reinstalled and wired to a simple fuse panel on the inside of the cockpit wall near the engine. They worked.

We also needed a stern light (white) for operating under sail, and in addition a mast-head light when running under power. The former, I located on a small block on the deck aft at the middle of the transom rail, running the wire under the deck to the fuse panel.

The mast light (required for running under power) was another matter. It was designed to shine forward in an arc of 110 degrees on each side of the bow. Therefore, the top or forward side of the foremast was the appropriate place for this light.

Securing the stern cleats turned out to be particularly challenging. Anita is inside the lazarette holding the nut while I screw in the bolt from above. Claustrophobic?

The mast light wire is usually led down through the center of a hollow mast. However, our masts were not hollow, and I was not in a position skills-wise, tools-wise, or time-wise to rout a channel in our new solid foremast for the wire. We would have to make do, as many vessels made do, with an external wire running down along the top of the mast and then taped to one of the shrouds down to a fitting in the deck. I bored a hole in the top of the foremast for the socket of the wing-tip masthead light fitting and then a smaller hole out the side for the wire. The fitting was screwed to the masthead and bedded in Caulk- Tex. The wire led out the hole, along the mast to the "hounds" where the stays looped around the mast, and from there down one of the port stays to a brass connector in the deck. The connector was, in turn, wired to the fuse panel inside. We tested the light at the top of the mast with a battery, but had no way to test the connection aboard the boat. Presumably it worked….

As these words are being written, now almost 50 years after the event, it strikes me how often the passive voice is employed to describe what we were doing in those frantic weeks and months. It is almost as if these things were being done by themselves. But, of course, that is not true. Nothing like this happens by itself. Although we did experience moments of "serendipity" during the construction of our dream ship, all of the myriad tasks required in the construction of a 7-ton auxiliary schooner got done because we incessantly planned, schemed, organized, ordered, cut, bored, screwed, pasted, painted, chiseled, sanded, sanded some more, sweating, grimacing, cursing, with puny and inadequate tools, but with the energy of youth and the strength of purpose to get the job done.

One question that had been on my mind for a long time was how we were going to move *Serendipity* from the field behind my parents' home in Wilbraham to Graves Yacht Yard in Marblehead by the sea. Although boats were moved overland in the 1960s, the Brownell trailer had not yet been invented. Overland moves involved the use of custom made cradles and "low-bed" trailers of the kind used to move bulldozers, cranes and other heavy equipment. Wilbraham was far from the sea, and persons with the equipment and experience to move a 7-ton schooner some 36' long, including bowsprit, were not easy to find.

We did have a cradle – of sorts. Starting with the 4 x 4 and 4 x 6 oak cross ties onto which we had levered the cast iron keel back in the spring of 1965, we had progressively added lengthwise hemlock skids below and above the beds on each side and bolted them all together. As the hull developed, we made three props from the cross ties up to pads on the hull surface on each side. The whole thing was a bit Rube-Goldberg but it would have to do.

We resorted to the Yellow Pages to try to find a trucker in the Springfield, Massachusetts, area who could move *Serendipity* to the sea. But all of the riggers and heavy equipment haulers we called turned us down. Many were already committed at the time we wanted to move the boat. Others were not familiar with boats and did not want to get involved. We asked them if they knew of anyone else who might be able to do it and interested in taking it on.

We finally hit a kind of pay dirt in a rigger and house-mover from West Springfield. Roger Sherman Rigging was willing to consider our job. They sent Charley Beshaw, one of their senior riggers, to check out our project and give us a quote. Charley looked over the boat and cradle pretty carefully and measured the height from the bottom of the cradle to the highest point on the cabin. This was so that he could check clearances under highway bridges and other overhead obstacles, including the pear tree on my parents' lawn between the back garden and the street. Yes, he thought that he could do it. How would he get the boat and cradle up onto his flatbed trailer? We should leave that to him, he said. He had the necessary equipment and could do the job.

When did we want to go? Could he come on August 28? That would be a Monday. I was due to go to work in Maine the following Tuesday, the day after Labor Day. If he could move us to Marblehead on Monday, the 28th, we could be launched on Tuesday, the 29th, and leave for Maine on Wednesday, the 30th. That would give us two or three days to make the trip. It might just work. But there was no room for error . . .

Then he gave us the quote for coming to the site, getting the boat onto his trailer, and delivering it to Graves in Marblehead. We would have to pay, of course, for his crew to come and load the boat on the truck. We confirmed by a telephone call to Graves that they would be able to unload the boat from the trailer with their crane. The cradle would return with the truck to Wilbraham, there to await its future fate.

The first quote was a few hundred dollars. I blanched. We did not have money like that in the budget. Charley explained that the cost was increased by the requirement that he be accompanied by another person riding "shotgun" in his tractor and that the trailer be followed by a car with a sign warning of an oversized load while on the Massachusetts Turnpike en route to Marblehead. Could we save money by performing these functions ourselves? Charley thought so, and the quote was materially reduced. I would ride shotgun in the tractor with Charlie and Anita would drive our car behind with the necessary sign tied on the trunk.

Charlie Beshaw said that he could come on the appointed day. There was hope, but no certainty. For I had been around this kind of business long enough to know that sometimes people, even with the best of intentions, do not fulfill even the most serious of telephone commitments. We could only hope and call him up a day or two in advance and remind him. We were coming down to the wire.

285

There was a continuous stream of visitors and on-lookers. Fortunately, Mother intercepted them as they came and gave them the tour. Some people actually thought that we were about to sail off around the world. "Where are you going first?" This notion may have been fostered by a local news story which had appeared the preceding year. The reporter had assumed that our eventual fantasy of perhaps sailing "someday" around the world was imminent. The tone, however, of the onlookers had changed. By now, the naysayers were clearly muted. It was no longer a question of "if", but "when". And that "when" was not far away.

In odd moments, we swaged Nicopress sleeves on the quarter-inch stainless steel rigging cable purchased months before from Al Pendleton. The take-up on the turn buckles did allow us a good deal of room for error. Nonetheless, it was a little nerve-wracking to try to estimate the lengths of the stays with nothing more than a rigging plan at the scale of 1/2 inch to the foot.

Jim and Mary Ann Baxter and Arthur Thomas came from New York to help out for a weekend as we frantically tried to finish up. We sanded the old dirty sealer off the spars and replaced it with new fresh varnish. We wished that we had varnished them in the first place.

Of course, we had the bare minimum of tools. For $15, I had bought a nut and bolt swaging clamp from S & F Tool

Company in Costa Mesa, California. It was all we could afford. I must have taken up on those two bolts, first one and then the other, at least a thousand times as the tool gradually squeezed the copper sleeves around the slippery steel wire to form the loops, large and small, by which standing our rigging would be attached to the masts and turnbuckles respectively.

We turned to the booms and gaffs. I had fashioned jaws for them during the winter, but we had left them covered with nothing but a coat of sealer. This sealer had a soft finish, and in the ensuing months dust had settled on the spars and stuck to the finish. They were a mess. Before we could varnish them, we had to sand each spar down to bare wood and start all over again building up a finish with a new coat of sealer and then three coats of spar varnish. One summer weekend, Arthur Thomas and our friends Jim and Mary Ann Baxter came out and sanded for most of the time they were there. It was a real pain in the neck that we could have avoided by varnishing the spars at the time we received them or by at least covering them up for storage.

Arthur took the dying Craftsman rotary and also sanded the primer on the bottom preparatory to application of the bottom paint, which we had held to the end to preserve its anti-fouling potency.

Practically on the eve of departure, we addressed a problem that had been simmering in the back of my consciousness ever since we had cast the iron keel back in the spring of 1965. When we had picked up the keel from the Reid Foundry in Amesbury, it weighed only 4,200 pounds instead of the 4,800 pounds prescribed by the design plans. The difference turned out to be due to a mistake I had made in interpreting the dimensions of the forward end of the iron keel. My pattern was too narrow at the forward end. There had been an ambiguity in the plans, and I had resolved it – the wrong way. At the time we figured this out, we had decided to live with the keel we had rather than rebuild the pattern and have a new keel cast.

Now, as we were approaching the launching of our dream ship, we were confronted with the image of it floating decidedly bow-high due to a lack of ballast in that end of the iron keel. The solution that we had discussed with Mr. Crockett at the time, and were now confronted with implementing, was addition of "inside ballast" forward – some form of concentrated weight inside the hull that would take the place of the weight missing from the forward end of the ballast keel.

The most concentrated form of weight that we could consider was lead – used to ballast sailing craft for hundreds, if not thousands of years. The problem with lead, though, was that it was expensive. Lead ingots cost about 20 cents a pound at that time. We would need some 600 pounds, which would be about $120, a large sum at that stage of the project. We could, to be sure, get scrap lead for free from several sources. George Merwin, our plumber, had a quantity of old lead pipes that he had removed from houses he re-plumbed over the years. Somewhere we got hold of some lead wheel weights from balancing of tires. But how would we form these into something that could rest compactly and comfortably in the limited space below the floor forward? George Merwin came to the rescue again.

In the "old days" (back before the 1970's), domestic sewer pipe was made of rough cast iron. The various pipe pieces had male ends and female "hubs" into which the male ends loosely fit. The joints were sealed by jamming oakum into the hub around the male pipe end, and then pouring molten lead on top of the okum to complete the seal. Every plumber had the capacity to melt lead for this purpose. Usually it was a portable gas-fired device that heated a cast iron kettle shaped like a large ladle up to a temperature that would melt lead

Melting scrap lead for additional forward ballast. New lead ingots were expensive. We scrounged scrap lead where we could and used bread pans to form crude ingots from the molten metal.

inside the kettle. The plumber could then pour the molten lead from the kettle into the joint.

George Merwin had such a device, and he was glad to lend it to us and show me how to use it. Of course, it was somewhat dangerous. There was always a risk that a few drops of water falling into the molten lead could cause it to spatter onto one's clothing, hands, even face. We were not well equipped with safety clothing or eye protection. We just had to be careful. . . .

The next question was how we would form the bits and pieces of scrap lead that we had into useful ingots to fit into the bilge. After some head-scratching, we settled on bread-pans. We had a handful of old bread-pans at home, and bought a couple of cheap new ones at the hardware store. They should produce large ingots of 30-50 pounds that we could somehow fit in place under the forward floorboards in order to provide the necessary "trimming ballast."

289

We went to work, melting our lead scraps and pouring the molten metal into the bread pans to make ingots. But we were still far short of the 600 pounds of ballast that we needed to bring *Serendipity's* bow down to her design trim. At this point, my father reiterated a suggestion he had made before. How about old metal type? In those days, much of the printing was done with metal type plates that were cast into the configuration of the text to be printed, and were discarded after use. This type was made largely from lead, with traces of antimony and tin, cast onto a steel backing plate. When first suggested, we dismissed the idea of trying to melt up type-metal as impure and too difficult to recover.

But at this point we were desperate. We were several hundred pounds shy of what we needed. Maybe we should try the type-metal after all. . . . A friend of my father's, Henry White, operated a small print shop in southern Connecticut. Maybe Uncle Hank could get some used type metal which we could melt up and use for ballast.

Father was as good as his word. Yes, Hank could get some used type metal. How much did we want? "As much as you can bring." One day that summer, Uncle Hank showed up in Wilbraham with a car trunk full of sheets of cast type. It was of no value to him. We could have it *gratis*.

Gratefully, we tried to figure out how we would convert these sheets of metal-backed type into useful pigs of ballast for our bilge. The sheets were large, 11" x 17" or so. The type metal itself had been poured on a thin sheet of steel. They stacked like large sheets of cardboard or paper about 1/4" thick. We found, however, that they could be cut into small chunks with the saber saw. Tasks like these we could do at night, when it was too dark to work outside, in order to conserve every possible productive moment.

We also found that we could melt the leaden type off the steel backers, which we fished out of the kettle with tongs. The type-metal was practically as heavy as the pure lead, would not rust, and was available. Into the bread-pans it went. Between scrap lead and type metal we ended up with a little more than 500 pounds of various-sized ingots.

It took two days to melt the type metal and cast the pigs. We did it in batches, working on other tasks during the time it took for the pot full of type metal to melt. As the type metal melted, we fished the steel backing plates out with pliers and added more solid chunks until the pot was full of silvery looking molten metal.

It was not until after we had poured several ingots that we discovered a property of the bread-pans that turned out to be important. When we went to turn the cooled ingots out of their bread-pan moulds, we found that the old solid steel pans worked pretty well and released the ingots without too much problem. But the new tinned steel pans that we had bought from the hardware store were another matter entirely. The lead had apparently bonded with the tin coating on the pans so tenaciously that there was no way we could separate the ingots from the pans they were molded in. We tried everything, heat, prying, Liquid Wrench, whatever. Ultimately we had no more time to fool around with this. We would have to leave the pans on the ingots when we put them in the bilge. We were aware that the pans would rust, but there was nothing else to do. Maybe in time, they would rust off the ingots.... As it turned out, after several years the pans did rust away, but not before they had caused a big mess in the process.

At this point, we had little time for regrets over our mistakes. We were pressing ahead with the last details to get *Serendipity* ready to be taken away. We installed cleats on the deck, hardware on the cockpit lockers and companionway slide, and other fittings.

If we were going to take *Serendipity* to sea and to Portland, we would need some kind of dinghy. This would be our life-boat as well as our means of getting ashore at the ports we would visit en route. We could not afford a Dyer Dhow or

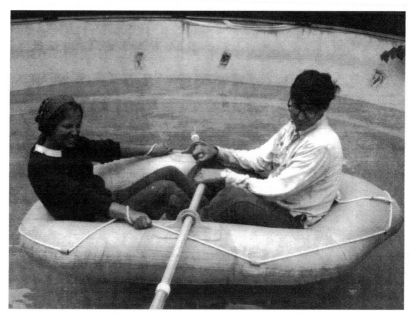

Our $32 dinghy was barely big enough for the two of us. We tested it in Art Taylor's above-ground pool and hoped that it would suffice to carry us between *Serendipity* and the shore.

other hard dinghy. Inflatables were in their infancy. We looked around, and settled on a blowup dinghy about 6 feet in length. We tried it out in our neighbor's pool. It would just fit the two of us. It cost $32. It seemed like a cost-effective way out.

At last, we were less than 48 hours away from launching. *Serendipity* stood there, gleaming green and red, truly a ship ready to sail. On sawhorses, nearby, lay the mighty spars, our ironwork attached, glistening with varnish. I hastily reinforced the oak skids and cradle which had supported *Serendipity* while she was being built. For it had to be strong enough to hold seven tons of ship for the transport to the ocean 100 miles away.

Of course, we were excited. The visitors marveled. Each step we took was visible, finishing and impressive. Every moment was occupied. At the same time, as the day approached, we became aware that we were coming to an end of an era. For the last 2-1/2 years, we had worked here in the

292

Here we are the day before departure. The new brass letters gleam on *Serendipity's* transom.

garden in Wilbraham. We had lived here and been sustained by the love, interest and support of my family and of the friends who had helped us in Wilbraham. But now the whole thing was coming to an end. We were going to leave our home.

To be sure, the fantasy was ever nearer. Soon we would be sailing the sea, shouldering the swell and sniffing the salt spray. But the garden behind the house at 477 Main Street would be empty. There would be nothing out there to admire. The tours would end. *Serendipity* would be gone.

My parents were game enough. Certainly the twinges which Anita and I felt could scarcely have matched the pangs of separation which my father and mother must have experienced in those final days. Dear and loving people that they were, they put aside their own feelings and joined with us in our celebration.

And so it came to be that *Serendipity* finally received her name. By that I mean, of course, that the gleaming brass letters, purchased long ago from Rostand, were finally affixed to her transom. We laid out the polished letters as best we could, in a gentle arc across the curved transom. It didn't take long to screw them on. We stood back. We looked up.

SERENDIPITY
PORTLAND, ME

It was almost a reverent moment.

It was late afternoon, the day before we were scheduled to leave. We had taken down the temporary A-frames, removed the staging and pushed aside the scrap pile. We had dismantled the planing bench, so that the movers could approach the cradle unencumbered. How wonderful she looked! I knew where every mistake was as well as every ineptitude and every flaw. But my eyes then saw them not. The exhaustion, frustration, chagrin, impatience and annoyance, all floated away. There was only the fantasy, the anticipation, and perhaps that little bit of dread. Would she leak? Would she float upright? Would all the pieces fit together? Would we be able to sail away?

Chapter 13

As August 28 approached, things were at a fever pitch. Local curiosity generated a stream of visitors. In order to spare us the distraction, my mother took on the task of giving tours. The newspapers came. Were we going to sail this vessel around the world? Maybe someday. But first we had to sail her to Portland, Maine.

It is impossible to describe my level of stress and anxiety as the big day approached. Suppose it leaked? Suppose she floated with a list? Suppose the ballast we had installed was not sufficient and she floated bow-high? Suppose, suppose, suppose? What had we forgotten? What had we left out? Had I properly calculated the length of the shrouds and stays? What if they were too long? Too short?

Serendipity on her last morning in my parents' garden. The riggers have arrived and are getting ready to jack the cradle. Mr. Boland, who came to watch the whole thing, is in the foreground.

Would our sails from England fit our spars? Would, would, would? Would everything go together in Marblehead Harbor to become a real yacht – our dream ship?

The morning of Monday, August 28, 1967, dawned fair and clear in New England. We had been up late the night before packing our belongings into the "Red Baron", our venerable 1960 Mercedes sedan. The Red Rambler had met its fate in an automobile accident on the Maine turnpike in April. Although I walked away, the experience convinced me of the value of an armored vehicle in highway warfare. And in those days, high-depreciation Mercedes were cheap, especially after they had been more than 100,000 miles.

The car was crammed with our luggage, our books, our personal belongings, and our tools. For today we and *Serendipity* would leave Wilbraham, never again to return to live. There she was, gleaming in the sunlight of early day. The freshly painted green topsides and the robust red bottom, were accentuated by the delicate tracery of the white boot top. We certainly weren't expert painters, but the freshness and newness of it all made up for any irregularity in striking the waterline or cutting the margins along the cabins sides.

All of the equipment was ready. The smaller spars had already been carefully stowed away inside the cavernous, empty, unfinished cabin. The two great masts glowed richly and redly through several coats of "Bak-Spar" varnish.

The press had been there in advance. Two local papers had sent reporters and photographers in the days before the scheduled departure. So when we read the morning paper on August 28, we were greeted with pictures and articles.

The trailer truck was due at 9. We were ready long before. And so were the onlookers. Early that day groups of well-wishers and curiosity seekers had assembled to witness the loading of *Serendipity* onto the great truck that was to take our dream ship away. Mr. Boland, of course, was there, as were most of our near neighbors. Mr. Merrick came down

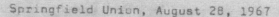

Wilbraham Vessel Ready for Launching

Mr. and Mrs. Peter Murray of 477 Main St., Wilbraham, Monday add finishing touches to their 30-foot, two-masted schooner Serendipity, before it is loaded on a trailer for Marblehead and then sailed to Portland, Me. It was built in 2½ years in their back yard and will sleep four. Murray, son of Mr. and Mrs. Samuel Murray of the same address, a graduate of Wilbraham Academy and Harvard Law School, will serve a year as clerk to a federal district judge in Portland.

This photo appeared in the Springfield morning paper on the day of our departure.

with a lawn chair and found a good vantage point in the shade. Neighbors, friends of my parents, people I didn't even know, dribbled in during the morning. Some were genuinely wishing us well on our way. Mr. Boland brought us an American flag which he presented tearfully. Others were merely curious to witness for themselves how this clumsy seven-ton vessel would be loaded aboard a truck and carried away. And maybe

297

there were even some who secretly hoped that something would go wrong . . .

Charlie Beshaw and his crew arrived promptly at 9. The truck was a great low flatbed, the kind which riggers use to haul diesel bulldozers, big items of construction equipment, massive machinery, and the like. On the forward end of the truck were a stack of 4" x 4" spruce or hemlock timbers. They almost looked like railroad ties, but were a lot lighter to handle. Three or four mechanical jacks, some load-binder chains, and half a dozen 4" round wood rollers about 8 feet long made up the kit. There was no crane, no sling, no automatic hydraulic cradle . . .

The riggers carefully jacked *Serendipity*, one side at a time, building a cribwork of four-by-four timbers under her cradle.

298

Charlie and his people went right to work. In order to reach the building site, Charlie had to back his long and awkward trailer along our driveway and then angle out over the back lawn beside the garage, wriggling right to avoid the apple tree and then out into the garden. He threaded the needle as deftly and surely as if he had done it every day of his life. Within a matter of minutes, the red truck and flat-bed trailer stood beside our ship.

Serendipity has been jacked to the level of the truck and is now supported by two cribworks. The last layer is a set of round rollers.

Loading *Serendipity* onto the trailer, although awesome to contemplate in advance, was scarcely more difficult. Hooking the old mechanical jacks under the edge of the cradle skid, Charlie jacked up first one side and then the other, four inches at a time, fore and aft, inserting the 4 x 4 timbers to build a crib work under our cradle. Gradually *Serendipity* was lifted higher and higher in the air. The two or three men who were with him worked as a smoothly coordinated team. I did the best that I could to hand people timbers, pump on the jacks when they let me, and to caution them - "be careful, slowly now . . ."

Rolling our 7-ton vessel from the cribwork over onto the trailer was a lot easier than I had imagined it would be. Two men gently pushed on the cradle and in a couple of minutes *Serendipity* was on the truck.

But they knew their business. It was barely an hour after the truck had arrived that *Serendipity's* cradle had been elevated by about three feet. The height of the cribwork now exactly matched the height of the bed of the truck.

What then happened caused not only my eyes, but those of the many onlookers, to bulge. Smoothly and efficiently the crew inserted a set of the rollers atop of the cribwork fore and aft. Then, as we watched, Charlie walked over to the cradle. He gently pushed it with one hand. The seven ton boat, cradle and all, rolled effortlessly to the right, over to the waiting bed of the truck. While the men swapped rollers, Charlie and I simply rolled *Serendipity* smoothly and quietly onto the truck that was to take her away.

The boat has been loaded, the cribwork dismantled, and Charlie Beshaw is ready to take *Serendipity* from the garden where she has grown from an iron keel and a pile of lumber into a dream ship.

The big red truck crept out of the garden, past the garage and into the yard. Too bad – it was too big to pass by the pear tree, and a branch fell casualty to the move. But otherwise everything went as smoothly as one could hope. The onlookers, fans and skeptics alike, were deeply impressed and moved their chairs to make way for the advancing truck and its load.

Although we had packed the spars, our gear, the rubber dinghy, and whatever we thought we would need to commission the boat and for the trip to Portland inside the hull, the masts would have to ride on the trailer alongside the cradle. We had already installed the shrouds, stays, halyards, topping

Here we are securing the masts, complete with standing rigging along the edge of the trailer. Charlie Beshaw, our resourceful rigger, is second from left.

lifts and lazy jacks.   It took some manpower to muscle the heavy masts onto the trailer and secure them to the cradle. The mainmast stuck out at the back. We put a red flag on it and hoped for the best.

By noon it was getting to be time to leave. We checked around the shop, the yard, and the house. Had we left anything behind? I patted my pocket for the official document, which would legitimize *Serendipity's* sailing on the sea. Did we have everything? We couldn't afford to leave anything in Wilbraham. We had to be self-sufficient, as we headed east by north.

And so we pull out onto Main Street, headed for Marblehead some 80 miles away. I am riding shotgun in the cab. Anita is driving the follow-up car.

The mass of onlookers, who had clustered in the yard between the garden and the street, parted so that the procession could begin. Slowly, ever so slowly, the great red truck crept out of the garden, bearing green *Serendipity* on its back. Although we successfully skirted the apple tree, the pear tree by the driveway was not so lucky. My parents rendered yet another sacrifice to the new age as a limb of our treasured pear tree caught in *Serendipity's* whisker chains and was snapped

303

off before we could prevent it. And then we were in the yard beside the house. A final round of pictures were taken. The last of the onlookers shook our hands. The naysayers melted away. There were tears. Heaven knows how my parents felt. Of course, they would be coming down to Marblehead early the next day for the launching. But *Serendipity* and their children, were leaving their home forever.

I rode up in the cab of the big truck. Anita followed in the Red Baron. And the little caravan set out for Marblehead 100 miles away. Fortunately, the truck was low enough, and

We are on the Massachusetts Turnpike, headed east. Anita is driving the "Red Baron," our elderly Mercedes sedan that replaced the Red Rambler which was totaled in an accident in April.

Serendipity, at 9-1/2 feet of beam, was narrow enough so that we did not have to take any extraordinary precautions. Charlie had checked the route in advance on special maps which showed the height of bridges, obstructions, etc. We would take the Massachusetts Turnpike (bridge clearance 13.5') to Route 128 around to Salem, and then on back roads to Marblehead. There was one limitation. We had to be off Route 128 by 4 p.m. The belt parkway during Boston rush hour was no place for an oversized load in those days.

We drove down the main street of Wilbraham.   I alternated between returning the waves of those who recognized us going by and peering anxiously through the small rear cab window. I had to make sure that the cradle was not shifting, that the masts were still lashed on tight, that nothing was going wrong . . .

Of course, I couldn't see anything except the cradle and the bottom of the bow from the cab. It was Anita, riding along behind, who noticed the fore hatch cover sliding off as we turned the corner to the toll booth at the turnpike. Rapid honks and flashing of lights brought us to a stop. I awkwardly climbed aboard and secured the hatch cover below. At that time, we had no latch to hold the hatch cover in place. Apparently a bounce on the highway had jounced it loose from the wood hatch frame on which it fitted.

The trip to Marblehead went smoothly. At least there were no untoward mishaps. But the routine nature of the move for Charlie Beshaw and his calm professionalism in handling *Serendipity* could not dispel the tremendous building anticipation and anxiety which had suffused my every fiber as the crucial day approached. I could feel the tension of my muscles, the constriction of my veins as my glands pumped adrenalin into my system. I was super-alert, sharp as a tack, on the balls of my feet. My eyes were wide, staring. I was ready to jump like a cat. The great challenge for which we had planned and schemed, built and labored, over the past 2-1/2 years, was approaching. As we sped down the highway, my mind was a riot as I imagined all of the things that could possibly go wrong.

Two and a half hours later, we were nosing our way into the Graves Yacht Yard in Marblehead. It was near the end of their day, but they agreed to unload the boat so that Charley could go home. In those days, Graves Yacht Yard at "Little Harbor" used an immense crane to haul and launch the boats, which were moved about the yard on greased skids over a

Straps are being rigged for the yard crane to lift *Serendipity* and her cradle from Charlie Beshaw's truck.

grid work of timbers set in a bed of stones. In order to reach the crane, we would have to back the truck through one of their large sheds.

As Charlie carefully backed the trailer through the shed into the launching area of the yard, the diesel engine on the crane was started. It rolled on a pair of tracks about eight feet apart. Soon it was in position, the immense boom positioned over the trailer. A giant frame with two slings hung at the end of the cable. It didn't take long to connect the slings under *Serendipity's* cradle. The diesel slowed under the load.

On the side of the cab of the crane was a huge dial scale. The needle climbed higher and higher, hitting nearly 14,000 pounds before *Serendipity* came off the truck. Charlie pulled the truck out from under, nearly wiping out the spreader

306

on the mainmast as he did so. But the new oak bent and did not break.

Back in the 1960s, boats were kept in cradles. Brownell stands, like Brownell trailers, were yet to be invented. So with *Serendipity* came her cradle. Graves agreed to keep the cradle for a time after the launching and then have it shipped to whatever boatyard we chose in Maine.

Relieved of his load, Charley and his truck left us to return back home. He had done a remarkable job in getting *Serendipity* from the field behind my parents' home here to Graves Yacht Yard in Marblehead on the edge of the sea – and all without a scratch. We were very grateful to him, his crew and his company.

So there we were at the end of the workday on August 28. Graves' people, already late for supper, left *Serendipity* on the cradle and went home. There would be enough time tomorrow to launch the boat and step the masts . . .

We checked everything once again. Then we drove off in the overloaded Mercedes to find shelter for the night. Passing up the flossy motels of the area, we checked in at a small tourist home and asked for the cheapest room. We had no money at this stage to spare for luxuries. The room was small and hot. But the rate was only a few dollars a night. What did it matter? Sleep was really out of the question.

My insomnia stemmed not only from lack of air conditioning on that hot August night. It was something far more serious. I was sure I was having a heart attack. Late that afternoon, when we had arrived at Marblehead, I had become aware of a growing ever-sharpening pain across the top of my chest. By suppertime, it felt as if my thorax had been banded with hot iron. Is this what people feel when they get angina? Was I having a coronary at the age of 24? Had I somehow grievously strained the musculature of my chest in the course of heaving the heavy masts around? Were my ribs broken?

I didn't dare say a word.   The vision of being hospitalized for some mortal ailment which would delay or frustrate the launching of *Serendipity* was unendurable. I tried to take deep breaths. But the bands around my lungs were too tight.   I breathed shallowly, almost panting.   And so I lay awake that night, waiting for the hours to pass until dawn showed gray. The concerns for the coming day alternated with fears for my own physical health. For in those days we did not know much about stress.

The workers at Graves Yacht Yard arrived each day around 7:30 a.m.   On Tuesday, August 29, we were there to greet them. Although the launching would not take place until near noon, we had to make sure that "everything was ready," just in case. I was still in pain. I thought that somewhere my ribs, my innards, something, was going to break. But I said nothing.

Graves would use the big crane to launch our dream ship.   At the appointed hour, the crane would come, pick *Serendipity* from her cradle in giant slings, and then, on its tracks, advance to the edge of the sea. The boom would swing out over the water and gently lower our dainty schooner into her new element.

They explained to us that mast stepping would be easier if we could step the fore at least while *Serendipity* stood yet in her cradle.   We had to kill the time between 7 and noon anyway. In a sense, it was fortunate that we did. The crane lowered the foremast down into its hole in the deck.   The squared butt seated firmly in the step. We quickly discovered another *faux pas*.

Although the shrouds, scaled up from the sail plan, fit within the take-up of the turnbuckles, the vital headstay was too short. Stretch as we might, even with the turnbuckle fully extended, we lacked about four inches. What were we going to do? We did not have enough extra stainless cable to make a new headstay. The bands tightened in my chest.

Although I had measured and calculated to the best of my ability, until we stepped the foremast at Graves we did not know whether it would fit in its step, whether it would stand straight, and whether the shrouds and stays were the right length.

Fortunately, we had some time yet before the launching. The man at Graves scrounged around in one of the many enticing junk piles in the sheds of that venerable institution. It didn't take them long to come up with an old piece of 1/4" wire-rope halyard or sheet from some racer of by-gone years. I had fortunately brought along the big red nippers and a couple of extra Nico-press sleeves. It took about an hour to make up a 6" link of cable to extend our head stay. Graves' crane obligingly took me aloft in the boatswain's chair so I could install the link at the head of the stay. There it would interfere less with the raising and lowering of the jib.

We readied our new manila rigging. In those days, Dacron was in general use for sailboat rigging. But our budget and my sense of nostalgia had militated in favor of traditional manila. Almost a year before, we had bought great coils of 7/16" and 5/16" manila rope from Al Pendleton at ridiculously low prices. During the winter, I had carefully measured off the likely lengths of the various halyards, sheets, etc., as scaled from the rigging plan. Thimbles and shackles had been spliced in at the appropriate places. The ends had been whipped. Now, as we waited for the tide to flood and our family to arrive, we rove our rigging through the blocks.

We were poorly equipped in the block department. Although wood blocks would have certainly dressed up our dream ship, in those days the only purveyor of wood blocks suitable for small yacht use was Merriman, then in Hingham, Massachusetts. Even then, Merriman's prices were high, several dollars a block. The Wilcox-Crittendon galvanized pulleys that we ultimately used cost less than $1 apiece. They were plain. They had no bearings. Often in order to get the block to "lie" correctly, it was necessary to string two or three shackles together. But they did the job. And the creak of our shiny new line as we rove the tackles, peak and throat, was the sound of music to our ears.

August 29, like August 28, was a beautiful day. Indeed, there was high pressure in New England all that week. At about 10 or 10:30, my family arrived including my parents, brother, sister-in-law and dog. *Serendipity* gleamed in her cradle. The fore mast stood proudly in place, set up with the shrouds and the newly lengthened headstay. The main mast lay on horses, rigging rove, ready to be stepped.

We had anticipated high tide that day by about an hour. There was plenty of water. We really didn't have to wait until noon. The people at Graves could see that we were anxious. By a little before 11, the sling frame had been rigged on the

310

Slowly the great crane advanced to the edge of the pier and then extended its boom to hold *Serendipity* out over the water.

crane. Advancing from the stern, the frame was positioned over the boat. The slings were attached. The newly erect foremast just cleared the frame forward. The crane motor "chucked" as the cable took the strain.

By now the pain in my chest was excruciating. Mentally, I brushed it aside. My mind raced. The goblins which had plagued us intermittently throughout the project came rushing in phalanxes to the fore. Suppose that we had left out a "stop-water" somewhere in the deadwood, and we had a leak that we could not find or fix? Or maybe our ballast forward would not be enough to bring the boat down onto her

311

waterline. What if she listed to port or starboard because of some asymmetry in her hull?

I had always feared for the symmetry of our ship. Many times during the build I had anxiously squinted, from forward, from aft, trying to satisfy myself that the proportions of our hull were truly fair. How much inaccuracy on one side or the other would cause our ship to sit uneven in the water? I fretted about a small distortion in the curve of the keel. Had I perhaps deviated an eighth, a quarter, a half an inch from the centerline in setting the stem or the horn timber? Had the moulds really been identical on both sides? If *Serendipity* did list, what could I do to take the list out? Would we be doomed to a lopsided caricature of a sailboat? Would the fantasy become a nightmare?

I had anticipated that we would float bow high. Although we had not loaded the ballast on board, we had the lead pigs in the floor of the back seat of the Red Baron ready for use. (It is amazing how badly we overloaded that car.) Of course, the question remained how much bow high would she float. Would only about 500 pounds of lead bring *Serendipity* down to her lines? Or had there been other inaccuracies, other mistakes? Would the anticipated angle between our struck waterline and the surface of the sea be a permanent disfigurement of our dream? My chest was a tight as a drum. I could scarcely speak. But we were ready. I gave the crane operator the signal.

Up she went, dangling from the boom of the massive crane. Reverently, almost as in a procession, we accompanied the great crane as it rolled along its rails bearing *Serendipity* from the yard to the edge of the Atlantic Ocean. The crane rolled out onto the old granite pier and came to rest. Now was the great and glorious moment.

We had been given several bottles of launching champagne by well-wishers. Prudently, we took the cheapest

312

Hanging from the crane, *Serendipity* is duly christened. We hadn't the wit to wrap the champagne bottle in plastic, so we were showered with glass.

one for the actual christening. We were saving the others to celebrate with when we got to Maine.

Ah, we were naive in those days. Anita and I boldly approached the bow of our vessel, suspended above and beside us at the edge of the pier. The family stood back a few feet with cameras at the ready. We held hands. Anita raised the bottle high, and then swung it. She intoned the magic words. "I christen thee '*Serendipity*'!" Cameras clicked, glass flew and my brother got a nasty cut on his hand. We were lucky that no one got it in the eyes. For we hadn't taken the simple precaution of putting our champagne bottle in a plastic bag.

The people of Graves were grumpy. We told them that we would sweep up the glass. Paul wrapped his hand in a handkerchief. We kicked the bigger shards aside. We turned our attention to the boom of the crane which was swinging out over the harbor.

Anita snapped pictures from the pier as I rushed down to the float. Slowly, gradually, the cable reeled out. The long red blade of *Serendipity's* keel approached the gray-green waters of the Atlantic Ocean. In a moment, they kissed. Then

Serendipity's keel touches the water for the first time. My heart was in my mouth. Would she float level? Would she leak?

gradually, ever so gradually, our dream ship became enveloped by its element.

Anxiously I peered as the hull sank lower and lower into the water. Would it just keep sinking? Or, when it floated, would it tilt? Then, with still an inch or two of red showing, I saw the slings slacken. *Serendipity* was afloat! The bow was clearly high, by three or four inches at least. But I could not detect any unevenness port and starboard. There was no list!

But was she leaking? In a moment I was aboard, clamoring below to check the seams. My caulking, learned quayside in Portland the previous summer, was untried. This was the test. Here and there I could see seams "weeping". Little rivulets of water were running down some of our green Cuprinol planks. For this, I was prepared. The weeping would disappear as the mahogany planks swelled in their element. There were no major leaks. *Serendipity* was tight!

With the help of the big crane, stepping the heavy main mast was a piece of cake. The yard crew is guiding it into position over the mast hole in the cabin top. The booms and gaffs are underfoot.

The feeling that we had on that August day can never be adequately described in words. It can never be replicated. It was once in a lifetime. Pride, wonder, satisfaction, gratitude, all spiced by anxiety and uncertainty, flooded us in repeated inundations that morning. Everyone's hand was shaken repeatedly until it was raw. The workers at the yard were clapped on the back. They were quick and generous in their admiration. They were also quick and cooperative in their work. The sling frame was unhitched and once again the big crane advanced to do its work, bearing the main mast, gleaming with varnish and dangling a confusion of wire and

My father takes the helm of *Serendipity* alongside the float at Graves. Although he must have seriously wondered if we would ever reach this point, he never expressed any doubt, but supported and encouraged us every step of the way...

rope rigging. With the accuracy of a surgeon, the great crane held the mast high over our floating hull and deftly inserted it in the tiny hole in the cabin trunk. The crane lowered the mast into its slotted step, where it was suitably blocked so that the main mast would be upright and parallel with the foremast.

316

Shrouds were secured all around. *Serendipity* was truly a schooner!

By noontime, *Serendipity* was alongside the float. All hands busily secured turnbuckles, bolted on pin-rails, secured shackles and untangled falls. The rigging on a schooner is a little complicated. There are so many tackles and falls, lazy-jacks, topping lifts, peak and throat halyards to unscramble. And this, of course, was the first time for us. The new manila line was tight. It kinked. But nothing would stop us at this point.

The triatic stays connect the two masts and provide forward support for the mainmast. They were secured by 3/8" turnbuckles to a mast band at the top of the foremast. Here I am taking up on the turnbuckle to tighten the lower triatic.

Father and Mother patiently held things, handed wrenches and unkinked lines. Paul pitched in with everything. A light and wiry friend of Paul's, Jimmy Severin, had come along to watch the launching and proved to be a monkey aloft. He was glad to shinny up the masts, even to the main truck, to reeve lines, and change shackles.

317

It was my job, however, to secure the triatic stays connecting the masts. We used the fore peak halyard, a four-part tackle, shackled to a crude boatswains chair that I had knocked together in the last days before we left. Everyone tailed onto the halyard as I clung to the mast. Creak, creak went our new galvanized blocks. Gradually I was hauled upward until I could reach the galvanized pipe eye band at the head of the foremast. Always a little acrophobic, I felt as if I was at the royal truck of the Flying Cloud! The two wire rope triadic stays were passed to me on rope messengers. We had estimated the length of these by scaling from the Crockett plans. Fortunately there was enough take-up on the turnbuckles to compensate for inexactitude in our measurements. Swaying aloft, I secured the jaws of the turnbuckles to the holes in the mast eye and was grateful to be lowered slowly to the deck.

Serendipity at Graves' float in Marblehead harbor. The masts have been stepped, but booms, gaffs, and sails have yet to be rigged.

This was better than Christmas ever had been. By early afternoon, we had brought out the beautiful cotton Jeckells sails. Everyone marveled at the intricate handwork and the

318

smooth softness of the fabric. We laced them to booms and gaffs, around and around like a barber pole. We laced them also to the mast. Wintertime reading of Eric Hiscock's *Voyaging under Sail* had convinced me that lacing was better than hoops for securing the luffs of gaff sails. Mast hoops in those days were virtually unobtainable, anyway. I carefully followed Hiscock's directions, passing the lacing around the mast, and then back around on the same side so that it would not bind upon raising or lowering.

Paul and I bend on the sails. We marvel at the softness of the long staple Egyptian cotton fabric and the intricate hemp handwork around the various eyes and reef-points.

We didn't have any lunch that day. I think Mother brought some sandwiches which were consumed by those who were interested. The pain in my chest had not let up with the launching. I would stop at nothing until we were under sail.

319

The pigs of lead were duly carried from the car and stowed forward around the foremast, nestling against the stem, the frames, and the forward end of the keel. I was pleased to see that with all 500 pounds aboard our waterline was approximately level. There was about an inch of red showing all around.

And so it was at about 3 o'clock that afternoon of August 29, *Serendipity* was rigged and ready. The pin-rails were bolted to the shrouds, the halyards were secured to the pins. The turnbuckles were taken up so that the stays were tight but not taut. The sails lay loosely flaked upon the booms. The sheets lay coiled on the deck, neatly secured to the shiny new bronze cleats.

At this point, James Wetherald, sales manager for Westerbeke, appeared. He lived in Marblehead and had graciously agreed to stop by and check the installation of the Volvo diesel before we set forth to Maine. All hands trooped aboard for the maiden voyage. There was Anita and me, my parents, my brother and sister-in-law, and Mr. Wetherald. We had only six lifejackets. We borrowed the seventh from the yard. The tightness in my chest was almost unendurable.

Wetherald carefully inspected the installation of the Volvo auxiliary under *Serendipity's* bridge deck and pronounced it "good". We got underway under power. The diesel thumped. I threw the great brass shift lever for the first time. We had the linkage rigged backwards. One pulled the lever aft in order to go forward. We could feel the propeller wash bubbling under the counter. Imperceptibly, we began to move. The float was inching by us. We were underway.

We put up the sails, fore, main and jib. The new manila cordage was bright and stiff. There was practically no wind, but at least the sails went up. The special English lacing in lieu of mast hoops seemed to work. We were a sailing ship!

The main purpose of the trial with Mr. Wetherald was to test the engine. It ran, but even when we opened the throttle, it seemed as if we were just idling along and moving mighty slowly. Wetherald came to the rescue. We had not properly calibrated the throttle cable when we attached the small throttle device that we had received with the engine from Sweden. In a few minutes, he was able to rectify the problem, and thereafter *Serendipity* stepped out right smartly under power. We put-putted among the anchored yachts dotting Marblehead harbor, exulting – yes, we had made it. We were afloat. We were going to Maine!

Serendipity set to sail

The Serendipity in the Murray back yard.

Loading the boat on the trailer on its way to launching.

Peter Murray and his wife Anita after completion of their schooner.

August 28 saw the launching of a 30 foot schooner built in the backyard of Peter Murray, of 477 Main St., Wilbraham. The boat took two and one-half years to build, at an estimated cost of $8,000. The boat was constructed while Mr. Murray was attending Harvard Law School. He worked on it during vacations and week-ends. The boat "Serendipity" was launched (and christened) at Marblehead, Mass. Mr. Murray and his wife, Anita, plan to sail the Serendipity to Portland, Me., where Mr. Murray will spend the next year as clerk to a Maine judge.

The boat weighs about seven tons and is equipped with an auxiliary engine which will propell the boat at six knots. The Serendipity is equipped to sleep four. Eventually, Mr. Murray hopes to sail around the world.

Here we are as captured by a newspaper photographer the day before departure. The photo appeared in the Springfield morning paper on the day we left.

Our plan, our scheme and our dream had been to leave Marblehead for Maine early the following morning. It would take us two days to sail the approximately 85 miles to Portland, Maine. On the afternoon of August 29, 1967, we were on schedule to do just that. The weather forecast for the following day was favorable – a gentle southerly wind that would waft us northeastward.

Then it was time for Mr. Wetherald to leave and the others to go home. We secured *Serendipity* to the float and shook hands with Mr. Wetherald. The Graves people had already gone home. For them, it was just another day's work.

The yard was deserted as my parents pulled out at about 5. They were taking the Red Baron with them. My father and my brother would drive it to Maine. Hopefully, we would find the car at Handy Boat Service in Falmouth when we would be sailing in there two or three days hence. And Anita and I were left alone.

In a way, it was a tremendous letdown. It was not as if there was no challenge left before us. The following morning, at the break of dawn, we were setting forth to sail to Maine. I repeatedly checked *Serendipity.* Who knows, the water might find its way in by some circuitous path to doom our vessel during in the night. The tightness and the pain had not left my chest.

We went over our preparations once more. Actually, we were ill-prepared to make any ocean trip, or even a coastwise cruise. *Serendipity* had no accommodations whatsoever, not even a head. We had bought a contraption consisting of a small folding aluminum frame, with a plastic seat over a suspended plastic bag. A supply of sandwiches, cookies, and fruit was stored in a picnic cooler. We had a siphon tap for water from the tank.

Serendipity had no lifelines. There were no coamings around our cockpit. The latter were called for in the plans but were dispensed with during construction. They looked difficult to make. And in those closing weeks, we had no time for anything which was not strictly necessary. We rationalized the

322

omission of the coamings by luxuriating on the broad quarterdecks on either side of the cockpit. Of course, we had no radio. We had no safety equipment other than six new lifejackets.

Our "dinghy" was a $32 blow-up plastic boat which we had got at a discount store. The two of us could just fit inside its single ring. It was hard to row with is jointed plastic oars. But we were ready to leave. We were ready to sail our dream ship to Maine.

That evening, we stayed in Marblehead. We were left at the B & B for another night of not much sleep.

Chapter 14

On the morning of Wednesday, August 30, we were up early – very early. The day was dawning and the sun was orange and still low in the sky. In those years, we were frequently the beneficiaries of the maxim, "Fortune favors the foolhardy". The weather, for instance, in that last week of August, 1967, was the only good weather New England saw in a summer known for fog and rain. Nineteen hundred sixty seven was the summer in which a well-known Portland yachting couple had suffered a fatal tragedy when their 30-foot yawl struck "Bold Dick" in the eastern part of Casco Bay. My friend, Peter Plumb, was serving as sailing instructor at the Biddeford Pool Yacht Club. He had complained of the bad weather for his sailing program and had marveled at the ability of cruising yachtsmen to find their way into his small harbor out of the pall of the fog.

But for us, there was no fog. To be sure, I was not totally inexperienced with Maine weather. My time in Prout's Neck had taught me to respect the fog. I had also learned something about getting around in it. And *Serendipity* was equipped with a gleaming Danforth "Corsair" compass mounted below a deadlight in the cockpit sole. The compass was far from accurate, though. The deviation came from the nearby Volvo engine. We had no chance to have the compass corrected before we were to leave. We also had the charts that we would need to make the trip to Portland. Somewhere we probably had dividers and a parallel rule. But that was it.

We left the White Haven B & B on foot, and walked first to a nearby donut shop for breakfast, and thence to the yard. There, in the gray twilight of early morning, was *Serendipity* lying at the float, ready for her maiden voyage. Somehow the tightness and the pain in my chest had gone. I was calm and cool – ready for our first adventure on our dream ship. There was no wind. We started "Steadfast" (the name we had given the Volvo diesel) and putt-putted out into the harbor. We were on our way.

Our route lay along Boston's North Shore to Cape Ann, which we would shortcut through the Annisquam Canal. From Annisquam, we would have a straight shot up by Newburyport, Portsmouth, New Hampshire, the Isles of Shoals, then York, Kennebunk and Cape Porpoise, Maine. With some luck we should be able to make it to Cape Porpoise, or maybe even Biddeford Pool, just beyond. Biddeford Pool was an attractive goal because the Plumbs were staying there that summer and could put us up overnight in default of suitable accommodations on *Serendipity*. Peter and his then-fiancee Pam had been a great help when we steam-bent *Serendipity's* 72 frames over Easter weekend, 1966. Since then Peter and Pam had married and he had gone to law school in New York. During that summer of 1967, he had a summer job as sailing instructor at the Biddeford Pool Yacht Club across Saco Bay from my own former station at Prout's Neck.

When we left Marblehead that day, *Serendipity* looked pretty well finished from the outside, but the inside was just an empty bare hull with the engine bouncing away under the cockpit aft. We had adapted a former bunk-bed ladder as our temporary companionway steps. The temporary floorboards below were composed of cheap pine 1" x 4" boards nailed to scrap wood cleats to form three removable sections. There were no berths, lockers, galley or head. Our $32 inflatable dinghy was rolled up and stowed below. We had a 12-pound Danforth "High Tensile" anchor, a bit of chain, and 300 feet of half-inch nylon for our ground tackle. We had a Freon foghorn. We had no radio, radar, or any kind of electronic navigational instrument. GPS navigation had not yet been developed. Marine radar was a still a bulky and expensive luxury item in the world of sailing yachts. Only the largest and

We approach the draw-bridge in the Annisquam River. Will it raise for us? Yes, it is going up!

most expensive yachts had it fitted. *Serendipity* did not. We did have a few government charts (the only charts then available) covering the waters between Marblehead and Portland.

The waters between Marblehead and Portland, Maine were not altogether strange to me even in 1967. Back in 1964, I had helped L. Mortimer Pratt sail the 53' *Meddler VI* overnight from Portland to Manchester, Massachusetts in order to avoid a potential hurricane. Saco Bay and the area around Cape Elizabeth were known to me from my days at the Prout's Neck Yacht Club. With compass and chart, we headed out on a beautiful day for *Serendipity's* maiden voyage to her new home in Portland, Maine.

We proceeded cautiously, chart in hand. We made sure to identify properly every landmark, every island and every ledge. "Ka-thunk, ka-thunk", the little Volvo pushed us ahead. The waters rippled smoothly to either side of the bow. We left a wake in the still surface of Massachusetts Bay.

326

The wind was calm as we put-putted out of the mouth of Marblehead Harbor, past Manchester and along the coast in the direction of Gloucester and Cape Ann. Just short of Gloucester Harbor, we turned to port to enter the Annisquam Canal. Would the swing bridge at the south entrance of the canal open for us? It was the height of commuter traffic. We approached and sounded our Freon horn. We waited, drifting quietly in the basin before the bridge. Nothing happened. We hooted again.

After some frustrating hesitation, evidently the bridge tender decided that we were serious or that the road traffic was not too heavy. The bridge began to move. Soon, being very careful to stay to the middle of the channel, we were putt-putting under the bridge into the calm waters of the canal. It is

Raising the foresail to catch the building southerly. We were under sail!

hard to describe the complex of feelings that went through me as we putted through that bridge opening – a sense of power, accomplishment, purpose, pride. We were really doing it. We were voyaging in *Serendipity*.

It remained calm as we powered north, sails still furled, past Ipswich and then Newburyport – a few miles off-shore. We could see the sand beaches as a light-colored line in the distance. By early afternoon, we could spy the Isles of Shoals up ahead. By then the waters were beginning to be ruffled by a gentle breeze from the south. It was time to raise sail! We made a lazy half-circle, bringing our bow into the southerly wind. Up went the sails, first the main, then the fore, and last the jib in the time-honored order in which schooners make sail. The ropes were stiff, and our new canvas was wrinkled, but that didn't stop us from squaring away before the gentle breeze. For the first time *Serendipity* was truly under sail. The Volvo, noisy and rackety in the echoing cavern of the cabin, was stilled. We drank lemonade, ate fruit, and steered by compass toward the Isles of Shoals just off the New Hampshire coast. We were voyaging under sail!

As is often the case, the southerly gently built throughout the afternoon. By late afternoon, we had scooted past the Isles of Shoals and saw Boon Island looming ahead. We were sailing briskly. We marveled at how smoothly *Serendipity* parted the waters, at the graceful billowing of the sails, at the gentle leaning of the masts away from the quartering breeze. Now and then, we would try running "wing and wing" with the wind behind us. We tested various settings of fore, of main, of jib. And we sailed on to the north-northeast.

We sailed past Boon Island, made famous by Kenneth Roberts' book of the same name. As the day went on, the southerly became a little "smoky" and items in the distance

The wind was light - just enough to waft us along on a broad reach.

appeared blurred by a little haze. No matter, we knew where we were and were confident that we could make it to Maine.

By late afternoon it seemed clear that we would not be able to make it to Biddeford Pool, so we decided to try Cape Porpoise. I had never visited Cape Porpoise. This was before GPS, electronic charts and the profusion of Maine Coast cruising guides that have since been published. Somehow we had to translate the cryptic lines on our chart into the fuzzy and indistinct shapes materializing in the mist ahead. But that was par for the course in those days. We matched the numbers and types of buoys that we came upon and altered our courses in order to enter the harbor as depicted on the chart.

It was about 6 p.m. when *Serendipity* sailed up the narrow, lobster trap-strewn entrance of Cape Porpoise Harbor. We were lucky enough to find a mooring. Although we had our sleeping bags and indeed an air mattress, we were not too eager to sleep aboard. If we were secure on a mooring we could leave *Serendipity* and sleep ashore that night.

I do not remember how we got ashore. Did we inflate our "rubber ducky" dinghy and paddle to the public float? Or did someone give us a lift? At any rate, we did get ashore and called the Plumbs from the public phone on the dock. They were happy to come and pick us up, feed us a good dinner, and put us up for the night.

That night we slept in relative comfort in sleeping bags on the floor of the Plumbs' tiny apartment over the Biddeford Pool Yacht Club. At dinner we celebrated. Peter and Pam presented us with a great launching gift – a pair of Perko polished brass gimbaled kerosene cabin lamps, complete with glass shades and "smoke bells" to catch the ascending carbon and spare the overhead.

That night a weather front went through. We awoke to a morning of drizzle and fog. The Plumbs brought us back to Cape Porpoise. They were eager to see *Serendipity* close up, and maybe even have a sail. Would we mind stopping at Biddeford Pool later that morning?

Mind? We were eager to show off our dream ship. We wore our new yellow "oilskins" as we brought *Serendipity* around to Biddeford Pool under power. The oilskins were stiff and heavy, a far cry from the fancy foul weather apparel in use today. Maine fog and rain was not new to us. We had, after all, spent two previous summers at Prout's Neck.

Fortunately, the fog was not thick. We could feel our way around Fortunes Rocks, Goose Rocks, and the various other "rocks" that make up the Biddeford Pool-Kennebunkport peninsula. Before noon we were putt-putting in the narrow gut at Biddeford Pool. We basked in the Plumbs' admiration of our new ship. The four of us motored around in the dripping fog as I demonstrated the sturdy reliability of the engine and how confidently *Serendipity* shouldered the swells outside the

Anita goes out in the bowsprit chains to furl the jib as we enter Biddeford Pool to pick up the Plumbs and show them the boat.

harbor mouth. We even put up the sails, although there was no real wind for sailing.

By early afternoon, the front came through, the rain stopped, it cleared and the wind started to blow cold and clean from the northwest. We were eager to move on in hopes of reaching Portland by nightfall. We bid the Plumbs good-bye on the docks of Biddeford Pool and pressed on.

The northwesterly was fair for a close reach across Saco Bay and on to Cape Elizabeth. We motored out of the snug gut at the Pool and spread our white wings outside. The wind was blowing smartly and it was cool – if not cold. What a sail we had that day! We were getting to know how our dream ship actually performed in the element for which she was designed. We were in familiar waters sailing past Prout's Neck and Bluff and Stratton Islands. Ahead loomed Richmond Island, well remembered.

Peter Plumb takes *Serendipity* around Biddeford Pool under power. The brass shift lever is by his leg in the (backwards) forward position.

What a thrill it was to catch a full reaching breeze in the great gaff sails of our schooner! We fairly foamed along through a three or four foot sea. The new manila sheets strained. We tugged at the tiller to overcome a newly discovered strong weather helm. Indeed, as we cut Cape Elizabeth close, we even fancied we saw a man standing on the rocks taking a picture of us!

As we headed more west of north to enter the channel at Portland, we found the breeze cold in our teeth. It was late afternoon coming on evening. We bucked a small harbor chop.

Although I had sailed a great deal in Saco Bay, the approach to Casco Bay was unfamiliar to me. We followed the chart, picking out the winking lights of the flashers and the flashing bi-colored beam of Spring Point as we chugged north into the deepening night. We were getting cold as we nosed around Little Diamond Island and followed the yacht channel, red to starboard, black to port, up toward the cluster of lights which marked Handy's Boat Services on the Falmouth shore. This last three miles seemed to take forever. It was truly night by the time we could pick out the outlines of Handy's dock against the background of too-bright shore lights which shined in our eyes.

Who was that standing on the edge of the dock, silhouetted against the floodlights and spotlights which made us squint? The bulky figure looked familiar. But it wasn't until we were right alongside, wearily making fast, that we realized. . . It was, indeed, my father. He had just arrived at Handy's to leave us the Red Baron and had come down on the dock to see if per chance we were coming in. Father, who with Mother had put up with so much for so long as we made our dream a reality, was on the dock in Maine to greet us. And so it was, on August 31, 1967, that we and *Serendipity* came home.

Serendipity sailing on Casco Bay on Labor Day weekend, 1967. The crew is Peter and Pam Plumb, Bill and Connie Hyde, and Anita and Peter Murray. The picture was taken by Judge Edward T. Gignoux from his motorboat *B+*. Two days later, I started my one-year clerkship in his chambers.

Epilogue

Over 50 years have passed since that slushy February morning in Cambridge when our dream ship coalesced into what became *Serendipity*. For 49 summers, she has sailed the New England coast, from Nova Scotia to Nantucket. A lot of water has passed under her keel. It would take another volume, at least as long as this one, to sketch in even lightly the adventures shared with her, the pleasures still savored and the memories which linger.

It would take a hefty volume, indeed, to record the major portion of my life and the lives of my family members that *Serendipity* has occupied. However, this account would not be complete without some brief mention of how she was ultimately completed. After all, when she was launched in August of 1967, she was far from finished. The cabin was still an empty dark cavern, punctuated by the parallel ribs and dimly lit by our two extravagant bronze marine windows. There was still a lot left to be done before we would have the cozy cruising yacht which had nurtured our imaginations as we struggled in the back yard in Wilbraham.

During that first fall of 1967, we enjoyed our new ship to the utmost. We quickly learned the advantages and disadvantages of our traditional schooner rig. How she scooted when we could start the sheets and reach or run! But how laborious, how difficult it was to beat to windward, especially against any kind of a chop or sea. Our traditional purism gave way to 20th century practicality when our course lay within 60 degrees of the wind, especially if there were any kind of a sea running. We got used to the thump, thump, thumping of the Volvo diesel.

Other expressions of traditional authenticity that did not last long were the manila cordage and cotton sails. The former, we found, stretched considerably when dry and stiffened and

335

shrank considerably when wet. When leaving the boat, it was hard to know how tight to set up the sheets and halyards. The glorious baby-soft cotton sails from Jeckells did not take kindly to exposure to the weather. Very soon speckles and spots of mildew began to appear. They offended our aesthetic senses. We tried to scrub the mildew off the sails in our tiny back yard on Pine Street. It was very difficult to eradicate. If the sails got wet, which they frequently did in fog or rain or from spray, the fine soft cotton became so hard and swollen that it was hard to manage with our stubby, clawing fingers. Three years was enough for the sails; the cordage was replaced at the same time. Dacron is a wonderful fiber, even if its stark whiteness contrasts a bit with the mellowness of *Serendipity's* traditional wooden hull and spars.

Building the interior was quite a job. That first year, we hauled the boat for the winter in a boatyard in Yarmouth, Maine, about 15 miles north of Portland. There, we set about roughing in the galley and the main double bunk. And so began another series of weekends working on the boat. This time Anita was carrying our next joint project, a baby boy, so she felt sick a lot of the time. She was not helped by squeezing into tight spaces and the odd smells of boatbuilding.

Vere B. Crockett's original interior lay-out was a traditional one for a vessel of *Serendipity's* size. The galley was aft to port, with the head opposite. Settee berths on either side of the main cabin were separated by a drop-leaf table running from the main mast forward. The forward cabin contained the usual Vee-berth.

Early on in our fantasizing, we had decided not to follow Mr. Crockett's layout. As newlyweds relishing the pleasures of connubiality, we agreed that a double bunk was a must for our cruising pleasure. And we wanted the head forward between the cabins rather than aft. Finally, the drop-leaf table seemed to be clumsy and obstructive of the center of the cabin. A small permanent dinette-a-deux would be much better. We had also learned enough by then to know that in Maine you cannot go cruising without a good wood or coal stove.

After a great deal of doodling and drawing, measuring and visualizing, checking and conferring, we arrived at our own original layout for *Serendipity's* main cabin. To port we would have the galley counter, with space for a couple of lockers and an icebox underneath. There would be a cutout for a little cast iron wood stove.

In the late 1960's, the Portland Stove Foundry Company was still in business. One of their many excellent products was a tiny yacht-sized "Ship's Stove", a knock-off from the famous Shipmate cast iron ranges. The Portland Stove Company version, however, was special. The entire stove, inside and out, was coated with porcelain enamel, color at the customer's option. That first winter in Maine, our Christmas present to ourselves was a gleaming red "No. 210" two burner wood range with a small 9" x 9" x 6" oven. Forward to port we would later on build a little dinette, with sitting space for two facing fore and aft.

Aft on the starboard side, I planned to work in a small hanging locker, partly under the bridge deck and partly in the corner of the cabin. Just forward of that would be the double berth. We would have a fold-out berth which could double as a settee. The berth would be hinged, so that at night it could slide out as far as the mast. It would be supported along the edge by fold-down legs. During the day, it could slide back and up to make a settee with upholstered back.

Our original notion was to have the frame sprung with a set of springs from an old cot. Although the rig was good in principle, we needed so much space underneath to accommodate the sag of our bodies that we had to discontinue it after a season of experimentation. Just forward of the berth on the starboard side was room for a tiny head. The forward cabin was unaltered from Crockett's plan.

337

Of course, in those days, we had little idea of what the actual measurements for these various interior elements should be. How high should the counter be? How about the hanging locker? What is the minimum size for a usable head? We had to guess as best we could. Many times we guessed wrong.

Fir plywood also was a new material for me to work with. Had I known how difficult it would be to keep any kind of a painted plywood surface presentable, I would have gone to mahogany plywood, even in those impecunious days. Ignorance is bliss, however. We cut and sawed, screwed and puttied during the spring of 1968 until we had a rather awkward galley counter, the hanging locker, and the double berth more or less finished. The head was added as a necessary afterthought just before launching in May. Much of the work was done in a cellar workshop under our small apartment at 87 Pine Street in Portland. On winter evenings, we turned out a mahogany companion ladder, cabinet doors, drawers, and even a little six-foot plywood dinghy. The rubber ducky had turned out to be useless.

The six foot dinghy, *Beak*, was William Atkin's, "Tiny Ripple" design. It was one of the many which had been published over the years in either *Rudder* or *Motorboating* (two publications which disappeared not long after we launched our dream ship). We picked it because, hypothetically at least, it could be taken aboard and stored on the cabin top between the masts. In point of fact we never did this. The dinghy, while cute, *barely* held two adults with about two inches of freeboard.

Although my salary as a U.S. District Judge's clerk was modest, nonetheless with my wife working as a librarian we were considerably better off than we had been during law school. Gear for *Serendipity* was a high priority. Thus we found ourselves able to afford the stove from the Portland Stove Foundry plus another pair of the beautiful bronze port lights and a set of eight cast manganese bronze lifeline stanchions from Rostand.   The latter we had found were a "must" after our first season of sailing.   There had been no dunkings, but a number of near misses.

By late May, 1968, we could work no longer.   We would launch *Serendipity* with our half-complete interior and enjoy our first full season of sailing and our first real cruise "down east" along the Maine coast.

That first summer's cruise of late June - early July 1968 is a story all of its own.   Brash, eager and inexperienced, we wanted it all.   For 16 days, we ranged up and down the Maine coast east of Portland.   We ultimately reached the fabled destination of Roque Island.

In our half-completed craft, with two portholes per side, and our shiny new red enameled stove burning charcoal briquettes by the bagful, we ventured forth in late June.   The weather was what one would expect at that latitude and time of year - changeable.   There were days of fog, in which we anxiously picked our way along, carefully scaling the mileage from buoy to buoy on the big yellow and blue nautical charts of the day.   We trusted our compass, suspected it, and then learned to trust it again.

There were days of "smokey southerlies", with calm mornings giving way to a ruffle of breeze toward noon.   By mid-afternoon, the hazy southerly would waft us along, from indistinct island to intricate passage, to a cozy lee.

There were days which were overcast, and threatened rain.   On one of those, we sallied forth from the comparative comfort of Winter Harbor out to the end of the Schoodic Peninsula. The point of decision was at hand.   Should we turn back at this easterly terminus of the well-traveled cruising grounds? Or should we press forward, to the unknown waters to the east?   The skipper wanted to go forward; the mate wanted to go back.   There were tears.   We pressed forward, to the eastward, under a leaden sky.   A wind from the southeast boded a change in the weather.

That night there were hard driving thunderstorms. We had found minimal shelter and a mooring in a cove on Beals Island beside the bridge to Jonesport. We lay awake cowering in our saggy sprung bunk, feeding briquettes to the stove. Would the lightning strike our stubby masts? In cozy Northeast Harbor, we would have been dwarfed by more tempting targets. Amid lobster boats in the exposed cove of Beals Island, we jutted perilously high into the rain-swept and crackling night . . . Although we slept little, we survived and sailed on to the fabled shores of Roque Island the following day.

We learned to love best of all the clear, cool northwesterly days that followed the passage of a cold front. The clouds, the rain, the sultry, hazy humidity were all swept away by the clear, cool breeze from the north. Those are the days when one can sail either east or west on the coast of Maine, when all the islands stand out like jewels on the sparkling sea, when spirits are high and the soul is refreshed as the eye is delighted by this panorama before it.

One of the highlights of that first cruise was a visit with V. B. Crockett, *Serendipity's* designer. Although we had spoken and corresponded with Mr. Crockett frequently during the building process, we had never met him in the flesh. We sailed our dream ship into Camden harbor with some trepidation. Would he be satisfied with our crude workmanship? What would he think of the little changes we had made in the interior? Would he see in our creation his own concept and design faithfully brought to fruition?

It turned out that Crockett was tickled to death to see us. A genial, fleshy, middle-aged man with thinning hair, he inspected *Serendipity* with a fine toothed comb. His eyes twinkled with benevolent amusement as he pronounced her "A-OK". We were proud and relieved. As it turned out, we were glad we had taken our newborn vessel to see him that summer. Two years later, Mr. Crockett passed away.

And so cruising in *Serendipity* became a part of our lives together. During the winter of 1968-69, we finished the forepeak, with a V-berth port and starboard. We put a door on our gaping head. How ingenious we were, or so we thought, to devise a door that could alternatively close the forepeak or the head, but not both at the same time. We did what we could in the shop. We fashioned drawers, and even precut plywood panels to rough measurements gleaned from the boat the weekend before.

Work on the boat itself, however, was a bit difficult. She was stored at the boatyard in Yarmouth, 15 miles or so from our little Portland apartment. We tried to foresee every eventuality. Each weekend, starting while the snow was still on the ground, we loaded the car with every tool or part that would be needed for that weekend's projects. We even brought picnic lunches. However, frequently the rage of frustration would rise, fists would clench and teeth would gnash, when I realized that some important part, fastening, tool, or bit of wood had been left behind.

Somehow, we got it done. The spring of 1969 saw another pair of bronze windows from Rostand. *Serendipity* now sported three per side, six in all. Here we decided to stop, although the original plans had called for five on a side. With six big bronze opening windows, the cabin was light and airy enough for us. We figured that we might as well enjoy the added strength of the un-pierced sections of cabin wall and the economy of fewer bronze ports. It was just as well. Very shortly after we received the 1969 order, we heard that Rostand, under pressure for many years, had gone bankrupt.

We finished off the cabin between the galley aft and the forward bulkhead. A simple dinette was arranged in the space to port. The head was finished to starboard. The berth was rebuilt with a solid paneled bottom to replace the sagging spring.

The little red stove earned its keep as well, especially when we gave up on charcoal briquettes. Small chunks of hardwood, shop scraps or diced fireplace logs, burned much cleaner and hotter without the grubby gray residue from the briquettes. The warmth from our little red cast iron friend dried our clothes, warmed our bodies, and comforted our souls.

Early on, we were also able to upgrade *Serendipity's* galvanized blocks to real wood-shell yacht blocks, albeit with galvanized straps and fittings. In 1968 or early 1969, I somehow learned of A. Dauphinee and Son, wooden block-makers of Lunenburg, Nova Scotia. Dauphinee was a relic of a bygone age, still subsisting in Nova Scotia's somewhat more traditional marine economy. I remember my excitement when I was able to obtain their descriptive pamphlet (printed sometime in the 1950s) showing the various fittings available with their 3", 3 1/2" and 4" wood-shell yacht blocks. They came with shells of ash or *lignum vitae*, an incredibly dense tropical hardwood traditionally used for the most expensive wood yacht blocks and fittings. After purchasing a sample to examine, we sprang for a whole set of 3" (for 3/8" rope) and 3 1/2" (for 7/16" rope) ash shell yacht blocks for *Serendipity's* halyards and sheets. We ordered the blocks by mail, and they eventually arrived, each one wrapped in newspaper, by international parcel post. They gleamed as we unwrapped them and marveled at the traditional workmanship of the wood shells and the sturdy galvanized fittings by which they would be attached to our booms and gaffs.

Indeed, our purchase of blocks for *Serendipity* in 1968 led to a business that I carried on for the next couple of years. "Traditional Sailing Yacht Hardware" was the name of a small mail-order business selling Dauphinee wood-shell yacht blocks as well as other traditional galvanized and bronze sailing yacht hardware items I had unearthed during the sourcing process for *Serendipity*. Interest in traditional sailing craft and wooden boatbuilding was just beginning to stir then, and the business grew rapidly. By 1970, it was taking good bit of my time. Finally, one of my senior partners came to me and asked if I wanted to be a lawyer or sell marine hardware? That did it. I promptly sold Traditional Sailing Yacht Hardware to an acquaintance and concentrated on lawyering – and on *Serendipity*, of course.

It was also in the early 1970s that we got a real dinghy to replace the tiny and tippy *Beak*. In those days, Jarvis Newman was molding 11-foot fiberglass rowing dinghies based on a traditional Whitehall-style rowboat model. They were nicely trimmed out in teak or mahogany. We gave ourselves the present of a green mahogany-trimmed Newman dinghy with 7' spruce oars – the *Beakson*. "Beak" and "Beakson" were endearing names originally given to chickens that I kept at home in Wilbraham during my early teens. Somehow they got transferred to *Serendipity's* tenders.

Although to some it seemed a little large in comparison with *Serendipity's* own length of only thirty feet, to me *Beakson* has always seemed to be just the right size. It has certainly performed superbly in terms of easy rowing, easy towing, carrying capacity, good looks and durability. We had quick, safe and comfortable communication with the shore and with other yachts whenever we needed it just by pulling *Beakson* in on her tow painter. To be sure, she was too large to take aboard. However, we had never found it necessary to take *Beak* aboard, and as things turned out we never had any problem just towing *Beakson* during our cruises up and down the Maine coast.

In those early years, we established a pattern, which has endured, at least in part, for decades. Annually, starting shortly after New Year, we, like many other owners of wooden boats in the Northern Hemisphere, would turn our energies to "getting the boat ready". In reality, *Serendipity* has never really been finished. Every season of sailing has sprouted new notions of how some feature of our dream ship can be improved.   For instance, early on we decided to fit a fisherman's staysail for better light weather performance on the wind. Although the new sail blanketed our gaff-topsail, it did improve performance to windward. Of course, we have had to strike it on each tack to avoid fouling the fore.

Each year as the grip of winter loosened on New England, we would venture forth to the boatyard. Of course, we always would have the routine maintenance of a wooden boat. Each year we have had to scrape and paint the bottom, sand and paint the topsides and deck, and varnish the masts. We have found that all of the major exterior surfaces have to be painted or varnished each year. It has been worth the trouble. *Serendipity* has gleamed anew every season.

In the late 1970s, we changed the color of the deck and cabin top from "Mint Green" to the more authentic Petit "Sandtone", a light buff. We continued to varnish the cabin sides, spars, and trim, even though the clear finish betrayed some of our many mistakes for all to see.   The hull has consistently remained dark green and the bottom red.

In those early years, we learned to love the coast of Maine and to know many of its bays, sounds, harbors, and coves. One summer we cruised south to Cape Cod, Martha's Vineyard and Nantucket, which we found over-developed, crowded and exposed. We quickly decided that Maine was much better.

Our two children, Peter and Anne, both were introduced to *Serendipity* as infants. We survived the squirmy ages of 1-3 with the aid of various kinds of harnesses and special lifejackets. At about that time, we purchased and renovated an old military home on Cushing Island. We spent those summers there when the children were still too young to go to school. *Serendipity* got a new mooring in Whitehead Passage and we temporarily left the Portland Yacht Club.

344

Times change. It became Anita and my lot to part one from another. In 1975 we separated, and in 1976 we were divorced. In the settlement, *Serendipity* came with me.

Some of the old patterns, however, continued. The crew of *Serendipity* became three. My first cruise alone with the children was in June of 1977, when Peter was 8 and Anne was 6. We cruised for four days to Boothbay Harbor and back. What an adventure!

Over the succeeding years, summer cruises for father and children became more or less of a tradition. Many summer weekend visits were similarly spent on *Serendipity*. Later, although occasionally more ambitious trips took precedence, in most years even busy teenagers found time for a few days on *Serendipity* with Dad. Each cruise has been faithfully logged. There is little point, however, in reproducing these personal reminiscences here. Suffice it to say that the delight of those cruises created lasting good memories.

Serendipity has aged gracefully. As the children became young adults, annual maintenance, upgrading and "improvements" to *Serendipity* kept her young. Mr. Travers' Caulk-Tex is truly a magnificent product. For the first 20 years of her life, *Serendipity* never had a serious leak and never was re-caulked, or even stripped to bare wood.

The Volvo diesel engine lasted about 13 years. Raw-water-cooled, it built up salt until it began to overheat routinely. The belt-driven starter-dynamo was never very efficient. And the Volvo was always noisy and vibrated a good deal despite various changes in rubber mounts and flexible couplings. In 1980, it finally gave up the ghost and was replaced by a two-cylinder Universal 16 horsepower job - a "marinized" version of the Japanese Kubota tractor diesel, which worked very well for many years. Our original George Merwin copper pipe jacketed exhaust system did not last long at all. The solder joints cracked under even damped engine vibration. Fortunately, I was able to replace it with a stainless steel and rubber hose jacketed version that gave good service for a longish time.

For a many years, the notion of a major voyage in a 30' miniature schooner had remained a rather implausible dream. After all, the children were small, there was always school, and I had to keep my nose to the grindstone to keep obligations up to date and put aside monies for college. But times do change. Children certainly grow faster as they get older. And suddenly, in the winter of 1984-85, I realized that it could be done. Peter would be graduating from high school in 1987. If he wanted to take a year off before he went to college, maybe, just maybe, we could go sailing for six months or a year . . . in *Serendipity*.

And so between 1984 and 1987, *Serendipity* was rebuilt, strengthened, improved, and re-equipped. We had moved into a large brick home in Portland that had a yard. By then the Brownell trailer had come into use. No more trips to the boatyard to work on *Serendipity!* Bucky Wooster, a talented boat trucker, would bring Serendipity home to West Street in the fall and set her up on stands right beside my house. I had a large woodworking shop in the basement. Conditions for boat work could not have been better.

An early improvement in this major rebuilding phase was to the V-berth and cabinetwork in the forward cabin. By now we could afford mahogany marine plywood to replace the fir plywood with which we had started. My craftsmanship had marginally improved. The original V-berth was torn out and replaced with overlapping berths to accommodate larger teenaged bodies.

In the spring of 1986, I tore apart the cockpit. We, (meaning "I" with help from Peter and Anne) replaced the original 22-gallon Monel fuel and water tanks with new ones. They were designed to take advantage of all of the available space under the deck and each held 35 gallons. My friends at Goudy and Stevens Yacht Yard in East Boothbay, Maine fabricated the new tanks to my custom measurements from stainless steel.

In order to increase our water capacity even further, I installed 15-gallon rubber flexible tanks on each side under the cockpit and next to the engine. These changes essentially tripled our water capacity and nearly doubled our fuel.

When we had originally built *Serendipity*, we had run out of time and had omitted the cockpit coamings specified on Crockett's plans. These were designed to protect the cockpit and its occupants from stray waves and spray and to provide some support for our backs when sailing. For nearly 20 years, we had sailed without coamings. This omission was rectified in the spring of 1986 when we fashioned and installed handsome mahogany coamings that we edge-bolted down through the deck and the deck beams underneath. We finished them "bright," meaning varnished.

We replaced the three original cockpit scuppers with two 1½" scuppers led to seacocks through the hull and recycled two of the former scuppers to drain the bridge deck corners inside the coamings, where water would otherwise collect. Large scuppers were a safety feature. If the cockpit were to be filled by a "rogue" wave, it would be important that it drain rapidly to relieve the boat of the excess weight of a cockpit full of water. We installed a watertight hatch in the cockpit floor to give access to the storage there behind the engine. All of these changes were in preparation for The Trip, which we were planning to commence in June, 1987.

From the time *Serendipity* was launched, we had relied on a Danforth 12-pound "High-Tensile" anchor for most of our anchoring needs. Under ideal conditions, it held pretty well. It was backed up by a 35 pound "fisherman" style anchor from Manhattan Marine for kelpy or rocky bottoms where the Danforth would not hold. After reading a great deal about the comparative virtues of various kinds of anchors and ground tackle, we went to a 35-pound CQR plow anchor from

Simpson-Lawrence, in Glasgow, Scotland on 200 feet of 5/16" high tensile chain. To get the chain pulled in and this anchor raised, we purchased and installed a bronze lever-actuated 2-speed anchor windlass from New Zealand.

In 1986, we also built a strong boom gallows frame to replace a shaky earlier version and installed an Aries wind-vane self-steerer. If we were going to traverse oceans with a crew of two, we would need some form of relief at the helm. Small tiller-linked autopilots for sailboats were just coming into general use and had not proven their reliability to my satisfaction. They also consumed precious battery power. Some maintained that a wind vane self-steerer would not work on a schooner because of the overhanging main boom and the strong weather helm. We scrupulously followed the instructions in the installation and crossed our fingers.

In my readings on long-distance sailors, their yachts and their voyages, there were several instances of the use of a large square-sail hoisted on its own yard for down-wind sailing. I crafted a hollow 14' yard in the cellar workshop during the winter. My friend Graham Stone, who had supplied *Serendipity's* first suit of Dacron sails, cut and sewed a suitable 14' x 14' square sail for it. We could carry the sail rolled up on yard on deck ready to be hoisted by a pair of "lifts" attached to eyes on either side of the top foremast band.

During the summer of 1986, Peter, Anne and I took a "shakedown cruise" to Nova Scotia. Bill Alcorn was with us for the first stage – overnight from Portland to Lunenburg, NS. Everything worked. In particular, the steering vane appeared to be able reliably to hold course on most points of sailing, even with the wind well aft. The square sail hoisted and drew, although we came to the conclusion that it was a bit small for the job and that a 16' yard would give us more meaningful sail area. We made our landfalls as expected – even in the fog.

While in Nova Scotia, we met Arthur Dauphinee, the maker of *Serendipity's* wood-shell blocks. Although we had done a lot of business together during the days of Traditional Sailing Yacht Hardware, we had never met face to face. He turned out to be a delightful and droll kind of fellow following an obsolete trade in an ancient workshop.

We returned to Maine overnight *a trois*. Despite some *mal de mer*, we made our landfall at Mount Desert Rock as planned. Our Nova Scotia cruise strengthened our confidence in our ability to cover greater distances of open water.

In the winter of 1986-1987, we reconstructed *Serendipity's* galley, tearing out the old fir plywood and replacing it with mahogany marine ply, which was devoid of voids, was easier to work, and took a much better finish. The old red cast iron wood-stove had lost most of its enamel. Moreover, we were headed for the tropics, scarcely a good place for a wood range. I bought a stainless steel and brass "Taylor's" pressurized kerosene stove. Although propane was available at the time and was being increasingly installed in yachts, it was a dangerous fuel. If there were a leak, heavier-than-air propane gas might accumulate in our bilge and cabin. The slightest spark could blow us all to smithereens. Pressurized kerosene, although more complicated to use, would provide a good hot flame without the risk of explosion.

Our original ice-box had been a small side-loading "RV-type" that only held about 10 pounds of ice. For sailing in the tropics we would need a real ice box, top loading and with lots of insulation. I designed a top-loading icebox and built it into the counter aft just ahead of the new flexible tanks. It would hold up to 50 pounds of ice and was insulated with 4-6" of rigid foam panels. The icebox itself, I molded out of fiberglass. There was a little hinged top covered in the same red formica as the rest of our countertop.

Activity in the last 6 months leading up to our planned June 1987 departure, took on much of the same character as our frantic efforts to get *Serendipity* ready for launching 20 years before. There was so much to do to transform our cozy traditional coasting schooner into a world voyager! In the spring of 1967, I purchased and installed a single sideband radio transceiver that would supposedly transmit and receive hundreds of miles at sea. One of the backstays was interrupted by insulators to form the antenna. We used wide copper straps to ground the rigging to the iron keel in case of lightning striking while we were on the high seas. I had read of wind and wave-powered electric generators that could keep our batteries charged without having to run the engine. As a result, I purchased an Ampair wind and water dual-mode generator and installed the necessary electrical circuits and brackets to hook it up for use in either mode.

Back in 1987, the predominant electronic navigation system was 'Loran C", originally developed in World War II. We had used Loran C, with its special overprinted charts, for the Nova Scotia trip and it had performed acceptably. A new worldwide navigation system, GPS, was just coming into use. However, in the early days of GPS there were no graphical chart plotters on which on could simply follow progress and plot courses and waypoints right on electronic navigational charts. Early GPS readouts were latitude-longitude, which one had to then transpose to a paper chart to learn one's position. Nonetheless, the touted accuracy and reliability of GPS made a strong case for adding a GPS receiver along with our Loran C device to our increasingly crowded cabin. I bought and installed a Danish Robertson GPS, which did indeed work as advertised.

Because a large part of our forepeak would be filled with supplies, rubber dinghy, etc., we decided to install an upper bunk above the former pull-out bunk in the main cabin. The idea was that Annie would bunk forward, and that Peter M. and I would share the main cabin. When not in use, the upper bunk laid back against *Serendipity's* side. It worked, although it sure made the main cabin seem crowded.

As the date of departure approached, I was still trying to line up some kind of insurance, at least for liability (P & I), to cover us during our world voyage. The reluctant insurance companies all required a comprehensive condition survey. So Jan Bijouwer, dean of Maine's ship surveyors, showed up at 89 West Street to poke, prod and survey the condition of the vessel we were about to embark in for the high seas.

During the survey, he tapped on the keel bolts. Although rusty on the surface, the sounds they made convinced him that they were OK. He drew several screws. Much to my relief, the 2" x 12 bronze screws that we had driven home 20 years before to secure *Serendipity's* planking to her frames were still almost like new. So far so good. Then, oops! Mr. Bijouwer examined our bowsprit, with its great knot clearly visible under several years of varnish. "This will never do!" Although the bowsprit had performed flawlessly in all sorts of weather, fair and foul, for 20 years, Mr. B. was convinced that it could fail at any time. If we were going to get a "clean survey", it would have to be replaced.

So there we were, weeks before our planned departure, with a bowsprit to replace. To find a piece of white oak of the requisite size and quality seemed almost impossible. After a bunch of calls, my friend Bill Alcorn, an expert on lumber grades, suggested that Douglas Fir might be almost as good. Bijouwer agreed. Richardson Dana, a local Portland lumber wholesaler, had some 10" x 10" Douglas Fir in stock. In a trice, we removed our old oak bowsprit and roughed out a blank for a new one of Douglas Fir. It took no more than 48 hours to replace the old condemned spar with a new one of gleaming Douglas fir, whereupon we received Jan Bijouwer's blessing. Not that it did much good. In the end, all insurance companies declined hull coverage, although we did get some limited coverage for liability.

Serendipity's cordage had long been a bit of a problem. The manila rope that we had started with, had been discarded after the first couple of seasons. For a long time, we had used standard spun Dacron line, but its white color always rubbed me a bit the wrong way. Shortly before we were ready to leave, I learned of Toplicht, in Hamburg, Germany, a veritable cornucopia of traditional sailing yacht hardware. Toplicht sold a special German polypropylene rope that closely resembled manila, but did not share its drawbacks. It was called Spleitex. Its only limitations were that although strong, it was light in weight and did not have the heft of traditional cordage. It was also prone to deterioration in the sun. Toplicht sent samples. Based on these, I outfitted *Serendipity* with Spleitex halyards, sheets and running rigging. It looked good, felt like real rope, and was likely to last at least for our planned trip.

And so it was on June 24, 1987, *Serendipity* and its crew of Anne, Peter and me, left the Portland Yacht Club on a voyage half way around the world. We were heavy laden with all our new equipment, including rubber Avon dinghy with tiny motor, inflatable life raft in its fiberglass canister, our new and larger square-yard and square-sail, hundreds of pounds of provisions, fuel and water. Our plan was for the three of us to sail south during that summer, and then for Peter and me to sail on to Australia or New Zealand during the ensuing months.

The story of that adventure would fill its own book, and will not be recapitulated here. Suffice it to say that the three of us sailed on the open ocean to Bermuda in July. At that point, recurring seasickness convinced Annie that she had enough of open water sailing, and she returned to Maine.

Peter Marshall and I continued on, through squalls and calms, to reach the British Virgin Islands in the Caribbean in August. By then we too were convinced the blue-water sailing under tropic skies was not necessarily for us. Too hot. Too boring. We shipped *Serendipity* home on a freighter and returned home ourselves by air. In a matter of days, Peter Marshall and I turned around to take the next several months traveling around the world by air, which is also a story in itself.

Serendipity and her crew in Hamilton Harbor, Bermuda. Peter Marshall Murray (left) and Anne Murray (right) made many cruises with me for over a decade. Our adventures together will remain a happy memory for all of my days.

When we returned from our world trip at the end of 1967, Peter was off to NOLS for a "Semester in the Rockies". I unpacked the provisions, extra equipment and gear with which *Serendipity* was still crammed and started the process of reconverting her from a world voyager to a traditional schooner yacht to cruise the coast of Maine. All of the sophisticated equipment came off, wind vane, GPS receiver, single sideband, wind and water electric generators. These items, along with the scores of special ocean charts purchased for the voyage I disposed of as best I could, or simply stored in our cellar pending future disposition. *Serendipity* rose to her original water line, which I had raised when she had been so loaded down for our world voyage. The cabin became lighter and airier once more.

The reconversion back to Maine cruising did require some source of warmth to replace the red cast iron range of former years. The Taylor's kerosene stove had performed very well, and I decided to keep it for cooking and baking. After some casting around, I found a Dickinson solid fuel fireplace that would fit in a small niche I was able to carve out of a corner of the head at one end of our bunk. It would burn bits of wood and provide a cheery fire-place feel along with drying warmth on cool or foggy days.

By the summer of 1988, *Serendipity* had been retransformed from a somewhat overloaded world voyager to a graceful traditional Maine coast schooner yacht. But it was clear to me that the beloved era of cruising the Maine coast with my children had come to an end. *Serendipity* had lost her crew. Peter Marshall was on his way to college, and Anne would be going in the following fall. They were going on to make their own lives, which would not include sailing the Maine coast with their father. That summer, I could not foresee that in a very few months, something would occur that would bring new life to my love affair with *Serendipity* and many more years of cruising adventures.

In early November, 1988, during the course of an unsuccessful campaign for a seat in the Maine Legislature, I met a potential voter named Deborah Clark. After the end of the campaign, I got to know her better and fell deeply in love with her. It was not long before I wondered, "Was this a person with whom I could cruise together on the Coast of Maine in *Serendipity*?" On July 1, 1989, aboard *Serendipity* anchored in a little cove off Great Diamond Island, I asked Debby to marry me. She said "yes." Later that summer, we made our first cruise together along the Maine Coast. Debby's children, Cam and Alison, twins then aged 10, came with us as far as East Boothbay, Maine, where they were going to stay with their father for the week that Debby and I would be sailing. The cruise started inauspiciously with a thunderstorm off Halfway Rock. Ultimately we had an enjoyable cruise along the coast. It was a special pleasure for me to share with my beloved some of the beauty and wonder of sailing the coast of Maine.

Debby at the helm with Mount Desert Island on the horizon. Maine Coast cruises with Debby have become the high points of each summer for me over the last 25 years.

This first cruise with Debby in 1989 was the start of the third and longest phase of cruising in *Serendipity*, a phase which has continued to the present day. We married in November 1989 and practically every summer since have spent at least a week together cruising the coast of Maine. Debby already had some cruising experience and quickly learned the ropes aboard a traditional gaff-rigged schooner. Over time, she has given *Serendipity* her own particular stamp with new curtains, cushions and other interior appointments without changing her essential character. She has tolerated my annual rites of preparation and painting in the spring and hauling and preparing for winter in the fall. As long as we lived together at West Street, she cheerfully agreed to share our back yard with *Serendipity* every winter.

Starting soon after my return from our world cruise, I started to upgrade *Serendipity* as a traditional sailing yacht.

This consisted chiefly of replacing her galvanized hardware and fittings, which were beginning to rust, with bronze. It was a gradual process. By the end of the 1980's, however, the wooden boat revival was in full swing, and many sources of hardware and supplies for traditional wood sailing yachts had sprung up. Therefore, it was a lot easier to find appropriate hardware for *Serendipity* than it had been twenty-plus years before.

Early on, I ordered a new set of ash-shell yacht blocks from Arthur Dauphinee, this time with bronze straps and fittings. The old makeshift galvanized eye-bands were replaced with cast bronze ones from Bristol Bronze, a purveyor of bronze marine hardware copied from the old Herreshoff and some of the Rostand patterns. Bronze belaying pins from Nova Scotia replaced the old galvanized ones. Gradually rusty grey steel was replaced with bronze, which quickly turned green in the salt air. *Serendipity* looked more like a real yacht rather than a scaled-down version of an old commercial fishing schooner.

In the early 1990s, we replaced the engine once more, this time with a three-cylinder Universal (Kubota) diesel that was lighter and shorter than the two-cylinder model that it had replaced. Like the others, it has given good service with regular maintenance and occasional repairs. Over the years, these engines have taught me a bit about how they work, so that it is possible for me to make many routine repairs and adjustments without the need of a diesel mechanic.

Although the second twenty-five years of *Serendipity's* life to date may have been somewhat less eventful than the first, she has continued to bring immense pleasure and satisfaction. Debby's years as *Serendipity's* crew far outnumber those of any prior crew members, and our book of shared cruising experiences has become thick. We have sailed together as far as Grand Manan, New Brunswick, several times to Roque Island, and have covered and re-covered all the intervening coast of Maine. Over the years, we have revisited many favorite spots first discovered with one of the earlier crews, and have found many more that we now call our own. Some of our cruises are documented with careful notes, most are not.

Now at age 50, *Serendipity* is still going pretty strong. Her hull is tight and true. We have had practically no rot – just a spot on one of the garboards and on a single other hull plank – quickly replaced with "Dutchmen" (partial replacement planks). The white oak frames are as hard as iron, and show no rot at all. Several of them, however are cracked. I have screwed on bronze straps bridging the cracks, and installed three laminated sister frames. Our fiberglass-covered deck, on most wooden boats a source of rot and deterioration, is as good as new thanks to Mr. Travers' Liquid Marine-Tex. Masts and spars, stripped and refinished at infrequent intervals belie their age and are shiny and bright.

Over the years, we have had to "wood" (sand down to bare wood) *Serendipity's* bottom twice and her topsides and deck once each. The Travers Caulk-Tex kept her hull tight for decades, much to the amazement of wooden boat friends and colleagues who had to do re-caulk and re-putty their craft on a nearly annual basis. When it finally became brittle, we merely re-puttied with a new (and inferior) product with similar properties.

Serendipity's color scheme has remained pretty constant since I started painting the deck "Sandtone" in the mid-1970's. For years, we struggled to maintain the beauty of her varnished mahogany cabin sides, despite various blemishes and imperfections. We finally had to give up and go to paint. The white cabin sides complement the green hull, buff deck and varnished trim so nicely that I wonder why I did not paint them years earlier.

The key to *Serendipity's* continued good condition has been the work that we have done each year to keep her fully up to snuff. Without regular and frequent maintenance, any wooden boat will quickly start to go to pieces. *Serendipity* has been far too dear to us for us to let that happen. Hence, the annual ceremonies of scraping, sanding, fixing and painting. But it has been worth it.

For many years in the off seasons *Serendipity* was a fixture behind our garage in Portland's West End. When we moved to the East End in 2013, we were able to find a neighboring lot for *Serendipity* as well. This has been important. Having the boat right beside our home and my shop makes it feasible for me to continue to do most of the annual

Serendipity at her summer mooring in Whitehead Passage. She gladdens the view from my study at our summer home on nearby Cushing Island.

maintenance and make occasional improvements. In recent years, however, first Ray Tremblay and more recently Eric Hanna have done most of the spring painting.

Back in 1965, as I looked at the pages of the little booklet in Harvard Square, how could I have ever imagined that the dainty dream ship which entranced me then would develop into such a major part of the lives of our family? How could I have foreseen the remarkable challenges of her building and launching, and the many adventures that she would bring us? How could I have foreseen that 50 years later, she would still be with us, sitting daintily at her mooring, beckoning us to a sail, a cruise or another adventure?